Aspects

of

FICTION

A *Handbook*

ASPECTS

OF

FICTION

A HANDBOOK

Howard E. Hugo
The University of California, Berkeley

LITTLE, BROWN
AND COMPANY
Boston and Toronto

SECOND PRINTING

Published simultaneously in Canada
by Little, Brown & Company (Canada) Limited

PRINTED IN THE UNITED STATES OF AMERICA

FOREWORD

MISS MARGERY SHARP, herself an English novelist lately turned critic, has recently reminded us that the novel "squats at the foot of Parnassus." Her charming turn of phrase underscores two qualities of the novel as a form: its late arrival on the literary scene, and—until the last few decades, at least—the treatment it has generally received as a medium somehow less dignified and respectable than other more traditional genres, such as the epic, the drama, and lyric poetry.

I think this judgment may be quite simply explained. The number of terms in the *Glossary*—epic, romance, fabliau, novella, etc.—pointing to the novel's antecedents stress its relative modernity. And, the novel does occasionally seem a jostling parvenu when placed amid the more glorious company of Homer's epics, Sophoclean and Shakespearean tragedy, even the lyric poems of a Keats or a Shelley. Its birth and development are closely associated with the emergence of the middle class as the dominant social group in European and American society, with the rise of literacy and the smell of printer's ink—indeed, the entire commercial world of book-publishing. (After all, it is the one literary form designed specifically to be *read*, not heard as with poetry, or heard and seen as with the drama.) To return to Miss Sharp's metaphor, none of these phenomena can be said to exude "Parnassian" elegance.

Nor do the themes of many of the world's greatest novels follow epic aspirations "to justify the ways of God to men," or delineate those nervous probings into ultimate reality to which we are made witness with the loftiest dramatic tragedies: *Oepidus Rex* and *King Lear* would be two excellent examples. I have just quoted Milton's well-known line from *Paradise Lost*. One might facetiously suggest that another line from his epic, deservedly less-known than the one just cited—"A while discourse they hold; / No fear lest dinner cool"—is more emblematic of the cozier universe of the novel. True, there are books like some of Dostoevsky's and Thomas Mann's—to mention two authors with serious metaphysical concerns—that propound questions of epic and tragic profundity. But in general the region of the novel is rich in small-talk and commonplace activity, where meals (I refer again to Milton's vegetarian banquet) are frequent, since they are a handy and convenient device by which an author can assemble his principals. In contradistinction, we cannot imagine Hamlet *eating*. . . .

Some time ago a French critic commented that the only new pleasures invented since Greek times have been smoking and the reading of novels. Yet this hedonistic praise also points to the novel's unfortunate lack of aristocratic and classical forebears. Throughout classical antiquity, for instance, writers seemed to have felt that mere story-telling in itself was undignified. The Roman *satira* never attained any major status, and stood with respect to the other more serious literature of the day, in about the same way as serialized fiction in *The Saturday Evening Post* stands in relation to the works of Faulkner and James Joyce. Classical authors simply made the narrating of a story part of the epic or the drama—(*e.g.*, the account of the founding of Rome in the *Aeneid*, or the lamentable tale of a king ignorant of his parentage in *Oedipus Rex*). It might be added that for all their word-coining genius, the Greeks had no name for "novel": a reasonable deficiency, since the form did not exist with them. When E. M. Forster amusingly notes that "Aristotle had read few novels and no modern ones—the *Odyssey* but not *Ulysses*" (the second title, of course, refers to Joyce's novel) he is hinting at Homer's work being a novel without being so-named officially, *avant la lettre*. But the English novelist and critic is being witty, and his humor must not obscure the fact that the *Odyssey* is, after all, an epic and not a novel. That Aristotle, figuratively the father of all critics, was condemned by an historical accident *not* to mention a genre that had *not* yet been conceived, places the novel in a poor light.

Not until lately has the novel enjoyed the analytical scrutiny lavished on its more eminent predecessors. Older academicians have been disturbed by its upstart-newness. I recall a former teacher of mine at a small New England college, describing the intellectual distress of that institution's President, when the suggestion was humbly made that a course on the novel be given. This was some thirty-five years ago! This dismay was not unique. One feels that the upholders of the genteel tradition regretted, out of a possible snobbism, the departure of the captains and the kings and the aristocratically prominent from the *dramatis personae* (the cast of characters) of most novels. For from the very start, the heroes and heroines of prose fiction were chosen from the ranks of the middle class that comprised its reading public. Even the names we recall seem of the earth, and the earthy:

Moll Flanders, Joseph Andrews, Elizabeth Bennett, Becky Sharp, David Copperfield—these culled from Defoe, Fielding, Jane Austen, Thackeray, and Dickens. True, there have been authors like Henry James, Edith Wharton, Marcel Proust, etc., who showed a marked preference for describing the upper classes in the modern world. But even the pleasure of momentarily dwelling in the leisurely environment of James or Wharton is scarcely equal to the thrill that the groundlings must have experienced at the sight of imaginary royalty in Shakespeare's plays.

There has also always been the lingering sentiment that to read non-fiction (biography, history, etc.) is potentially instructive and uplifting, that to read fiction is merely entertaining; and I refer to the French critic previously cited. A number of the texts in this volume are defenses, in some cases labored ones, of the basic morality of the novel: that it instructs as well as delights, that it shows virtue rewarded and vice properly punished, and so on. I might add that these moral apologies are encountered more frequently in the eighteenth and early nineteenth centuries, when novelists were still conscious of their second-class citizenship within the republic of letters. And the very nature of the entertainment could be also suspect, because of a pervasive convention in the novel used as a controlling device all the way from Richardson to Henry Miller: namely, love between the sexes. (This concern is actually rarer in great dramatic tragedy, for instance, than one would immediately believe.) Charges of immorality, mainly sexual, have been spasmodically levelled at the stage; such salvoes resound with far more sullen regularity against the novel, and we only have to think of the recent D. H. Lawrence and Henry Miller trials, where the issue hung on pornography vs. literature. Stage decorum, or even certain physical limitations, puts stringent curbs on how much of the manifestations of the "tender" passion may be actually presented to the eyes of the spectators. On the contrary, the novel offers an almost limitless franchise, even if this critic tends to feel that the best writers, like Stendhal, concerned with physical passion, have won their literary triumphs through suggestion rather than by description. (Take the great amorous moment in Stendhal's *The Red and the Black*: "When he left Madame de Rênal's bedroom a few hours later, we might have said in the style of the novel, that he had nothing more to desire.")

To its late appearance, its lack of classical forebears, the homely and ordinary quality of its customary themes, the possibility that it is mere entertainment (and often entertainment of a dubious moral nature), add two more strictures, and the earlier case against the novel as a serious form *seems* complete. The first is simple and takes little explaining. Novels are, or seem to be, easier to read than poetry or the drama. This same apparent facility even carries over to the student with the urge to write, who says, "Poetry is too complicated and difficult and since I don't know much about the technique of the stage, I think I'll write a novel." Such *apparent* simplicity of comprehension can be annoying to the teacher or critic who feels that his role as explicator is diminished. The feeblest instructor can always take recourse to metrics with poetry or stagecraft with the drama when the ideas come weakly. With the novel there is only the all-too transparent device of retelling the story. And related to this pedagogical stricture which has tended to thwart the novel's rise up Parnassus, to return to Miss Sharp's image, have been certain tendencies in professional literary criticism, roughly summed up in the phrase *New Criticism.* The lay reader need only know that this movement, dominant in America since the 1930's, stressed a kind of scientific objectivity toward the poetic statement (quite separate from and to the exclusion of other human and historical elements in the literary work); and that the leading exponents of the *New Criticism* generally dealt with poetry (mainly the short lyric), where they were happiest with their analysis. The amorphous quality of the novel, its frequent panoramic hugeness and scope, did not seem congenial to such study; its popularity among the uninitiated readers made it suspect for these most professional of critics. That the novel so often contains autobiographical elements makes it hard to study without some knowledge of the author or the world he labors to describe.

Our time has seen some of the highest mountain peaks finally conquered; and no wonder that classical Parnassus, figuratively speaking, has had the novel slowly scaling its flanks. Hence Miss Sharp's picture of the squatting novel perhaps needs to be modified, since much of what I have been discussing no longer appears valid to us in the 1960's.

For this tardy but real success there are at least two additional reasons, besides the obvious disappearance of many early strictures about the novel's respectability, morality, and so forth. The first has to do with novelists themselves, who starting in the mid-nineteenth century exhibited increasing self-consciousness about their craft, and lavished a technical care on their works that previously was associated with poets and playwrights. An examination of the contents of this volume, where the selections are presented chronologically, demonstrates this point. You will note that most of the earlier pieces mainly offer apologies for the novelist's "humble offering," or vouch for the authenticity of his sources and information after the manner of the pseudo-historian he often conceived himself to be. We can already detect a serious concern for the novel as an artifact by the time we

reach Stendhal discriminating between Sir Walter Scott and *La Princesse de Clèves* in 1830, thus showing an awareness of two distinct
schools of novel-writing, or Flaubert's letters in the 1850's with their
acute analysis of technical problems in writing *Madame Bovary*.

Allied to this preoccupation on the part of the writers has been
a similar swelling of interest on the part of the critics. How seldom,
if ever, did Sainte-Beuve or Matthew Arnold—to single out two of the
leading nineteenth-century critics—speak of novels! Yet today, a hundred years later, most of our best critics are turning their attention to
the genre, finding it truly to be what Henry James once described as
"the most independent, most elastic, most prodigious of literary forms."
I mentioned earlier that the advocates of the *New Criticism* did not
find the sheer mass of the novel congenial to their analytic tastes. Yet
even as the original bleak austerity of the first apostles of that movement has softened, so has the area of their critical scrutiny broadened.
And if no one work of criticism has yet achieved for the novel what
Aristotle's *Poetics* accomplished for the drama, one might still hazard
that various contemporary critics, by showing us the possibilities and
limitations of the form, are in effect forming a *Poetics* of the novel.

Here follow a few explanations for the selections and the method
by which they are presented. The chronological pattern was chosen for
its simplicity and also for those readers who like myself dislike indices:
here the reader can open the book, for example, at approximately
the mid-point and be fairly sure of stumbling upon a late nineteenth-
century author. It might have been desirable to group the writings
under categorical headings (*i.e.* historical antecedents, style, morality
and fiction, structural problems, story and plot, character, and so on).
But here the danger lies in over-simplifying the contents of any single
selection, if we rigorously force it into a specific classification. Miriam
Allott's fine book, *Novelists on the Novel* (London: Routledge &
Kegan Paul, 1959)—to which this editor is indebted—establishes
various categories and then cites relatively short passages to substan-
tiate the headings; its purpose, however, was somewhat different from
my own. As an aid to the reader, each item in the Table of Contents is
followed by a brief "argument" (after the fashion of certain seven-
teenth- and eighteenth-century writers) to suggest the main lines of
thought, although these phrases are intended in no way to suggest all
the ideas found in an essay, but merely point to the leading ones.

Excerpts annoy equally editors and readers, but obviously the
limitations of space dictated this necessity. In some instances the
pruning, hopefully judicious, may have damaged the trunk of the tree.
And while many of the critical commentaries represent a high level of

belle-lettristic excellence, it was not my purpose to select writings for their intrinsic literary merit, where deletions could seriously damage the organic unity of a text. A case may also be made for excising those portions of essays where relevance to strictly novelistic concerns seems remote. This is particularly true for some of the older writers. Thus, the entire *Foreword* of Balzac's *Human Comedy* is a fascinating document, while his eloquent testimony to the virtues of Throne and Altar and his lament *passim* for the damages wreaked by the Revolution of 1789 are ancillary to the main points he raises about the conception and execution of his monumental series of novels. Similarly, Zola throughout *The Experimental Novel* never tires of praising the indefatigable Dr. Claude Bernard, the workings of the "new" deterministic universe, and the wonders of the scientific method applied to all human activity. Yet we find more interest in his precise efforts to coördinate science and literature.

Perhaps more serious is the omission of those documents which more specialized readers might legitimately want to see included. As a lame defense, the editor at one time contemplated a volume three times as large as this: a prospect that rightfully caused the publishers to shudder. The aim finally was to strike a happy balance between the familiar and the unfamiliar; the old and the contemporary; English, American, and Continental authors—as well as to range over as many aspects of the novel as could conveniently be touched upon.

My own translations aimed more at accuracy of meaning than at felicity of expression. My intention was nicely expressed several centuries ago by the Elizabethan translator, Philemon Holland, when he pleaded: "If the sentence be not so concise, couched and knit together as the originall, loth I was to be obscure and dark: have I not englished everie word aptly?" It seemed far more important to concentrate on an exact and modern rendering of the ideas than on niceties of style and the subtler nuances of phrases.

I wish to express my gratitude to friends and colleagues who were generous with suggestions.

H. E. H.

ONTENTS

THE NOVELIST

Encased in talent like a uniform,
The rank of every poet is well known;
They can amaze us like a thunderstorm,
Or die so young, or live for years alone.

They can dash forward like hussars; but he
Must struggle out of his boyish gift and learn
How to be plain and awkward, how to be
One after whom none think it worth to turn.

For, to achieve his lightest wish, he must
Become the whole of boredom, subject to
Vulgar complaints like love, among the Just

Be just, among the Filthy filthy too,
And in his own weak person, if he can,
Must suffer dully all the wrongs of Man.

W. H. Auden (1907-   )

Reprinted from *The Collected Poetry of W. H. Auden*, by permission of Random House, Inc. Copyright 1940, by W. H. Auden.

The Preface to *Joseph Andrews*

A S IT IS possible the mere English reader may have a different idea of romance from the author of these little volumes, and may consequently expect a kind of entertainment not to be found, nor which was even intended, in the following pages, it may not be improper to premise a few words concerning this kind of writing, which I do not remember to have seen hitherto attempted in our language.

The Epic, as well as the Drama, is divided into tragedy and comedy. Homer, who was the father of this species of poetry, gave us a pattern of both these, though that of the latter kind is entirely lost; which Aristotle tells us, bore the same relation to comedy which his *Iliad* bears to tragedy. And perhaps, that we have no more instances of it among the writers of antiquity, is owing to the loss of this great pattern, which, had it survived, would have found its imitators equally with the other poems of this great original.

And farther, as this poetry may be tragic or comic, I will not scruple to say it may be likewise either in verse or prose: for though it wants one particular, which the critic enumerates in the constituent parts of an epic poem, namely metre; yet, when any kind of writing contains all its other parts, such as fable, action, characters, sentiments, and diction, and is deficient in metre only, it seems, I think, reasonable to refer it to the epic; at least, as no critic hath thought proper to range it under any other head, or to assign it a particular name to itself.

Thus the *Telemachus* of the Archbishop of Cambray appears to me of the epic kind, as well as the *Odyssey* of Homer; indeed, it is much fairer and more reasonable to give it a name common with that species from which it differs only in a single instance, than to confound it with those which it resembles in no other. Such are those voluminous works, commonly called Romances, namely, *Clelia, Cleopatra, Astræa, Cassandra,* the *Grand Cyrus,* and innumerable others, which contain, as I apprehend, very little instruction or entertainment.

Now, a comic romance is a comic epic poem in prose; differing from comedy, as the serious epic from tragedy: its action being more extended and comprehensive; containing a much larger circle of incidents, and introducing a greater variety of characters. It differs from the serious romance in its fable and action, in this; that as in the one these are grave and solemn, so in the other they are light and ridiculous: it differs in its characters by introducing persons of inferior rank, and consequently, of inferior manners, whereas the grave romance sets the highest before us: lastly, in its sentiments and diction; by preserving the ludicrous instead of the sublime. In the diction, I think, burlesque itself may be sometimes admitted; of which many instances will occur in this work, as in the description of the battles, and some other places, not necessary to be pointed out to the classical reader, for whose entertainment those parodies or burlesque imitations are chiefly calculated.

But though we have sometimes admitted this in our diction, we have carefully excluded it from our sentiments and characters; for these it is never properly introduced, unless in writings of the burlesque kind, which this is not intended to be. Indeed, no two species of writing can differ more widely than the comic and the burlesque; for as the latter is ever the exhibition of what is monstrous and unnatural, and where our delight, if we examine it, arises from the surprising absurdity, as in appropriating the manners of the highest to the lowest, or *è converso*; so in the former we should ever confine ourselves strictly to nature, from the just imitation of which will flow all the pleasure we can this way convey to a sensible reader. And perhaps there is one reason why a comic writer should of all others be the least excused for deviating from nature, since it may not be always so easy for a serious poet to meet with the great and the admirable; but life everywhere furnishes an accurate observer with the ridiculous.

I have hinted this little concerning burlesque, because I have often heard that name given to performances which have been truly of the comic kind, from the author's having sometimes admitted it in his diction only; which, as it is the dress of poetry, doth, like the dress of men, establish characters (the one of the whole poem, and the other of the whole man), in vulgar opinion, beyond any of their greater excellences: but surely, a certain drollery in style, where characters and sentiments are perfectly natural, no more constitutes the burlesque, than an empty pomp and dignity of words, where everything else is mean and low, can entitle any performance to the appellation of the true sublime.

And I apprehend my Lord Shaftesbury's opinion of mere burlesque agrees with mine, when he asserts, There is no such thing to be found in the writings of the ancients. But perhaps I have less abhorrence than he professes for it; and that, not because I have had some little success on the stage this way, but rather as it contributes more to exquisite mirth and laughter than any other; and these are probably more wholesome physic for the mind, and conduce better to purge away spleen, melancholy, and ill affections, than is generally imagined. Nay, I will appeal to common observation, whether the same companies are not found more full of good-humour and benevolence, after they have been sweetened for two or three hours with entertainments of this kind, than when soured by a tragedy or a grave lecture.

But to illustrate all this by another science, in which, perhaps, we shall see the distinction more clearly and plainly, let us examine the works of a comic history painter, with those performances which the Italians call Caricatura, where we shall find the true excellence of the former to consist in the exactest copying of nature; insomuch that a judicious eye instantly rejects anything *outré*, any liberty which the painter hath taken with the features of that *alma mater*; whereas in the Caricatura we allow all licence—its aim is to exhibit monsters, not men; and all distortions and exaggerations whatever are within its proper province.

Now, what Caricatura is in painting, Burlesque is in writing; and in the same manner the comic writer and painter correlate to each other. And here I shall observe, that, as in the former the painter seems to have the advantage; so it is in the latter infinitely on the side of the writer; for the Monstrous is much easier to paint than describe, and the Ridiculous to describe than paint.

And though perhaps this latter species doth not in either science so strongly affect and agitate the muscles as the other; yet it will be owned, I believe, that a more rational and useful pleasure arises to us from it. He who should call the ingenious Hogarth a burlesque painter, would, in my opinion, do him very little honour; for sure it is much easier, much less the subject of admiration, to paint a man with a nose, or any other feature, of a preposterous size, or to expose him in some absurd or monstrous attitude, than to express the affections of men on canvas. It hath been thought a vast commendation of a painter to say his figures seem to breathe; but surely it is a much greater and nobler applause, that they appear to think.

But to return. The Ridiculous only, as I have before said, falls within my province in the present work. Nor will some explanation of this word be thought impertinent by the reader, if he considers how wonderfully it hath been mistaken, even by writers who have professed it: for to what but such a mistake can we attribute the many attempts to ridicule the blackest villainies, and, what is yet worse, the most dreadful calamities? What could exceed the absurdity of an author, who should write the comedy of Nero, with the merry incident of ripping up his mother's belly? Or what would give a greater shock to humanity than an attempt to expose the miseries of poverty and distress to ridicule? And yet the reader will not want much learning to suggest such instances to himself.

Besides, it may seem remarkable, that Aristotle, who is so fond and free of definitions, hath not thought proper to define the Ridiculous. Indeed, where he tells us it is proper to comedy, he hath remarked that villainy is not its object: but he hath not, as I remember, positively asserted what is. Nor doth the Abbé Bellegarde, who hath written a treatise on this subject, though he shows us many species of it, once trace it to its fountain.

The only source of the true Ridiculous (as it appears to me) is affectation. But though it arises from one spring only, when we consider the infinite streams into which this one branches, we shall presently cease to admire at the copious field it affords to an observer. Now, affection proceeds from one of these two causes, vanity or hypocrisy: for as vanity puts us on affecting false characters, in order to purchase applause; so hypocrisy sets us on an endeavour to avoid censure, by concealing our vices under an appearance of their opposite virtues. And though these two causes are often confounded (for there is some difficulty in distinguishing them), yet, as they proceed from very different motives, so they are as clearly distinct in their operations: for indeed, the affectation which arises from vanity is nearer to truth than the other, as it hath not that violent repugnancy of nature to struggle with, which that of the hypocrite hath. It may be likewise noted, that affectation doth not imply an absolute negation of those qualities which are affected; and, therefore, though, when it proceeds from hypocrisy, it be nearly allied to deceit; yet when it comes from vanity only, it partakes of the nature of ostentation: for instance, the affectation of liberality in a vain man differs visibly from the same affectation in the avaricious; for though the vain man is not what he would appear, or hath not the virtue he affects, to the degree he would be thought to have it; yet it sits less awkwardly on him than on the avaricious man, who is the very reverse of what he would seem to be.

From the discovery of this affectation arises the Ridiculous, which always strikes the reader with surprise and pleasure; and that in a higher and stronger degree when the affectation arises from hypocrisy, than when from vanity; for to discover any one to be the exact reverse of what he affects, is more surprising, and consequently more ridiculous, than to find him a little deficient in the quality he desires the reputation of. I might observe that our Ben Jonson, who of all men understood the Ridiculous the best, hath chiefly used the hypocritical affectation.

Now, from affectation only, the misfortunes and calamities of life, or the imperfections of nature, may become the objects of ridicule. Surely he hath a very ill-framed mind who can look on ugliness, infirmity, or poverty, as ridiculous in themselves: nor do I believe any man living, who meets a dirty fellow riding through the streets in a cart, is struck with an idea of the Ridiculous from it; but if he should see the same figure descend from his coach and six, or bolt from his chair with his hat under his arm, he would then begin to laugh, and with justice. In the same manner, were we to enter a poor house and behold a wretched family shivering with cold and languishing with hunger, it would not incline us to laughter (at least we must have very diabolical natures if it would); but should be discover there a grate, instead of coals, adorned with flowers, empty plate or china dishes on the sideboard, or any other affectation of riches and finery, either on their persons or in their furniture, we might then indeed be excused for ridiculing so fantastical an appearance. Much less are natural imperfections the object of derision; but when ugliness aims at the applause of beauty, or lameness endeavours to display agility, it is then that these unfortunate circumstances, which at first moved our compassion, tend only to raise our mirth.

The poet carries this very far:

> None are for being what they are in fault,
> But for not being what they would be thought.

Where if the metre would suffer the word Ridiculous to close the first line, the thought would be rather more proper. Great vices are the proper objects of our detestation, smaller faults, of our pity; but affectation appears to me the only true source of the Ridiculous.

But perhaps it may be objected to me, that I have against my own rules introduced vices, and of a very black kind, into this work. To which I shall answer: first, that it is very difficult to pursue a series of human actions, and keep clear from them. Secondly, that the vices to be found here are rather the accidental consequences of some human frailty or foible, than causes habitually existing in the mind. Thirdly, that they are never set forth as the objects of ridicule, but detestation. Fourthly, that they are never the principal figure at that time on the scene: and, lastly, they never produce the intended evil.

Having thus distinguished *Joseph Andrews* from the productions of romance writers on the one hand and burlesque writers on the other, and given some few very short hints (for I intended no more) of this species of writing, which I have affirmed to be hitherto unattempted in our language; I shall leave to my good-natured reader to apply my piece to my observations, and will detain him no longer than with a word concerning the characters in this work.

And here I solemnly protest I have no intention to vilify or asperse any one; for though everything is copied from the book of nature, and scarce a character or action produced which I have not taken from my own observations and experience; yet I have used the utmost care to obscure the persons by such different circumstances, degrees, and colours, that it will be impossible to guess at them with any degree of certainty; and if it ever happens otherwise, it is only where the failure characterised is so minute, that it is a foible only which the party himself may laugh at as well as any other.

As to the character of Adams, as it is the most glaring in the whole, so I conceive it is not to be found in any book now extant. It is designed a character of perfect simplicity; and as the goodness of his heart will recommend him to the good-natured, so I hope it will excuse me to the gentleman of his cloth; for whom, while they are worthy of their sacred order, no man can possibly have a greater respect. They will therefore excuse me, notwithstanding the low adventures in which he is engaged, that I have made him a clergyman; since no other office could have given him so many opportunities of displaying his worthy inclinations.   (1742)

TOBIAS SMOLLETT (1721-1771)
The Preface to *Roderick Random*

F ALL KINDS of satire, there is none so entertaining and universally improving, as that which is introduced, as it were,
occasionally, in the course of an interesting story, which
brings every incident home to life; and, by representing familiar scenes
in an uncommon and amusing point of view, invests them with all
the graces of novelty, while nature is appealed to in every particular.

The reader gratifies his curiosity in pursuing the adventures of a person in whose favour he is prepossessed; he espouses his cause, he sympathises with him in distress; his indignation is heated against the authors of his calamity; the humane passions are inflamed; the contrast between dejected virtue and insulting vice appears with greater aggravation; and every impression having a double force on the imagination, the memory retains the circumstance, and the heart improves by the example. The attention is not tired with a bare catalogue of characters, but agreeably diverted with all the variety of invention; and the vicissitudes of life appear in their peculiar circumstances, opening an ample field for wit and humour.

Romance, no doubt, owes its origin to ignorance, vanity, and superstition. In the dark ages of the world, when a man had rendered himself famous for wisdom or valour, his family and adherents availed themselves of his superior qualities, magnified his virtues, and represented his character and person as sacred and supernatural. The vulgar easily swallowed the bait, implored his protection, and yielded the tribute of homage and praise even to adoration; his exploits were handed down to posterity with a thousand exaggerations; they were repeated as incitements to virtue; divine honours were paid, and altars erected to his memory, for the encouragement of those who attempted to imitate his example; and hence arose the heathen mythology, which is no other than a collection of extravagant romances. As learning advanced, and genius received cultivation, these stories were embellished with the graces of poetry; that they might the better recommend themselves to the attention, they were sung in public, at festivals, for the instruction and delight of the audience; and rehearsed before battle, as incentives to deeds of glory. Thus tragedy and the epic muse were born, and, in the progress of taste, arrived at perfection. It is no wonder that the ancients could not relish a fable in prose, after they had seen so many remarkable events celebrated in verse, by their best poets; we, therefore, find no romance among them, during the era of their excellence, unless the *Cyropædia* of Xenophon may be so called; and it was not till arts and sciences began to revive, after the irruption of the Barbarians into Europe, that anything of this kind appeared. But when the minds of men were debauched, by the imposition of priestcraft, to the most absurd pitch of credulity, the authors of romance arose, and, losing sight of probability, filled their performances with the most monstrous hyperboles. If they could not equal the ancient poets in point of genius, they were resolved to excel them in fiction, and apply to the wonder rather than the judgment of their readers. Accordingly they brought necromancy to their aid, and instead of supporting the character of their heroes by dignity of sentiment and practice, distinguished them by their bodily strength, activity, and extravagance of behaviour. Although nothing could be more ludicrous and unnatural than the figures they drew, they did not want patrons and admirers, and the world actually began to be infected with the spirit of knight-errantry, when Cervantes, by an inimitable piece of ridicule, reformed the taste of mankind, representing chivalry in the right point of view, and converting romance to purposes far more useful and entertaining, by making it assume the sock, and point out the follies of ordinary life.

The same method has been practised by other Spanish and French authors, and by none more successfully than by Monsieur

Le Sage, who, in his *Adventures of Gil Blas,* has described the knavery and foibles of life, with infinite humour and sagacity. The following sheets I have modelled on his plan, taking the liberty, however, to differ from him in the execution, where I thought his particular situations were uncommon, extravagant, or peculiar to the country in which the scene is laid. The disgraces of Gil Blas are, for the most part, such as rather excite mirth than compassion: he himself laughs at them; and his transitions from distress to happiness, or at least ease, are so sudden, that neither the reader has time to pity him, nor himself to be acquainted with affliction. This conduct, in my opinion, not only deviates from probability, but prevents that generous indignation which ought to animate the reader against the sordid and vicious disposition of the world.

I have attempted to represent modest merit struggling with every difficulty to which a friendless orphan is exposed, from his own want of experience, as well as from the selfishness, envy, malice, and base indifference of mankind. To secure a favourable prepossession, I have allowed him the advantages of birth and education, which, in the series of his misfortunes, will, I hope, engage the ingenuous more warmly in his behalf; and though I foresee that some people will be offended at the mean scenes in which he is involved, I persuade myself the judicious will not only perceive the necessity of describing those situations, to which he must of course be confined, in his low state, but also find entertainment in viewing those parts of life, where the humours and passions are undisguised by affectation, ceremony, or education; and the whimsical peculiarities of disposition appear as nature has implanted them. But I believe I need not trouble myself in vindicating a practice authorised by the best writers in this way, some of whom I have already named.

Every intelligent reader will, at first sight, perceive I have not deviated from nature in the facts, which are all true in the main, although the circumstances are altered and disguised, to avoid personal satire.

It now remains to give my reasons for making the chief personage of this work a North Briton; which are chiefly these: I could at a small expense bestow on him such education as I thought the dignity of his birth and character required, which could not possibly be obtained in England, by such slender means as the nature of my plan would afford. In the next place, I could represent simplicity of manners in a remote part of the kingdom, with more propriety than in any other place near the capital; and, lastly, the disposition of the Scots, addicted to travelling, justifies my conduct in deriving an adventurer from that country.

That the delicate reader may not be offended at the unmeaning oaths which proceed from the mouths of some persons in these memoirs, I beg leave to premise, that I imagined nothing could more effectually expose the absurdity of such miserable expletives, than a natural and verbal representation of the discourse in which they occur.   (1748)

JEAN-JACQUES ROUSSEAU (1712-1778)
From the Preface to the Second Edition of *Julie, or the New Héloïse*

Discussion about Novels between the Editor and a Man of Letters

 HERE is your manuscript. I have read the whole thing.

    R.   The whole thing? I mean, you can rely on having few imitators.

N.   *Vel duo, vel nemo.*

R.   *Turpe et miserabile.* But I want a positive judgment.

N.   I don't dare.

R.   You dare everything by that one word alone. Explain yourself.

N.   My judgment of it depends on the answer you are going to give me. Is this correspondence real or fictitious?

R.   I don't see the importance of this at all. In order to say whether a book is good or bad, who cares about knowing how it was created?

N.   It matters a great deal as far as the former is concerned. A portrait always has its price, provided that it bears a resemblance, no matter how odd the original may be. But in an imaginary picture, every human figure must have traits common to men, or the picture is worthless. Both of these presumed to be good, there still is this difference: that the portrait is of interest to few people, the picture must please the entire public.

R.   I follow you. If the letters are portraits, they will be of no interest; if they are pictures, they imitate badly. Is that it?

N.   Precisely.

R.   Thus I extract all your answers before you answer me yourself. For the rest, since I can't give you satisfaction for your question, we'll have to pass over it to resolve my own. Let us suppose the worst: my Julie. . . .

N.   Oh! If she ever lived!

R.   Well?

N. But certainly this was not merely fiction.

R. Suppose it is.

N. In that case, I know of nothing more tedious. These letters are not letters at all; this novel is no novel at all; the characters are people from another world. . . .

N. A Christian woman, a pious woman who doesn't even teach her children the catechism, who dies without wishing to pray to God; yet whose death provides a pastor with moral edification and converts an atheist. . . .

R. Sir!

N. As for the interest, it is for those who don't count, it is worthless. Not one wicked action, not one bad man who causes the virtuous to be fearful; events that are so natural and so simple that they are too much so; nothing unforeseen, no theatrical surprises. Everything is anticipated a long time in advance; everything occurs as it has been anticipated. Is it worth the trouble to keep account of what everyone can see everyday in his house or in his neighbor's?

R. That's because you want ordinary people and unusual events. I think I prefer the opposite. Moreover, you judged what you have read as if it were a novel. It isn't one at all: you said so yourself. It's a collection of letters. . . .

N. Which aren't really letters at all. I think I also said that. What an epistolary style! How stilted it is! So many exclamations! So much affectation! What pomposity in telling about the most ordinary things! What big words for such petty reasoning! Rarely any sense, any exactness: never any finesse, strength, or profundity. A diction that is always up in the clouds, and thoughts that always creep on the ground. If your characters are in nature, admit that their style is little that is natural.

R. I have to admit, that from your point of view, it must seem this way to you.

N. Do you think that the public will see it otherwise? And haven't you asked my opinion? . . .

R. . . . I return to my letters. If you read them as the work of an author who wants to be pleasing or who persists in writing, they are detestable. But take them for what they are, and judge them within their own class. Two or three simple young persons, but impressionable, discuss among themselves their hearts' concerns; they do not dream of dazzling each other's eyes; they know and love each other mutually so much that self-esteem has nothing to do with them. They are children; do they think as grown men? They are foreigners; do they write correctly? They are solitary souls; do they know the

world and society? Replete with the one sentiment that occupies
them, they are in a frenzy and think themselves philosophizing. Do
you want them to know how to observe, judge, and reflect? They know
nothing about all that; they know how to love; they relate everything
to their passion. Is the importance that they give to their mad ideas
any less amusing than all the wit they might display? They talk of
everything; they are wrong about everything; they know nothing but
themselves; yet in making themselves known to each other, they fall
in love. Their errors are worth more than the knowledge of the wise
man; their honest hearts, even in their mistakes, bear throughout the
prejudices of a forever confident and a forever betrayed goodness.
They do not accept discouraging truths; finding nowhere what they
feel, they fall back upon themselves, creating for themselves a little
world that differs from ours. There they make up a spectacle that is
truly new. . . .   (1761)

(Translated by H. E. Hugo)

DENIS DIDEROT (1713-1784)
From *In Praise of Richardson*

BY A novel, up to now has been meant a tissue of chimerical
and frivolous events, the reading of which was dangerous
both for taste and for manners. I wish indeed that we might
find another name for Richardson's works, which elevate the mind,
touch the soul, exude throughout them a love for the good, and which
also are called novels.

Everything that Montaigne, Charron, La Rochefoucauld and
Nicole put into maxims, Richardson has put into action. But an intelligent man who reads Richardson's works reflectively remakes most
of the moralists' sentences; and yet with all these sentences he would
not retouch one page of Richardson.

A maxim is an abstract and general rule of conduct whose
application we are left to make. By itself it does not implant any
sense-impression on our minds; but if we see someone who acts, we
put ourselves in his place or near him, we get excited for or against
him; we identify ourselves with his role, if he is virtuous; we part
from him with indignation if he is unjust and vicious. Who has not
shuddered at the character of a Lovelace, a Tomlinson? Who has not
been struck with horror by the pathetic and genuine manner, the
candid and dignified way, and the profound skill by which the former
plays all the virtues? Who has not said to himself, from the bottom
of his heart, that he would have to flee from society to take refuge

in the depths of the forest, if there were many men of similar dissimulation?

O Richardson! Despite ourselves, we take part in your books; we mix in the conversation; approve, blame, admire, become irritated, and get angry. How often have I surprised myself, like children that we take to the theater for the first time, by crying out: "Don't believe him, he is deceiving you! . . . If you go there, you are lost!" My soul was held in a state of perpetual agitation. How good I was! How wise I was! How happy I was about myself! When I finished reading, I was like a man at the end of a trip undertaken to do good.

In the space of a few hours I had undergone a vast number of situations, scarcely available throughout the length of the longest life imaginable. I heard genuine discussions about the passions; I watched self-interest and self-esteem played and judged in a hundred different ways; I became the spectator for a multitude of incidents; I felt that I had acquired experience.

This author never makes the blood flow along the wainscoting. He never carries you off to distant lands, nor does he expose you to be eaten by savages. He never shuts himself up in clandestine areas of debauchery, nor does he stray in the regions of fairy-land. The background is the world in which we live; the foundation of his drama is truthful; his actors are completely real; his characters are chosen from the core of society; the events are to be found amid the customs of all civilized countries; the passions he depicts are those that I myself feel; the same things are there that move my own, and they have the energy that I understand. What his characters endure and what afflicts them are the same kind that unceasingly trouble me; he shows me the general pattern of the things that hem me in. Without his craftsmanship—my troubled soul yielding toward chimerical tendencies —the illusion would be merely momentary and the impression weak and transitory. . . .

. . . I still recall the first time that Richardson's works fell into my hands. I was in the country. How delightfully this reading moved me! I felt my happiness was curtailed with each page. Soon I underwent the same sensation that men in an excellent business must feel, having lived together for a long time, when they are about to separate. When I finished, it seemed to me suddenly that I was all alone.

He carries the torch down to the bottom of the cave; he teaches us to discern the subtle and dishonest motives that hide and mask themselves behind other honest motives, and then speedily show themselves to be the prime ones. He puffs on the sublime-looking phantom who appears at the entrance to the cave, and we are aware of the hideous Moor behind the mask.

He knows how to make the passions talk, occasionally with the violence they own when they cannot restrain themselves, other times with that artificial and moderate tone they affect. . . .

. . . O Richardson, Richardson! In my eyes the only man, I will always be your reader! Compelled by pressing needs, if my friend became poverty-stricken, if my mediocre fortune did not suffice to give my children the necessary wherewithal for their education, I would sell my books; but you would remain, you would stay on the same shelf with Moses, Homer, Euripides and Sophocles; and I would read you each in turn.

The more beautiful one's soul is, the more one's taste is exquisite and pure, the more one understands nature, the more one loves the truth—the more one values Richardson's works.

I have heard my author reproached for his details which some call excessively lengthy. How these reproaches annoy me!

Bad luck to the man of genius who breaks down the barriers that custom and time have prescribed for artistic production, and who tramples down protocol and its formulae with his feet! For many a long year after his death he will be forgotten, until the justice that he deserves is rendered him.

However, let's be fair. For people carried away by a thousand distractions, where the twenty-four hours of the day are not enough for the amusements they are accustomed to indulge in, Richardson's books may seem too long. For the same reason these people no longer have any opera, and incessantly they only play detached scenes from comedy and tragedy at the other theaters.

My dear fellow citizens, if Richardson's novels seem too long for you, why don't you abridge them? Be consistent. You scarcely go to see a tragedy save for the last act. Jump immediately to the last twenty pages of *Clarissa*.

Richardson's details are displeasing and must be so for a frivolous and dissipated man; they are meant for the quiet and solitary man, who knows the vanity of noise and worldly amusements, and who likes to dwell in a shadowy retreat, beneficially to cultivate his compassion in the silence. . . .

. . . I've often had the notion while dreaming about Richardson's works, that I'd bought an old chateau; that one day going through the rooms, I noticed a cupboard in the corner that had not been opened for a long time; and that having broken into it, I discovered the letters of Clarissa and Pamela all in a jumble. After reading a few, with what eagerness I would have sorted them by order of their dates! How chagrined I would have felt, if there had been any missing! Can you imagine what I would have suffered if some bold hand (I almost say sacrilegious) had blotted out a line?

You who have only read Richardson's works in your elegant French translation, and who think you know him, are mistaken.

You do not know Lovelace, you do not know Clementine, you do not know the unfortunate Clarissa; you do not know Miss Howe, her dear and sweet Miss Howe, because you have never seen her hair in confusion and stretched out on her friend's coffin, her arms writhing, lifting up her tear-filled eyes to heaven, filling the Harlowe house with her piercing cries and hurling her imprecations against the entire cruel family; you do not know the effect of these circumstances which your small taste would eliminate, since you have not heard the dismal sound of the parish bells, borne by the wind to the Harlowe house to arouse soothing remorse in those stony souls; since you have not seen the shuddering they manifested at the sound of the wagon-wheels bearing the corpse of their victim. Then the mournful silence reigning in their midst was broken by the sobbing of the father and mother; then the real torture of these wicked souls began, then the serpents aroused themselves within their hearts and gnawed them. Happy those who are able to weep! . . .

. . . Richardson's works will please everybody more or less, always and everywhere; but the number of readers who will reap the whole reward will never be great. You need a very firm taste; and furthermore, the variety of events is so great, the relationships so multiplied, the behaviour is so complicated; there are so many facts given to you and so many kept back, and then so many characters and types of character! Scarcely had I gone through a few pages of *Clarissa* when I counted fifteen or sixteen characters. Soon the number doubled. There are about forty in *Grandison*; but what fills me with amazement is that each has his own ideas, expression, and manner; and these ideas, expression, and manner vary according to the circumstances, interests and passions even as you see the various aspects of the passions change on the same face. A man of good taste would never take a letter by Mme. Norton for a letter written by one of Clarissa's aunts, or a letter by one aunt for that of another or by Mme. Howe, nor a note by Mme. Howe for a note by Mme. Harlowe; even though it might be that these characters are in the same situation, filled with the same feelings, relative to the same thing. In this immortal book, like nature in springtime, you never find two leaves of the same greenness. What an immense variety of subtlety! If it is hard for the reader to grasp them, how much harder it must have been for the author to discover and describe them!

Oh Richardson! I would dare to say that the truest history is full of lies, and your novel is full of truth. History depicts a few individuals; you paint the human race. History attributes to a few individuals what they have never said nor done; everything you attribute to men has been said and done; history merely encompasses a part of the duration of time and a small point on the earth's surface; you encompass all times and all places. The human heart which ever has been, is, and shall be the same, is a model you have copied. If we taxed a better historian with severe criticism, is there any who could sustain it better than you? In this regard, I again dare to say that history is often a poor novel; and that the novel, as you have made it, is good history. Oh nature's painter! You never lie. . . .   (1761)

(Translated by H. E. Hugo)

FANNY (Francis) BURNEY (1752-1840)
Author's Preface to *Evelina*

IN THE republic of letters, there is no member of such inferior rank, or who is so much disdained by his brethren of the quill, as the humble Novelist; nor is his fate less hard in the world at large, since, among the whole class of writers, perhaps not one can be named of which the votaries are more numerous but less respectable.

Yet, while in the annals of those few of our predecessors, to whom this species of writing is indebted for being saved from contempt, and rescued from depravity, we can trace such names as Rousseau, Johnson,[1] Marivaux, Fielding, Richardson, and Smollett, no man need blush at starting from the same post, though many, nay most men, may sigh at finding themselves distanced.

The following letters are presented to the public—for such, by novel writers, novel readers will be called,—with a very singular mixture of timidity and confidence, resulting from the peculiar situation of the editor; who, though trembling for their success from a consciousness of their imperfections, yet fears not being involved in their disgrace, while happily wrapped up in a mantle of impenetrable obscurity.

To draw characters from nature, though not from life, and to mark the manners of the times, is the attempted plan of the following letters. For this purpose, a young female, educated in the most secluded retirement, makes, at the age of seventeen, her first appearance

[1] However superior the capacities in which these great writers deserve to be considered, they must pardon me that, for the dignity of my subject, I have to rank the authors of *Rasselas* and *Eloïse* as Novelists.

upon the great and busy stage of life; with a virtuous mind, a cultivated understanding, and a feeling heart, her ignorance of the forms, and inexperience in the manners, of the world, occasion all the little incidents which this volume records, and which form the natural progression of the life of a young woman of obscure birth, but conspicuous beauty, for the first six months after her ENTRANCE INTO THE WORLD.

Perhaps were it possible to effect the total extirpation of novels, our young ladies in general, and boarding-school damsels in particular, might profit by their annihilation; but since the distemper they have spread seems incurable, since their contagion bids defiance to the medicine of advice or reprehension, and since they are found to baffle all the mental art of physic, save what is prescribed by the slow regimen of Time, and bitter diet of Experience, surely all attempts to contribute to the number of those which may be read, if not with advantage, at least without injury, ought rather to be encouraged than contemned.

Let me, therefore, prepare for disappointment those who, in the perusal of these sheets, entertain the gentle expectation of being transported to the fantastic regions of Romance, where Fiction is coloured by all the gay tints of luxurious Imagination, where Reason is an outcast, and where the sublimity of the Marvellous, rejects all aid from sober Probability. The heroine of these memoirs, young, artless, and inexperienced, is

No faultless Monster, that the world ne'er saw,

but the offspring of Nature, and of Nature in her simplest attire.

In all the Arts, the value of copies can only be proportioned to the scarceness of originals; among sculptors and painters, a fine statue, or a beautiful picture, of some great master, may deservedly employ the imitative talents of younger and inferior artists, that their appropriation to one spot, may not wholly prevent the more general expansion of their excellence; but, among authors, the reverse is the case, since the noblest productions of literature are almost equally attainable with the meanest. In books, therefore, imitation cannot be shunned too sedulously; for the very perfection of a model which is frequently seen, serves but more forcibly to mark the inferiority of a copy.

To avoid what is common, without adopting what is unnatural, must limit the ambition of the vulgar herd of authors; however zealous, therefore, my veneration of the great writers I have mentioned, however I may feel myself enlightened by the knowledge of Johnson, charmed with the eloquence of Rousseau, softened by the pathetic powers of Richardson, and exhilarated by the wit of Fielding, and humour of Smollett; I yet presume not to attempt pursuing the same ground which they have tracked; whence, though they may have cleared the weeds, they have also culled the flowers, and though they have rendered the path plain, they have left it barren.

The candour of my readers, I have not the impertinence to doubt, and to their indulgence, I am sensible I have no claim; I have, therefore, only to entreat, that my own words may not pronounce my condemnation, and that what I have here ventured to say in regard to imitation, may be understood, as it is meant, in a general sense, and not be imputed to an opinion of my own originality, which I have not the vanity, the folly, or the blindness, to entertain.

Whatever may be the fate of these letters, the editor is satisfied they will meet with justice; and commits them to the press, though hopeless of fame, yet not regardless of censure.   (1778)

MADAME DE STAËL (1766-1817)

The Conclusion from *Essay on the Art of Fiction*

BJECTIONS have always been made against novels about love, that they describe passions that are then engendered in the reader, and that there are times in life when such a danger would triumph over any other beneficial results. Yet such a disadvantage is not true of novels where the subjects are entirely different passions. If we trace from its inception the apparent symptoms of some dangerous tendency, we may be able to guard both ourselves and others from it. A person often possesses ambition, pride, and avarice without being aware that he has succumbed to them. Love waxes when it observes its own emotions. The best expedient for combating the other passions is to reveal them. If their traits, their power, their methods and their results were revealed and popularized, so to speak, via novels as a history of love, we would enjoy firmer rules and more delicate principles in both society and in our daily conduct. Like novels, purely philosophical writings can predict and relate in detail all the possible nuances of action, but the dramatization of an ethical situation still has a great advantage. The latter can engender feelings of indignation, spiritual exaltation, sweet melancholy—various results of romantic situations—and culminate by supplementing experience. The impression resembles our bearing witness to real facts; yet since it is constantly aimed at a single goal, it misleads the mind less than does the inconsistent picture of the events that surround us. Finally, there exist those for whom duty has never held sway over their passions, and for whom we might ward off criminal tendencies by developing within them the opportunity for self-amelioration. These persons who are only capable of attaining humanity by dint of this emotional faculty, which is so to speak the physical pleasure of the soul, are doubtlessly little worthy of our esteem. Yet the effect of tales that are touching, if they became popular, might guarantee our not meeting creatures in our country whose characters make for the most unbelievable moral problem of all time. Any gradation from the known to the unknown breaks off when we come to conceive the impulses that have guided France's executioners. It must be that no trace of humanity, no recollection of a single instance of pity, no flexibility of mind, can have developed in their souls through any kind of situation or kind of writing, to make them capable of such unending cruelty—alien to all of nature's impulses—and which has given mankind its first unrestricted idea, the perfect idea of crime.

There are works like Pope's *Epistle from Abelard*, *Werther*, *The Portuguese Letters*, etc.; the world possesses a work, the *New Héloïse*, where the chief value is the eloquence of passion, and where no matter how moral the aim may be, what stands above all is the omnipotence of the heart. We cannot classify such a type of novel. This century has seen a soul and a genius capable of achieving it. It cannot be called a genre, nor can it be a goal to be aimed at. But would you like to prohibit such miracles of language, such profound utterances that satisfy all the impulses of passionate persons? Enthusiastic readers of this kind of talent are few in number, but these works are always beneficial for their admirers. Let fiery and sensitive souls enjoy them: still they cannot express their feelings in words. The emotions that excite them are scarcely to be understood and are ceaselessly condemned. These readers think themselves alone in the world; and they would soon despise their very temperament which isolates them, were it not that a few melancholy and passionate works cause them to hear a voice in life's desert, and make them discover a few rays of sunshine in solitude which have been lost to them in society. Their pleasure in retirement puts them at rest, far from futile attempts at deceiving hopes. When the entire universe, remote from this unhappy soul, is in a state of disturbance, an eloquent and tender piece of writing remains by him like the most faithful friend, and a friend who understands him the best. Yes, that book is the right one that provides only one day of distraction from sadness; it serves the very best of mankind. No doubt we can find troubles that stem from defects in character; but there are so many troubles that arise from either having superior intelligence or sensibility of the heart; so many we could better support if we owned these qualities to a lesser degree! Even before we become acquainted, I respect the heart that suffers; I am delighted with fiction where the sole intent is to assuage the heart by capturing its attention. In this life that must be endured rather than felt, he who can distract a man from himself and from others, who can suspend the course of passions to replace them with independent delights, would be the donor of the only true happiness of which human nature is capable, if the influence of his talent might last forever. (1795)

(Translated by H. E. Hugo)

FRIEDRICH SCHLEGEL (1772-1829)
From A *Letter on the Novel*

T THE beginning of our last conversation you maintained that Friedrich Richter's novels were not really novels but rather a medley of sickly wit; that the fable was meagre, too poorly represented to pass for a fable, and only vaguely to be guessed at; that even if his plots were all taken together and reduced to sheer narrative, they would at best amount to confessions; and that the subjectivity of the man was much too conspicuous and a dubious one to boot.

I pass over the last point, since it is in turn but a matter of subjectivity. The "medley of sickly wit" I admit, but declare myself in favor of it and maintain boldly that such grotesques and confessions are the only remaining romantic productions in our unromantic age.

Let me on this occasion set forth what has been on my mind for a long time.

I have often been amazed and secretly enraged at the mass of books continually brought to your house by the servant. How can you even touch those filthy volumes with your hands? And how can you permit those rude and confused phrases to enter through your eyes into the sanctuary of your soul? To waste your fancy by the hour on persons with whom to converse face to face you would be ashamed! Truly, it serves nothing but to kill time and spoil the imagination! Nearly all the bad books from Fielding to La Fontaine you have read! Ask yourself what profit you have derived. Your own memory despises the vile stuff which an unfortunate juvenile habit has made you to crave, and what must be so industriously procured is promptly forgotten again.

But perhaps you will recall that there was a time when you loved Sterne, when you took pleasure in adopting his vein, half imitating, half burlesquing it. I still have some playful little notes from you in that manner, which I shall carefully preserve. Sterne's humor, then, must have left a distinct impression on you. It constituted a form, a clever if not an ideally beautiful one, and thereby engaged your fancy. An impression thus clearly retained, and thus capable of being used by us in jest or in earnest, is never lost. And is there anything more thoroughly valuable than that which in any way serves to excite or to nourish the play of our spiritual refinement?

You yourself are surely aware how pure the pleasure you took in Sterne's humor was, how totally different in nature from the mere suspense of curiosity which a thoroughly bad book will at times elicit from us at the very moment when we recognize it as such. Ask yourself, then, whether your enjoyment was not related to that derived from the contemplation of the kind of witty and playful painting which we call arabesque.

In the event that you cannot pronounce yourself altogether indifferent to Sterne's sentimentality, I am sending you a book of which I wish to inform you, however, lest you refer to it without circumspection in the presence of strangers, that it has the misfortune, or good fortune, to be somewhat infamous. It is Diderot's *Fataliste*. I think that it will please you, and that you will find in it an abundance of wit free of all sentimental admixtures. It shows a sensible plan and sure workmanship. Without exaggeration I can call it a work of art. I admit it is no sublime poetry but only—an arabesque. Precisely for this reason, however, it is of no mean pretensions to my interest, for I regard the arabesque as a distinct and fundamental poetic form or manner of expression. . . .

I have been engaged in delineating certain characteristic distinctions between the Romantic and the Classical. I would ask you, however, not to conclude from this automatically that I regard the Romantic as completely identical with the Modern. I think it differs from the latter in about the same way in which the paintings of Raphael and Correggio differ from the copperplate engravings currently in fashion. To get a clear impression of the difference, read *Emilia Galotti* and then compare it to Shakespeare, in whom I would locate the true center, the very core of the romantic imagination. There, among the earlier of the modern writers, in Shakespeare, in Cervantes, in Italian poetry, in the age of chivalry, of love and fairy legend, whence we derive both the matter and the name, there I seek and find the truly Romantic. That age has hitherto remained the only one capable of providing a serious antithesis to the great works of classical antiquity; only these forever unfading blossoms of fantasy are worthy to wreathe the statues of the ancient gods. And certain it is that the best of modern poetry tends, in the spirit, and even in the manner, in their direction—unless perhaps it showed signs of a return to the antique. Just as our poetic art began with the romance, so that of the Greeks both arose from, and again dissolved into, the epic.

There is only this difference, that the Romantic is not so much a genre as it is an element of all poetry, which may be more or less prominent, but must never be wholly absent. If you grant me these premises, you will see why I must postulate that all poetry should be romantic; why, on the contrary, I detest the romance as soon as it claims to be a specific genre.

You demanded yesterday, when the dispute grew most lively, that I give a definition of the novel, and you did so with an air as though you could not expect to receive a satisfactory answer. I do not think this problem altogether unsolvable. A romance (or novel) is a romantic book. You will call this a meaningless tautology. But I should like, first of all, to call your attention to the basic fact that a book is generally regarded as a complete work, an independent whole. Consequently, it differs from a play, which is designed to be seen, whereas the novel was from the beginning designed to be read. From this fundamental distinction we can deduce almost all the differences in the manner of representation of the two forms. The play, too, like all poetic art, should be romantic, but a romance it can be called only in the sense of "applied romance." In the novel, on the contrary, mere dramatic continuity of the fable is as yet by no means sufficient to create an integrated work of art—unless there be a relation of the whole composition to a unity higher than that of the letter (which can be, and often is, transcended): a unity of idea, a spiritual center. Apart from this, there is so little difference between the drama and the novel that in fact drama so radical and historical as, *e.g.*, Shakespeare treats it, is the very foundation of the novel.

You maintained, indeed, that the romance was directly related to the narrative, even to the epic, genre. In answer to this, I may remind you, however, that a song can be just as romantic as a story. I cannot even imagine a novel other than composed of narrative, song, and other forms. Cervantes never wrote otherwise, and even so generally prosaic a writer as Boccaccio decorated his collection with a setting of songs. There may be novels where no elements of this kind do or can exist. The reason for that, however, is to be sought in the character solely of the individual work, not of the genre. Such a novel constitutes merely an exception to the rule. So much by way of preliminaries; my real objection to your argument is this: nothing is more contrary to the epic style than that the influence of personal moods should become in the least visible, let alone that the author should abandon himself so completely to his humor, and play with it so freely, as we see it happen in the most admirable novels.

Subsequently you must have either forgotten or abandoned your original proposition, when you would have it that all these classifications led to nothing, that there was only one poetry, and that the sole consideration was whether something was beautiful—only pedants would ask for labels.

You know what I think of those classifications that are always being bandied about. Nonetheless I realize the absolute necessity for every virtuoso to confine himself to a very distinct purpose; and in my historical researches I have hit upon some archetypal forms which admit of no further analysis. Thus, to cite an example, it appears to me that in the sphere of romantic poetry even novellas and fairy tales are, as it were, infinitely opposed to one another. And I should like nothing better than to see an artist rejuvenate each of these genres by reducing them to their archetypes.

If such exemplars saw the light of day, I would be encouraged to develop a theory of the novel that would be a theory in the truest sense of the word: a spiritual intuition of the object, with a mind calm, serene, and undivided, as is fitting when we contemplate the momentous play of divine ideas in festive joy. Such a theory of the novel would have to be in itself a romance, able to reproduce each eternal tone of fantasy in a fantastical way, and to render the chaos of the world of chivalry more confused. There the ancient beings would live in new and different shapes; there would the sacred shade of Dante rise from his underworld, Laura walk celestially before our eyes, and Shakespeare hold familiar discourse with Cervantes; and there Sancho once again would jest with Don Quixote.

Those would be true arabesques, and arabesques I maintained, in the beginning of my letter, to be, along with confessions, the only romantic products of nature of our age.

That I should have included the confessions will no longer appear strange to you once you have admitted that true history is the basis of all romantic poetry; and if you but reflect on it, your own recollection will easily convince you that the best in the best of novels is nothing more than a personal confession of the author, more or less disguised, the harvest of his experience, the quintessence of his singularity.

Although none of the so-called novels are in the least reconcilable to my ideas of romantic form, I value them nonetheless exactly according to the measure of personal observation and represented reality they contain. In this respect I can welcome even the successors of Richardson, no matter how misguided their efforts may be. We learn from a Cecilia Beverly at least how one went about being bored in London at the time when it was fashionable to do so, and how a lady was expected out of sheer delicacy finally to fall prostrate and bruise herself bloody. The swearing, the squires, etc., in Fielding appear as though directly taken from life, and the [*Vicar of*] *Wakefield* gives us a deep insight into a country parson's view of the world; indeed, if Olivia could only have regained her lost innocence at the end, this novel would perhaps be the best of all the English novels.

But how niggardly and piecemeal is the little bit of reality doled out in all these books! Compared to them, would not any traveller's tale, any collection of letters, any autobiographical account make a better novel to him who reads in a romantic way?

Especially confessions tend to transform themselves into arabesques in the majority of cases, whereas novels rise to this level, if at all, only at the end, when wealth and credit return to the bankrupt merchants, when the starvelings are fed, the amiable knaves become honest, and the fallen virgins regain their virtue.

The *Confessions* of Rousseau are, in my opinion, a first-rate novel, the *Héloïse* but a very middling one.

I am sending you here the autobiography of a famous man, which, as far as I know, you have not yet seen: the *Memoirs of Gibbon*. It is an infinitely cultured and an infinitely droll book. It will meet you halfway—indeed, the comic novel latent in it is almost full-fledged. The grandeur of these historical periods will convey to your eyes, as vividly as you could wish, the Englishman, the gentleman, the virtuoso, the scholar, the bachelor, the well-bred elegant in all his graceful absurdity. You can search through many bad books, and many insignificant people, before you will find so much laughing-matter gathered together in one spot.   (1800)

(A *Letter on the Novel* is part of the *Conversation about Poetry*. Translated by Ernst Bernhardt-Kabisch.)

MARQUIS DE SADE (1740-1814)

From A *Sketch about Novels*

E NAME as a novel a *fictitious* work composed out of the most extraordinary adventures in men's lives.

But why does this genre bear the name of novel [roman]?

Among what people should we seek its origins, and who are the most famous?

And finally, what are the rules we should follow in order to attain perfection in writing a novel?

Here are the three questions we propose to treat. Let us start with the etymology of the word.

The races of antiquity teach us nothing about the name for this composition. It seems to me that we have merely to apply ourselves in discovering what the name has come to mean for us, and what meaning we still use.

As we all know, *Romance* language was a mixture of Celtic and Latin idioms employed during the first two generations of our monarchs. It is quite reasonable to suppose that the works of the genre we now discuss, written in this tongue, derived their name from the language. We ought to say *"une Romane"* when we explain a work concerned with amorous adventures, even as we speak of a *Romance* when we speak of plaintive ballads of the same sort. It is fruitless to seek another etymology for this word. Since common sense provides nothing else, it is simplest to adopt this one.

Let us pass to the second question. *Among what people should we seek its origins, and who are the most famous?*

Common belief says that we find it with the Greeks. From thence it passed over to the Moors to be borrowed by the Spaniards; next to our troubadours from whom our authors of chivalric romances received it.

Much as I respect this chain of influences, and indeed I have often accepted it, still I am loathe to accept it rigorously. Surely such a relationship must have been difficult during those centuries when travelling was seldom undertaken and any communication was faulty. Certain customs, fashions, and tastes are never transmitted; inherent to all mankind, they are born quite naturally to every man. Wherever men exist we find traces of these same customs, fashions, and tastes. . . .

Before broaching our third and last question, *"What are the rules of the art of writing a novel?"* it seems to me that we ought to answer the eternal objection of certain peevish persons who—wanting to set themselves forth as being moral, when often their hearts are far from this condition—inquire without respite: *what good are novels?*

What good are they, oh you perverse hypocrites? After all, you are the ones who ask this ridiculous question. They are useful because they describe you, and describe you the way you are—you proud types who wish to flee from the painter's brush because you fear what the results might be; the novel being, if I make myself clear, *a picture of secular customs* and therefore as essential as is history, for the philosopher who wishes to understand mankind. For the latter's graving-tool only engraves men after they reveal themselves, and then they are no longer really themselves. Ambition and pride hide their faces with a mask that only displays these two passions to us and not the man himself. On the contrary, the paint-brush of the novel gets inside, grabs a man when he relinquishes this mask, to sketch him more interestingly, which is to say more genuinely. Here is the usefulness of novels. Oh you cold censors who do not like novels, you are like that legless cripple who said, "Why do people paint portraits?"

Therefore if it is true that the novel has some utility, let us not be afraid to trace here some of the principles that we deem necessary to bring this genre to perfection. I understand perfectly well that it will be hard for me to accomplish this task without handing out weapons to be used against me: do I not become doubly guilty of not having *done well*, if I prove that I know what has to be done to *do well*. Very well! Let us leave these foolish considerations, and may they sacrifice themselves to the love of art.

The most essential knowledge that the novel demands is most certainly that of the heart. Hence all the well-read people will doubtlessly agree with us about this important knowledge, at the same time saying that we only acquire it through *unhappiness* and *voyaging*. You have to have seen people from every country to understand them well, and you have to have been their victim in order to know how to appreciate them. The hand of someone unfortunate, by praising the character of the man who crushes him, places him at the proper distance he must be in order that men can be studied. He views them from there, the way a passenger watches the waves furiously breaking on the reef where the storm has thrown him. But no matter in what situation nature or fate may have put him, if he wants to know mankind, he should speak but little when he is with them; you learn nothing when you talk, you only learn when you listen; and that is why babblers are usually fools.

Oh you who wish to travel down this thorny career! Do not lose sight of the fact that the novelist is a man born from nature; nature made him in order that he might be its painter. If he doesn't become his mother's lover as soon as she has brought him into the world, may he never write anything, and we shall never read him. But if he experiences this burning thirst to paint everything, if he partly opens nature's womb with a shudder to find his art there and pulls his models thereout, if he is feverish with his talent and has the enthusiasm of genius, may he follow the hand that guides him; he has comprehended man, and he will paint him. Overcome by his imagination, to which he surrenders, may he embellish all that he sees: the fool plucks the rose and picks it to pieces, the man of genius breathes upon it and paints it. Here is someone we shall read. . . .

Avoid any moral affectation: people don't look for this in the novel. If the characters required for your project are occasionally compelled to reason, may this always be unaffected and without any pretention to do so. The author should never moralize, only the character; and only allow him to do this when circumstances force him.

Once at the denouement, let this be natural—never forced, never contrived, but always born out of the circumstances. I do not demand from you, like the authors of the *Encyclopedia*, that it should *conform to the wishes of the reader*. What pleasure is left for him if he has guessed everything? The denouement should always be of such a kind that the events have prepared, that probability demands, and that imagination inspires. . . .

Finally I must answer the reproach that has been made to me, when *Aline and Valcourt* appeared. They said that my brush-strokes were too strong; I gave excessively odious traits to vice. Do you want to know why? I don't want vice to be liked. I do not undertake, like Crébillon and Dorat, the dangerous project of making women fall in love with the characters who deceive them; to the contrary, I want the women to detest them. It is the sole way that might prevent them from being duped. Thus, in order to succeed, I made those of my heroes who follow a career of vice so frightful that surely they inspire neither pity nor love; in so doing, might I say, I become more moral than those who think that they are allowed to beautify their heroes. The pernicious creations of these authors resemble those fruits in America that contain death within and brilliant colors without. Such treachery in nature, for which it is not up to us to disclose the reason, is not suitable for man. Never, I repeat, never would I paint crime except in Hell's own colors. I want people to see it laid bare so that they fear it, detest it; and I know no other method to reach this than to show crime in the full horror that characterizes it. Woe to those who bedeck it with roses! Their points of view are not as pure as mine, and I shall never copy them. In view of these ideas, may people no longer attribute to me the novel about *Julie*; I have never written such works, and I certainly never shall. It is only imbeciles and wicked people who, despite the authenticity of my denials, can still suspect me and accuse me of having been the author. The only weapon with which I fight their calumnies shall henceforth be scorn to the most sovereign degree.   (1800)

(Translated by H. E. Hugo)

MARIA EDGEWORTH (1767-1849)

The Preface to *Castle Rackrent*

THE PREVAILING taste of the public for anecdote has been censured and ridiculed by critics who aspire to the character of superior wisdom; but if we consider it in a proper point of view, this taste is an incontestable proof of the good sense and profoundly philosophic temper of the present times. Of the numbers who study, or at least who read history, how few derive any advantage from their labours! The heroes of history are so decked out by the fine fancy of the professed historian; they talk in such measured prose, and act from such sublime or such diabolical motives, that few have sufficient taste, wickedness, or heroism, to sympathize in their fate. Besides, there is much uncertainty even in the best authenticated ancient or modern histories; and that love of truth, which in some minds is innate and immutable, necessarily leads to a love of secret memoirs and private anecdotes. We cannot judge either of the feelings or of the characters of men with perfect accuracy, from their actions or their appearance in public; it is from their careless conversations, their half-finished sentences, that we may hope with the greatest probability of success to discover their real characters. The life of a great or of a little man written by himself, the familiar letters, the diary of any individual published by his friends or by his enemies, after his decease, are esteemed important literary curiosities. We are surely justified, in this eager desire, to collect the most minute facts relative to the domestic lives, not only of the great and good, but even of the worthless and insignificant, since it is only by a comparison of their actual happiness or misery in the privacy of domestic life that we can form a just estimate of the real reward of virtue, or the real punishment of vice. That the great are not as happy as they seem, that the external circumstances of fortune and rank do not constitute felicity, is asserted by every moralist: the historian can seldom, consistently with his dignity, pause to illustrate this truth; it is therefore to the biographer we must have recourse. After we have beheld splendid characters playing their parts on the great theatre of the world, with all the advantages of stage effect and decoration, we anxiously beg to be admitted behind the scenes, that we may take a nearer view of the actors and actresses.

Some may perhaps imagine that the value of biography depends upon the judgment and taste of the biographer; but on the contrary it may be maintained, that the merits of a biographer are inversely as the extent of his intellectual powers and of his literary talents. A plain unvarnished tale is preferable to the most highly ornamented narrative.

Where we see that a man has the power, we may naturally suspect that he has the will to deceive us; and those who are used to literary manufacture know how much is often sacrificed to the rounding of a period, or the pointing of an antithesis.

That the ignorant may have their prejudices as well as the learned cannot be disputed; but we see and despise vulgar errors: we never bow to the authority of him who has no great name to sanction his absurdities. The partiality which blinds a biographer to the defects of his hero, in proportion as it is gross, ceases to be dangerous; but if it be concealed by the appearance of candour, which men of great abilities best know how to assume, it endangers our judgment sometimes, and sometimes our morals. If her Grace the Duchess of Newcastle, instead of penning her lord's elaborate eulogium, had undertaken to write the life of Savage, we should not have been in any danger of mistaking an idle, ungrateful libertine for a man of genius and virtue. The talents of a biographer are often fatal to his reader. For these reasons the public often judiciously countenance those who, without sagacity to discriminate character, without elegance of style to relieve the tediousness of narrative, without enlargement of mind to draw any conclusions from the facts they relate, simply pour forth anecdotes, and retail conversations, with all the minute prolixity of a gossip in a country town.

The author of the following Memoirs has upon these grounds fair claims to the public favour and attention; he was an illiterate old steward, whose partiality to *the family*, in which he was bred and born, must be obvious to the reader. He tells the history of the Rackrent family in his vernacular idiom, and in the full confidence that Sir Patrick, Sir Murtagh, Sir Kit, and Sir Condy Rackrent's affairs will be as interesting to all the world as they were to himself. Those who were acquainted with the manners of a certain class of the gentry of Ireland some years ago, will want no evidence of the truth of honest Thady's narrative; to those who are totally unacquainted with Ireland, the following Memoirs will perhaps be scarcely intelligible, or probably they may appear perfectly incredible. For the information of the *ignorant* English reader, a few notes have been subjoined by the editor, and he had it once in contemplation to translate the language of Thady into plain English; but Thady's idiom is incapable of translation, and, besides, the authenticity of his story would have been more exposed to doubt if it were not told in his own characteristic manner. Several years ago he related to the editor the history of the Rackrent family, and it was with some difficulty that he was persuaded to have it committed to writing; however, his feelings for "*the honour of the family*," as he expressed himself, prevailed over his habitual laziness, and he at length completed the narrative which is now laid before the public.

The editor hopes his readers will observe that these are "tales of other times"; that the manners depicted in the following pages are not those of the present age; the race of the Rackrents has long since been extinct in Ireland; and the drunken Sir Patrick, the litigious Sir Murtagh, the fighting Sir Kit, and the slovenly Sir Condy, are characters which could no more be met with at present in Ireland, than Squire Western or Parson Trulliber in England. There is a time when individuals can bear to be rallied for their past follies and absurdities, after they have acquired new habits and a new consciousness. Nations, as well as individuals, gradually lose attachment to their identity, and the present generation is amused, rather than offended, by the ridicule that is thrown upon its ancestors.

Probably we shall soon have it in our power, in a hundred instances, to verify the truth of these observations.

When Ireland loses her identity by an union with Great Britain, she will look back, with a smile of good-humoured complacency, on the Sir Kits and Sir Condys of her former existence.   (1800)

JOHN DUNLOP (1785-1842)

From the Introduction to *The History of Fiction*

THE ART of fictitious narrative appears to have its origin in the same principles of selection by which the fine arts in general are created and perfected. Among the vast variety of trees and shrubs which are presented to his view, a savage finds, in his wanderings, some which peculiarly attract his notice by their beauty and fragrance, and these he at length selects, and plants them round his dwelling. In like manner, among the mixed events of human life, he experiences some which are peculiarly grateful, and of which the narrative at once pleases himself, and excites in the minds of his hearers a kindred emotion. Of this kind are unlooked-for occurrences, successful enterprise, or great and unexpected deliverance from signal danger and distress. As he collected round his habitation those objects with which he had been pleased, in order that they might afford him a frequent gratification, so he rests his fancy on those incidents which had formerly awaked the most powerful emotions; and the remembrance of which most strongly excites his tenderness, or pride, or gratitude.

Thus, in process of time, a mass of curious narrative is collected, which is communicated from one individual to another. In almost every occurrence of human life, however, as in almost every scene of nature, something intervenes of a mixed, or indifferent description, tending to weaken the agreeable emotion, which, without it, would be more pure and forcible. For example, in the process of forming the garden, the savage finds that it is not enough merely to collect a variety of agreeable trees or plants; he discovers that more than this is necessary, and that it is also essential that he should grub up from around his dwelling the shrubs which are useless or noxious, and which weaken or impair the pure delight which he derives from others. He is careful, accordingly, that the rose should no longer be placed beside the thistle, as in the wild, but that it should flourish in a clear, and sheltered, and romantic situation, where its sweets may be undiminished, and where its form can be contemplated without any attending circumstances of uneasiness or disgust. The collector of agreeable facts finds, in like manner, that the sympathy they excite can be heightened by removing from their detail every thing that is not interesting, or that tends to weaken the principal emotion, which it is his intention to raise. He renders, in this way, the occurrences more unexpected, the enterprises more successful, the deliverance from danger and distress more wonderful. "As the active world," says Lord Bacon, "is inferior to the rational soul, so *Fiction* gives to mankind what history denies, and, in some measure, satisfies the mind with shadows when it cannot enjoy the substance: For, upon a narrow inspection, *Fiction* strongly shows that a greater variety of things, a more perfect order, a more beautiful variety, than can any where be found in nature, is pleasing to the mind. And as real history gives us not the success of things according to the deserts of vice and virtue, *Fiction* corrects it, and presents us with the fates and fortunes of persons rewarded or punished according to merit. And as real history disgusts us with a familiar and constant similitude of things, *Fiction* relieves us by unexpected turns and changes, and thus not only delights, but inculcates morality and nobleness of soul. It raises the mind by accommodating the images of things to our desires, and not, like history and reason, subjecting the mind to things."

From this view of the subject, it is obvious that the fictions framed by mankind, or the narratives with which they are delighted, will vary with their feelings, and with the state of society. Since Fiction may be regarded as select and highly coloured history, those adventures would naturally form the basis of it which had already come to pass, or which were most likely to occur. Accordingly, in a warlike age, it would be peculiarly employed in tales of enterprise and chivalry, and, in times of gallantry, in the detail of love adventures.

The History of Fiction, therefore, becomes, in a considerable degree, interesting to the philosopher, and occupies an important place in the history of the progress of society. By contemplating the fables of a people, we have a successive delineation of their prevalent modes of thinking, a picture of their feelings and tastes and habits. In this respect prose fiction appears to possess advantages considerably superior either to history or poetry. In history there is too little individuality; in poetry too much effort, to permit the poet and historian to portray the manners living as they rise. History treats of man, as it were, in the mass, and the individuals whom its paints are regarded merely, or principally, in a public light, without taking into consideration their private feelings, tastes, or habits. Poetry is in general capable of too little detail, while its paintings, at the same time, are usually too much forced and exaggerated. But in Fiction we can discriminate without impropriety, and enter into detail without meanness. Hence, it has been remarked, that it is chiefly in the fictions of an age that we can discover the modes of living, dress, and manners of the period. "Finally," says Borromeo (in the preface to the *Notizia de Novellieri Italian*), "we should remark the light that novels spread on the history of the times. He who doubts of this may read the *Eulogium of Bandello*, and he will be satisfied that his *Novelliero* may be regarded as a magic mirror, which distinctly reflects the customs and manners of the sixteenth century, an age fertile in great events; and it also acquaints us with many literary and political anecdotes, which the historians of the revolutions of our states have not transmitted to posterity. I, myself, can affirm that in these tales I have found recorded authentic anecdotes of the private lives of sovereigns, which would in vain be sought for in ordinary histories."

But even if the utility which is derived from Fiction were less than it is, how much are we indebted to it for pleasure and enjoyment! It sweetens solitude and charms sorrow—it occupies the attention of the vacant, and unbends the mind of the philosopher. Like the enchanter, Fiction shows us, as it were in a mirror, the most agreeable objects: recalls from a distance the forms which are dear to us, and soothes our own griefs by awakening our sympathy for others. By its means the recluse is placed in the midst of society; and he who is harassed and agitated in the city is transported to rural tranquillity and repose. The rude are refined by an introduction, as it were, to the higher orders of mankind, and even the dissipated and selfish are, in some degree, corrected by those paintings of virtue and simple nature, which must ever be employed by the novelist, if he wish to awaken emotion or delight.

And such seems now to be the common idea which is entertained of the value of Fiction. Accordingly, this powerful instrument of virtue and happiness, after having been long despised, on account of the purposes to which it had been made subservient, has gradually become more justly appreciated, and more highly valued. Works of Fiction have been produced, abounding at once with the most interesting details, and the most sagacious reflections, and which differ from treatises of abstract philosophy only by the greater justness of their views, and the higher interest which they excite. And it may be presumed, that a path, at once so useful and delightful, will continue to be trod: It may be presumed, that virtue and vice, the conduct of human life, what we are expected to feel, and what we are called on to do and to suffer, will long be taught by example, a method which seems better fitted to improve the mind than abstract propositions and dry discussions.

Entertaining such views of the nature and utility of fiction, and indebted to its charms for some solace and enjoyment, I have employed a few hours of relaxation in drawing up the following notices of its gradual progress. No works are perhaps more useful or agreeable, than those which delineate the advance of the human mind—the history of what different individuals have effected in the course of ages, for the instruction, or even the innocent amusement, of their species. Such a delineation is attended with innumerable advantages: It furnishes a collection of interesting facts concerning the philosophy of mind, which we thus study not in an abstract and introspective method, but in a manner certain and experimental. It retrieves from oblivion a number of individuals, whose now obsolete works are perhaps in detail unworthy of public attention, but which promoted and diffused, in their own day, light and pleasure, and form as it were landmarks which testify the course and progress of genius. By contemplating also not only what has been done, but the mode in which it has been achieved, a method may perhaps be discovered of proceeding still farther, of avoiding the errors into which our predecessors have fallen, and of following the paths in which they have met success. Retrospective works of this nature, therefore, combine utility, justice, and pleasure; and accordingly, in different branches of philosophy and literature, various histories of their progress and fortunes have appeared.

I have attempted in the following work to afford such a delineation as is now alluded to, of the origin and progress of fiction, of the various forms which it has successively assumed, and the different authors by whom the prose works in this department of literature have been most successfully cultivated and promoted. I say *prose* works, since such alone are the proper objects of this undertaking. It was objected to a former edition, that I had commenced the History of Fiction only in the decline of literature, and had neglected the most sublime and lofty efforts of mythology and poetry. But it never was my intention to consider fiction as connected with these topics (an inquiry which, if properly conducted, would form a work of greater extent than the whole of the present volumes, and which well deserves a peculiar treatise), but merely to consider the different fictions in prose, which have been given to the world under the name of romance or novel. That I have begun late, arises from the circumstance, that the works of which I have undertaken a description were late in making their appearance; and I am the more strongly induced to direct my inquiries to this subject, as I am not aware that any writer has hitherto presented a full and continued view of it, though detached parts have been separately treated with much learning and ingenuity.   (1814)

SIR WALTER SCOTT (1771-1832)
From *Miss Austen's Novels*

HE TIMES seem to be past when an apology was requisite from reviewers for condescending to notice a novel; when they felt themselves bound in dignity to deprecate the suspicion of paying much regard to trifles, and pleaded the necessity of occasionally stooping to humour the taste of their fair readers. The delights of fiction, if not more keenly or more generally relished, are at least more readily acknowledged by men of sense and taste; and we have lived to hear the merits of the best of this class of writings earnestly discussed by some of the ablest scholars and soundest reasoners of the present day.

We are inclined to attribute this change, not so much to an alteration in the public taste, as in the character of the productions in question. Novels may not, perhaps, display more genius now than formerly, but they contain more solid sense; they may not afford higher gratification, but it is of a nature which men are less disposed to be ashamed of avowing. We remarked, in a former Number, in reviewing a work of the author now before us, that "a new style of novel has arisen, within the last fifteen or twenty years, differing from the former in the points upon which the interest hinges; neither alarming our credulity nor amusing our imagination by wild variety of incident, or by those pictures of romantic affection and sensibility, which were formerly as certain attributes of fictitious characters as they are of rare occurrence among those who actually live and die. The substitute for these excitements, which had lost much of their poignancy by the repeated and injudicious use of them, was the art of copying from nature as she really exists in the common walks of life, and presenting to the reader, instead of the splendid scenes of an imaginary world, a correct and striking representation of that which is daily taking place around him."

Now, though the origin of this new school of fiction may probably be traced, as we there suggested, to the exhaustion of the mines from which materials for entertainment had been hitherto extracted, and the necessity of gratifying the natural craving of the reader for variety, by striking into an untrodden path; the consequences resulting from this change have been far greater than the mere supply of this demand. When this Flemish painting, as it were, is introduced—this accurate and unexaggerated delineation of events and characters—it necessarily follows, that a novel, which makes good its pretensions, of giving a perfectly correct picture of common life, becomes a far more *instructive* work than one of equal or superior merit of the other class; it guides the judgment, and supplies a kind of artificial experience. It is a remark of the great father of criticism, that poetry (*i.e.* narrative, and dramatic poetry) is of a more philosophical character than history; inasmuch as the latter details what has actually happened, of which many parts may chance to be exceptions to the general rules of probability, and consequently illustrate no general principles; whereas the former shows us what must naturally, or would probably, happen under given circumstances; and thus displays to us a comprehensive view of human nature, and furnishes general rules of practical wisdom. It is evident that this will apply only to such fictions as are quite *perfect* in respect of the probability of their story; and that he, therefore, who resorts to the fabulist rather than the historian, for instruction in human character and conduct, must throw himself entirely on the judgment and skill of his teacher, and give him credit for talents much more rare than the accuracy and veracity which are the chief requisites in history. We fear, therefore, that the exultation which we can conceive some of our gentle readers to feel, at having Aristotle's warrant for (what probably they had never dreamed of) the *philosophical character* of their studies, must, in practice be some-what qualified, by those sundry little violations of probability which are to be met with in most novels; and which so far lower their value, as models of real life, that a person who had no other preparation for the world than is afforded by them, would form, probably, a less accurate idea of things as they are, than he would of a lion from studying merely the representations on China teapots.

Accordingly, a heavy complaint has long lain against works of fiction, as giving a false picture of what they profess to imitate, and disqualifying their readers for the ordinary scenes and everyday duties of life. And this charge applies, we apprehend, to the generality of what are strictly called novels, with even more justice than to romances. When all the characters and events are very far removed from what we see around us,—when, perhaps, even supernatural agents are introduced, the reader may indulge, indeed, in occasional day-dreams, but will be so little reminded of what he has been reading, by any thing that occurs in actual life, that though he may perhaps feel some disrelish for the tameness of the scene before him, compared with the fairy-land he has been visiting, yet, at least, his judgment will not be depraved, nor his expectations misled; he will not apprehend a meeting with Algerine banditti on English shores, nor regard the old woman who shows him about an antique country seat, as either an enchantress or the keeper of an imprisoned damsel. But it is otherwise with those fictions which differ from common life in little or nothing but the improbability of the occurrences: the reader is insensibly led to calculate upon some of those lucky incidents and opportune coincidences, of which he has been so much accustomed to read, and which, it is undeniable, *may* take place in real life; and to feel a sort of confidence, that however romantic his conduct may be, and in whatever difficulties it may involve him, all will be sure to come right at last, as is invariably the case with the hero of a novel.

On the other hand, so far as these pernicious effects fail to be produced, so far does the example lose its influence, and the exercise of poetical justice is rendered vain. The reward of virtuous conduct being brought about by fortunate accidents, he who abstains (taught, perhaps, by bitter disappointments) from reckoning on such accidents, wants that encouragement to virtue, which alone has been held out to him. "If I were *a man in a novel*," we remember to have heard an ingenious friend observe, "I should certainly act so and so, because I should be sure of being no loser by the most heroic self-devotion, and of ultimately succeeding in the most daring enterprises."

It may be said, in answer, that these objections apply only to the *unskillful* novelist, who, from ignorance of the world, gives an unnatural representation of what he professes to delineate. This is partly true, and partly not; for there is a distinction to be made between the *unnatural* and the merely *improbable*: a fiction is unnatural when there is some assignable reason against the events taking place as described,—when men are represented as acting contrary to the character assigned them, or to human nature in general; as when a young lady of seventeen, brought up in ease, luxury, and retirement, with no companions but the narrow-minded and illiterate, displays (as a heroine usually does), under the most trying circumstances, such

wisdom, fortitude, and knowledge of the world, as the best instructors
and the best examples can rarely produce without the aid of more
mature age and longer experience.—On the other hand, a fiction is
still *improbable*, though not *unnatural*, when there is no reason to be
assigned why things should not take place as represented, except that
the *overbalance of chances is* against it; the hero meets, in his utmost
distress, most opportunely, with the very person to whom he had
formerly done a signal service, and who happens to communicate to
him a piece of intelligence which sets all to rights. Why should he not
meet him as well as any one else? all that can be said is, that there
is no reason why he should. The infant who is saved from a wreck,
and who afterwards becomes such a constellation of virtues and accom-
plishments, turns out to be no other than the nephew of the very
gentleman, on whose estate the waves had cast him, and whose lovely
daughter he had so long sighed for in vain: there is no reason to be
given, except from the calculation of chances, why he should not have
been thrown on one part of the coast as well as another. Nay, it would
be nothing unnatural, though the most determined novel-reader would
be shocked at its improbability, if all the hero's enemies, while they
were conspiring his ruin, were to be struck dead together by a lucky
flash of lightning: yet many *dénouements* which *are* decidedly unnatural, are better tolerated than this would be. We shall, perhaps,
best explain our meaning by examples, taken from a novel of great
merit in many respects. When Lord Glenthorn, in whom a most
unfavourable education has acted on a most unfavourable disposition,
after a life of torpor, broken only by short sallies of forced exertion,
on a sudden reverse of fortune, displays at once the most persevering
diligence in the most repulsive studies, and in middle life, without
any previous habits of exertion, any hope of early business, or the
example of friends, or the stimulus of actual want, to urge him, out-
strips every competitor, though every competitor has every advantage
against him; this is unnatural.—When Lord Glenthorn, the instant he
is stripped of his estates, meets, falls in love with, and is conditionally
accepted by the very lady who is remotely entitled to those estates;
when, the instant he has fulfilled the conditions of their marriage,
the family of the person possessed of the estates becomes extinct,
and by the concurrence of circumstances, against every one of
which the chances were enormous, the hero is re-instated in all
his old domains; this is merely improbable. The distinction which
we have been pointing out may be plainly perceived in the events of
real life; when any thing takes place of such a nature as we should
call, in a fiction, merely improbable, because there are many chances
against it, we call it a lucky or unlucky accident, a singular coincidence,

something very extraordinary, odd, curious, &c.; whereas any thing which, in a fiction, would be called unnatural, when it actually occurs (and such things do occur), is still called unnatural, inexplicable, unaccountable, inconceivable, &c., epithets which are not applied to events that have merely the balance of chances against them.

Now, though an author who understands human nature is not likely to introduce into his fictions any thing that is unnatural, he will often have much that is improbable: he may place his personages, by the intervention of accident, in striking situations, and lead them through a course of extraordinary adventures; and yet, in the midst of all this, he will keep up the most perfect consistency of character, and make them act as it would be natural for men to act in such situations and circumstances. Fielding's novels are a good illustration of this: they display great knowledge of mankind; the characters are well preserved; the persons introduced all act as one would naturally expect they should, in the circumstances in which they are placed; but these circumstances are such as it is incalculably improbable should ever exist: several of the events, taken singly, are much against the chances of probability; but the combination of the whole in a connected series, is next to impossible. Even the romances which admit a mixture of supernatural agency, are not more unfit to prepare men for real life, than such novels as these; since one might just as reasonably calculate on the intervention of a fairy, as on the train of lucky chances which combine first to involve Tom Jones in his difficulties, and afterwards to extricate him. Perhaps, indeed, the supernatural fable is of the two not only (as we before remarked) the less mischievous in its moral effects, but also the more correct kind of composition in point of taste: the author lays down a kind of hypothesis of the existence of ghosts, witches, or fairies, and professes to describe what would take place under that hypothesis; the novelist, on the contrary, makes no demand of extraordinary machinery, but professes to describe what may actually take place, according to the existing laws of human affairs: if he therefore present us with a series of events quite unlike any which ever do take place, we have reason to complain that he has not made good his professions.

When, therefore, the generality, even of the most approved novels, were of this character (to say nothing of the heavier charges brought, of inflaming the passions of young persons by warm descriptions, weakening their abhorrence of profligacy, by exhibiting it in combination with the most engaging qualities, and presenting vice in all its allurements, while setting forth the triumphs of "virtue rewarded") it is not to be wondered that the grave guardians of youth should have generally stigmatized the whole class, as "serving only to fill young people's heads with romantic love-stories, and rendering them unfit to mind any thing else." That this censure and caution should in many instances be indiscriminate, can surprise no one, who recollects how rare a quality discrimination is; and how much better it suits indolence, as well as ignorance, to lay down a rule, than to ascertain the exceptions to it: we are acquainted with a careful mother whose daughters, while they never in their lives read a *novel* of any kind, are permitted to peruse, without reserve, any *plays* that happen to fall in their way; and with another, from whom no lessons, however excellent, of wisdom and piety, contained in a *prose-fiction*, can obtain quarter; but who, on the other hand, is no less indiscriminately indulgent to her children in the article of tales in *verse*, of whatever character.

The change, however, which we have already noticed, as having taken place in the character of several modern novels, has operated in a considerable degree to do away this prejudice; and has elevated this species of composition, in some respects at least, into a much higher class. For most of that instruction which used to be presented to the world in the shape of formal dissertations, or shorter and more desultory moral essays, such as those of the *Spectator* and *Rambler*, we may now resort to the pages of the acute and judicious, but not less amusing, novelists who have lately appeared. If their views of men and manners are no less just than those of the essayists who preceded them, are they to be rated lower, because they present to us these views, not in the language of general description, but in the form of well-constructed fictitious narrative? If the practical lessons they inculcate, are no less sound and useful, it is surely no diminution of their merit that they are conveyed by example instead of precept; nor, if their remarks are neither less wise nor less important, are they the less valuable for being represented as thrown out in the course of conversations suggested by the circumstances of the speakers, and perfectly in character. The praise and blame of the moralist are surely not the less effectual for being bestowed, not in general declamation, on classes of men, but on individuals representing those classes, who are so clearly delineated and brought into action before us, that we seem to be acquainted with them, and feel an interest in their fate. . . .   (1821)

STENDHAL (Henri Beyle, 1783-1842)

Walter Scott and "La Princesse de Clèves"

THESE two names in fact set up the two poles of the novel. Must we describe the habits of characters, the landscape in which they find themselves, the shape of their faces? Or can't we do better to paint the passions and the various emotions that excite their souls? A great body of men of letters is interested in praising Sir Walter Scott and his style to the skies, and my reflections will be badly received. The dress and the leather collar of a mediaeval serf are easier to describe than the movements of the human heart. It is possible to paint badly or imagine badly a mediaeval costume. We have only a partial knowledge of the clothes and costumes they wore in Cardinal Richelieu's antechamber. But we throw aside with disgust a book where the author portrays the human heart badly, and gives the ignoble feelings of a lackey to some illustrious person, companion-at-arms to the son of Henry IV. We all recall Voltaire's remark. He was giving a lesson in tragic diction to a young actress, and she spoke an extremely lively passage coldly. "But, mademoiselle," exclaimed Voltaire, "you have to have the devil in you! What would you do if a cruel tyrant had just carried off your lover?" "Monsieur, I would take another one."

I do not insist that all the creators of historical novels think *as reasonably* as this prudent young girl; but the most susceptible will not accuse me of calumniating if I assert that it is infinitely less difficult to describe a character's costume picturesquely than it is to say what he feels and to make him speak. Let us not forget another advantage of the school of Sir Walter Scott. The description of the costume and *posture* of a character, no matter how subordinate he may be, takes at least two pages. The movements of the soul, which to begin with involve so much work to discover, and then are so difficult to explain with precision and with neither exaggeration nor timidity, scarcely furnish more than a few lines. Open at random one of the volumes of *La Princesse de Clèves*, take any ten pages, and afterwards compare them to ten pages of *Ivanhoe* or *Quentin Durward*. These last works have *historical merit*.

They teach a few small things about history to people who are ignorant about history or are wrong about it. This historical merit has given a great deal of pleasure, this I do not deny. But it is this same historical merit that will be the first to wither away. The century is moving a step toward the simple and genuine style, and these imprecise mannerisms of Sir Walter Scott will be as displeasing as they have been charming. Perhaps it might be judicious to sketch rapidly the future destiny of the popular novel.

Behold what a mob is interested in maintaining that Sir Walter Scott is a great man! No matter how many there are, I shall not borrow that mask of hypocrisy so popular in the nineteenth century. I say frankly that ten years will be enough to make half the Scottish novelist's reputation collapse. Among us Richardson had a reputation equal to his. Diderot said, "In exile or in prison I would only ask for three books: *Homer, the Bible,* and *Clarissa Harlowe.*" Richardson, just like Sir Walter Scott, had a greater reputation in Paris than in England.

Every work of art is a *beautiful lie:* we writers know this well. Nothing is more ridiculous than the advice given by fashionable people: *imitate nature.* Ha! I know perfectly well, what the devil, that we have to imitate nature; but how far? Here is the whole question. Two men of equal genius, Racine and Shakespeare, have shown an Iphigenia at the moment when her father is about to sacrifice her in Aulis, and an Imogen at the instant when the husband she adores is about to stab her in the mountains bordering Mitford Harbor.

These great poets *imitated nature.* But one aimed to please rustic gentry, still filled with a rude, harsh, openness of mind; the other sought the applause of those polished courtiers who—following the practise established by Lauzun and the Marquis de Vardes—wanted to please the king and deserve the praise of ladies. *Imitate nature* is thus advice devoid of meaning. Up to what point do you have to imitate nature in order to please the reader? That is the big question.

I believe I must insist on a puerile detail. If someone had taken down in shorthand everything that had been said in Aulis on the occasion of Iphigenia's murder, we would have five or six volumes, even if we limited all that was said to the characters chosen by Racine. The first thing would be to reduce these six volumes to eighty pages. But there is something else: almost everything said by Agamemnon and Calchas would today be completely unintelligible, or if we could understand them we would be horrified.

Thus art is nothing more than a beautiful lie, but Sir Walter Scott was too much the liar. He would have been more appealing to well-bred persons, who in the long run determine everything in literature, had he introduced a *greater number of traits of human nature* into his portrayal of passions. His impassioned characters seem to be *ashamed of themselves,* just like Mlle. Mars when she plays the role of a fool. When she comes on the stage, this great actress casts a sly little glance at the audience. "Don't believe that I am a fool," the glance says, "I am just as intelligent as you are; only let me know if I have pleased you and deserved your applause—my sole aim—by enacting the part of a fool well."

It has been said of a painter who shared Walter Scott's and Mlle. Mars' defect: *his colors lacked naïveté.*

I will go even further. The Scottish novelist's characters are so lacking in boldness and assurance that they have to express the most exalted sentiments. I confess that this chagrins me the most about Sir Walter Scott. Here we can all recognize the experience of an old judge. Behold the man who when he was welcomed to George IV's table, when the king was visiting Edinburgh, asked enthusiastically for the *glass* with which the King has just drunk the health of his subjects. Sir Walter obtained the precious goblet and put it in his frock-coat. But he forgot this high favor when he came home, threw off his coat breaking the glass, and was in despair. Would old Corneille or Ducis have understood such despair? In a hundred and forty-six years, Sir Walter Scott will not stand at that height where Corneille seems to us to be one-hundred and forty-six years after his death.   (1830)

(Translated by H. E. Hugo)

HONORÉ DE BALZAC (1799-1850)
From the Foreword to *The Human Comedy*

IN GIVING the title, *The Human Comedy*, to a work written for what will soon be thirteen years, it is necessary to go into the thought behind it, to consider the origins, to explain briefly the plan, all while trying to speak of these things in a detached manner. This is really not so difficult as the public might think. A small output gives us much self-esteem; a large one infinite modesty. Such an observation accounts for the self-examinations made by Corneille, Molière, and other great authors. If we cannot emulate their great ideas, at least we can share their feelings about their work.

From the start, the first idea for *The Human Comedy* was like a dream for me, like one of those impossible projects that we fondle and then let fly away; a smiling chimera that displayed its woman's face and immediately spread out its wings to ascend into a fantastic sky. But like many chimeras, the chimera turned into a reality with its own rules and tyrannies to which we had to submit.

This idea arose from a comparison between Humanity and Animality.

It would be wrong to think that the great quarrel which recently was stirred up between Cuvier and Geoffroi Saint-Hilaire stemmed from a scientific innovation. *Unity of composition,* under a different terminology, had already exercised the greatest minds of two preceding centuries. If we reread those most extraordinary works by writers of the occult who dealt with the sciences and their relationship with the infinite, such as Swedenborg, Saint-Martin, etc., and the writings of the finest geniuses in natural history such as Leibnitz, Buffon, Charles Bonnet, etc., we find in Leibnitz's monads, in Buffon's organic molecules, in Needham's vegetative force, in Charles Bonnet's *interlocking* of similar parts—rather bold to write in 1760, *the animal grows as does the plant*; we find, I say, the rudiments of the fine law of *each for itself*, on which is based the *unity of composition.* There is only one animal. The creator used but one and the same pattern for all organic beings. The animal is a principle which borrows its exterior form, or to speak more exactly the differences in its form, from the environment to which it is summoned to develop itself. Zoölogical Species result from these differences. The proclamation and vindication of this system, which is moreover in harmony with those ideas we conceive about divine power, will be to the eternal glory of Geoffroi Saint-Hilaire, Cuvier's victor concerning this point in the advanced sciences, and whose triumph was signaled in the last article written by great Goethe.

Influenced by this system well before the debates which it occasioned, I saw that under this analogy Society was similar to Nature. Does not Society make man, according to the environment wherein he enacts his role, into as many different men as there are zoölogical varieties? The differences between a soldier, a worker, an administrator, a lawyer, an idler, a scholar, a statesman, a shop-keeper, a sailor, a poet, a poor man, a priest, are—although more difficult to grasp—as extensive as those which distinguish the wolf, the lion, the donkey, the crow, the shark, the seal, the sheep, etc. Thus there have existed and there shall always exist Social as well as Zoölogical Species. If Buffon did a magnificent job in attempting to portray the whole of zoölogy in one volume, is there not a similar task to be done for Society? But Nature has placed limits on animalian varieties to which Society ought not to adhere. When Buffon depicted the lion, he dispensed with the lioness in a few sentences; whereas in Society the woman is not always found to be the female of the male. One couple can consist of two perfectly dissimilar persons. Often a shop-keeper's wife is worthy to be a prince's, and often a prince's is not worth an artist's. The Social Condition, because it is Nature and in addition Society, exhibits random chances with which Nature cannot take liberties. Thus the description of Social Species is at least double that of Animal Species, if we treat but the two sexes. Finally, there is little dramatic action be-

tween animals, rarely does confusion enter into their relations; they
merely struggle each with the other. Men also struggle among themselves, but their varying degrees of intelligence make the combat all
the more complicated. If a few scholars still do not admit that Animality is transmuted to Humanity through a huge current of life, surely
the grocer would become the Peer of France, and the nobleman occasionally drop to the lowest social rank. Then too, Buffon found life
excessively simple among animals. An animal owns few possessions,
he produces neither arts nor sciences: whereas man, owing to a law
which is still to be investigated, tends to implant his customs, his ideas,
and his life on all that he appropriates to his needs. Although Leuwen-
hoëc, Swammerdam, Spallanzani, Réamur, Charles Bonnet, Muller,
Haller, and other assiduous zoölogists showed how interesting were
the customs of animals, the habits of each animal are—at least in our
eyes—constantly the same; whereas the habits of a banker, artist,
bourgeois, priest and poor man are entire dissimilar and alter with the
changing tastes of civilizations.

Therefore the work to be done should have a tripartite form: men,
women, and things; that is to say, characters and the material embodi-
ments they make from their ideas; finally, mankind and life, because
life is our garment.

While reading the dry and repelling list of facts called *histories*,
who has not observed that in all ages writers have forgotten to give us the
history of customs, in Egypt, Persia, Greece, and Rome? Petronius's
piece on the private lives of Romans only irritates us, and doesn't
satisfy our curiosity. Having noted this immense gap in the field of
history, Abbé Barthélemy dedicated his life, in *Anarcharsis*, to redoing
the customs of the Greeks.

But how can one make the drama interesting to the three or four
thousand people who compose a Society? How can we at once please
the poet, the philosopher, and the masses, who want philosophy and
poetry in terms of striking imagery? If I conceived the importance
and the poetry of this history of the human heart, I did not see any
means for its execution; because, until our era, the most celebrated
story-tellers used their talents to create one or two typical characters,
to paint one facet of life. With this idea in mind I read the works of
Walter Scott. Walter Scott, that modern troubadour, had then imposed a grand manner upon a genre of writing unjustly labeled secondary. Truly, is it not harder to compete against Legal Status with
Daphnis and Chloë, Roland, Amadis, Panurge, Don Quixote, Manon
Lescaut, Clarissa, Lovelace, Robinson Crusoe, Gil Blas, Ossian, Julie
d'Etanges, my uncle Toby, Werther, René, Corinne, Adolphe, Paul
and Virginia, Jeannie Dean, Claverhouse, Ivanhoe, Manfred, Mignon,

than it is to assemble approximately-similar facts for all countries, investigate the spirit of obsolete laws, edit theories that have led races astray, or—like certain metaphysicians—explain existence? First, almost all these characters who live longer and more authentically than those generations in whose environment they are conceived, exist solely because they are a grand prospectus of the present. Created from the very bowels of their century, all the heart of mankind beats within their flesh, wherein is often contained an entire philosophy. Thus Walter Scott raised the novel to the philosophical value of history, this literary form which from century to century has encrusted with eternal diamonds the poetical crown of every country where letters are cultivated. There he instilled the spirit of antiquity, there he united simultaneously drama, dialogue, portraiture, landscape, description; he admitted wonder and truth, those elements of the epic; he caused poetry to be jostled by the familiarity of the humblest tongues. Yet having little dreamed of a system that would find its mode via the fire or the rationale of labor, he never imagined that he might connect his compositions each to each so to coördinate a complete history, of which each chapter might have been a novel, and each novel an epoch. I noticed this defect in liaison—which does not diminish the Scot's greatness—and I immediately envisioned the system that would be congenial for the execution of my work, and the possibility for this same execution. I might say that although I was amazed by the surprising fecundity of Walter Scott—always true to himself and always original—I did not despair; because I found the reason for this talent to be in the infinite variety of human nature. Chance is the greatest novelist in the world; to be prolific, one need only study. French Society was to be the historian, I was merely to be its secretary. By ennumerating vices and virtues, gathering together the principal facts about the passions, painting characters, choosing the outstanding events of Society, composing types by uniting the traits of several homogeneous characters, perhaps I might succeed to write the history forgotten by so many historians—that of customs. With much patience and courage I was able to realize the volume about France in the nineteenth century that we all have sorely grieved for; the same that Rome, Athens, Tyre, Memphis, Persia, India unhappily have not bequeathed us from their civilizations; and which inspired by Abbé Barthélemy, the courageous and patient Monteil attempted for the Middle Ages, but via a literary form of small appeal.

As yet the task was still nothing. Limiting himself to such a rigorous reproduction, a writer might become a more or less accurate painter, more or less happy, patient and courageous about types of humanity, the narrator of dramas about private life, the archeologist of society's possessions, namer of professions, registrar of good and evil. Yet in order to merit the praise that should make each artist ambitious, was I not to study the reasons or the reason for these social effects, to divine the hidden sense within this immense assembly of figures, of passions and events? Finally, after having sought—I do not say found—this reason, this social motivation, should not I have meditated about natural principles, to view where Societies divert from or are reconciled with eternal law, the true and the beautiful? Despite the scope of the premises, where they themselves might be a study, the work—in order to be an entity—demanded a goal. Thus depicted, Society was to support the reason for its own action.

The law of the writer, that which makes him what he is—I do not hesitate to say—makes him the equal and perhaps the superior of the statesman: this is a commitment however commonplace about human things, an absolute devotion to principles. Machiavelli, Bossuet, Leibnitz, Kant, Montesquieu represent knowledge which statesmen apply. Saint Peter and Saint Paul were systems put into execution by the Papacy. Bonald said, "A writer should have settled opinions in ethics and in politics; he should look to himself as a tutor for mankind, since mankind does not need masters in order to doubt." From the start I took these great lines as a rule, which is the law for both the monarchist as well as the democratic writer. . . .

In transcribing the whole of Society, grasping it in the hugeness of its restlessness, it happens and it must happen that such a composition presents more evil than good; that one portion of the fresco portrays a guilty couple and a critic deplores their immorality, without noting that the morality of another portion was intended to form a perfect contrast. Since the critics have not been aware of the general plan, I have excused them all the more; because you cannot impede criticism any more than you can prevent the intention, the language, and the judgment to practise it. Still, the time for impartiality has not yet been mine. Moreover, the author who does not know how to suffer the fire of criticism ought not to go about writing any more than a traveller should set off on a trip, counting on an ever-clear sky. On this point, I must still remind you that the most conscientious moralists strongly doubt whether Society can provide as many good as there are evil deeds; and in the picture I have made of it, there are more virtuous than reprehensible characters. There, censorable deeds, mistakes, crimes ranging from the slightest to the gravest, always receive their human or divine punishments, whether obvious or subtle. I have done better than the historian; I am freer. Cromwell dwelled on earth, without receiving any other punishment than that which the intellectuals have inflicted on him. Various schools still discuss this. Bossuet himself spared this famous regicide. The usurper William of Orange, another usurper Hugh Capet, died after long lives without having any more fears or suspicions than did Henry IV or Charles I. The lives of Catherine II and Louis XVI, placed in perspective, total up to no sort of ethical system, if they are judged from an ethical point of view that governs particulars; for as Napoleon said, there exists a small and a large morality for Kings and Statesmen. *Scenes from Political Life* are based on this fine observation. History has no law, like the novel, conducive to a beautiful ideal. History is or ought to be what was; while *the novel ought to be a better world,* as Madame Necker—one of the most distinguished minds of the last century—said. . . .

The *Scenes of Private Life* represent childhood and adolescence with their faults, just as *Scenes of Provincial Life* represent the age of passions, of calculations, of self-interests, and of ambition. Next the *Scenes of Parisian Life* offer a picture of tastes, of vices, and of all the unbridled things that stimulate particular customs in capital cities where the extremes of good and evil simultaneously meet. Each of these three parts has its own local color: Paris and the province, this social antithesis, provided an immense subject-matter. Not only men, but again the principal events in life, are formulated into types. There exist situations which exhibit themselves in all lives, typical phases, and this was one of the exactitudes for which I sought the most. I tried to give some idea of the different regions in our beautiful country. My work has its geography the way it has its genealogy, its families, its places and its things, its characters and its facts; just as it has its book of heraldry, its nobility and its middle class, its artisans and its peasants, its politicians and its dandies, its army, an entire world!

After having depicted social life in these three books, I had still to show exceptional persons who recapitulated most or all interests, those who in a way are outside ordinary law: hence the *Scenes of Political Life.* This vast portrait of Society accomplished and completed, was it then not necessary to show Society in its most violent condition; proceeding above and beyond itself, either for defense or for conquest? Hence the *Scenes of Military Life,* as yet the portion of my work least completed, but for whom room shall be kept in this edition, so that it can be a part of the work when it is concluded. Finally, *Scenes of Rustic Life* are after a fashion the evening of this long trip, if I may be allowed thus to name the social drama. In this book are to be found the purest characters and the application of the great principles of order, of politics, and of morality.

Such is the foundation rich with figures, comedies, and tragedies, on which the *Philosophical Studies* have arisen. Second Part of the work, where the social means for all the effects are demonstrated, where the devastation of the mind is portrayed, feeling by feeling, and of which the first work, "The Wild Ass's Skin," unites in one way the *Studies of Manners* with the *Philosophical Studies*, using a link of near-Oriental fantasy—where Life itself is portrayed grappling with Desire, the principle of all Passion.

With these are the *Analytical Studies*, about which I shall say nothing, because only one of them has been published, "The Physiology of Marriage."

From now and in the near future I should produce two other works of this genre. First the "Pathology of Social Life," next the "Anatomy of the Teaching Profession" and the "Monograph of Virtue...."   (1842)

(Translated by H. E. Hugo)

ALESSANDRO MANZONI (1785-1873)

From Part One, *On the Historical Novel*

On the Historical Novel, and in General on Literary Works which combine History and Invention

PLEASE NOTE: The author would have quite a task if he had to maintain that the doctrines set forth in the following discourse agree with the letter that precedes them. He can only say that if he has changed his mind, this was not to go backwards. The wise reader must judge for himself whether such movement forward has been toward truth, or a tumbling back into error; if the reader feels that the subject and the study merit any judgment whatsoever.

PART ONE

The historical novel is subject to two criticisms, different and indeed directly opposed. Since both deal with the very essence of this literary type, and not merely with accessory items, it seems to us that a good—if not the best—way to proceed without preamble to the heart of the problem, is to state these criticisms and to examine them.

Now there are those who complain about various historical novels, or parts of an historical novel, in that the factual truth is not distinct from the imaginary elements. Hence one of the principal effects of such a work is lacking: namely, the rendition of a true presentation of history.

To explain how valid such persons' criticism may be, we shall have to say more than they have, at the same time not saying anything not implicit and understood by their statement. And we think that we do no more than explain the logical motives for their complaint when we make them speak in the following fashion to him who is suffering (that is to say, the author):

"The purpose of your work was to set before my eyes, in a new and special form, a richer, more varied, more complete history than one generally finds in works to which this name is given, as if via autonamasia. The kind of history we expect from you is not a chronological account of mere political and historical facts, with once and a while some extraordinary event of a different sort. But we expect a more general representation of the state of human affairs in one period, in one place—naturally more limited than the scope found in the customary works about history, to use the accepted dictionary meaning of the word. There is the same difference between latter works and yours that there is between a geographical map on which mountains, rivers, cities, towns and the main roads are marked in a large area; and a topographical map where all this is more detailed (I mention the things that can go into a more restricted portion of the country), where in addition small hills, the less discernible rise and fall of the terrain, streams, canals, villages, isolated houses and back roads are marked. What you propose to reveal are customs, opinions—be they general, or peculiar to certain classes in society; the private effects of public events, or more properly speaking historical events; laws, the dictates of those in power—however these be made manifest; in short, all that a given society has owned as its most characteristic aspects; all walks of life; the relations of individuals with each other during a certain period. You succeed as well as you did through diligent study, and by your own good knowledge. And the pleasure you propose to provide stems naturally from acquiring such knowledge, and by getting it through a representation, may I say, at once animated and in action."

"Granting that much, when has confusion ever been a means to make things known? To know something is to believe something. In order to believe—when I know that what is offered to me is not consistently true—I realize I have to make distinctions. What! You want to teach me real things, and you don't give me the means by which I can recognize them as realities? Why did you ever decide that these real entities were to enjoy an extensive and central position within your composition? Why the title of "historian," tacked on as a distinction and an allurement? Because you know very well that it takes a strong and lively mind, as well as a specialized one, to understand what really has taken place and how it took place. After having directed and excited my curosity toward such an event, did you think you could satisfy me by showing me something that might have been true, but also might be a figment of your imagination?"

"Notice that in making this criticism, I mean as well to compliment you. I intend to be speaking to a writer who knows how to choose his arguments and how to develop them well. If it were a question of a boring novel, full of ordinary facts and appropriate to any period in time—and thus not remarkable about any one age—I would have shut the book without a second thought. But precisely because the facts, characters, manner and the consequences you offer strongly attract and hold my attention, you raise a desire in me all the more alive, restless, and may I add, more reasonable. And that is the desire to know if there I might see a genuine manifestation of humanity, nature, or Providence, instead of some possibility you were lucky enough to discover. When someone with a reputation for telling tall tales gives you a piece of interesting news, do you really believe it? Now you (writing, naturally, a novel) are like that fellow who narrates the true and the false in the same breath. If you make no distinction between one and the other, you leave me just as he does."

"Your two goals were to instruct and to delight. But these are so closely related that once you don't succeed in one you fail in the other. Your reader does not become entertained, exactly because he does not feel edified."

Certainly they might have stated their case better; but even thus expressing themselves, they are right—we must confess.

Yet as we remarked at the beginning, there are other persons who would prefer just the opposite. They complain that in various historical novels, or parts of historical novels, the author purposely distinguishes the factual from the fictitious, and they say that this destroys the unity that is the necessary condition for this or any other work of art. Let us examine in more detail on what they base their criticism.

"What is (I think they want to say) the essential element of the historical novel? The story. And what could possibly be more contrary to unity or continuity of impression of a story, to the connection, the coöperation, the 'friendly conspiracy' of each part that produces the total effect, than some parts being presented as true and others as imaginary products? The latter—if you know how to invent—will not be at all like the former, minus the truth and the special, incommunicable quality of reality. Now in giving this quality to those things which already possess it, you remove your story's whole reason for existence and you substitute for what the different materials have in common, something that renders them repugnant and inconciliable. If you expressly tell me or have me to understand in some way that a certain thing really is that way, you force me to reflect (even if this is not your intention, what difference does that make?) that nothing existed prior to this fact, and there shall be nothing subsequent to it. I must also reflect that what is invented has to be granted the feeling of assent given to a factual truth, and what is real has to get the due accord that we give to what is probably true. Thus I must conclude that the narrative form, applied equally to one and the other, is for the former proper and natural, and for the latter a convention and fictitious—which means a contradictory form for the whole."

"See whether this contradiction could be more curious! This unity, this homogeneity of the whole, you hold as most important, since you do all you can to attain it. The praise which Horace gives to the author of the *Odyssey*:

> He lies in such a way, he knows how to mix
> The true with the false, so that always
> The beginning corresponds to the middle, the
> Middle to the end . . .

you also try your hardest to merit, so that you choose from real and possible things so they might best correspond with each other. And with that purpose, why can't the reader's mind—subjugated and transported by art—take them as one thing, the way they are presented? Then you come along to undo your own work of art, in effect separating what you formally united. You yourself destroy that illusion which is the aim and goal of art, so difficult to create and to maintain, in the very act of creating it! Don't you realize that there is something repugnant between the conception and the execution? That little bits of copper and tin fitted together do not make a bronze statue?"

What shall we reply to these people? I don't actually know what we can say, save that they are right.

A friend of mine, dearly revered in my memory, related a strange scene at which he was present, at the home of the Justice of the Peace in Milan, and thus many years ago. My friend found the judge between two litigants, one of whom was defending his cause with warmth. When the latter had concluded, the judge said, "You are right." "But Your Honor," he immediately replied, "you ought to listen to me before deciding." The judge answered, "You are all too correct; out with it, I am carefully listening." Then the other litigant began to plead his cause with even more zeal. He did so well that the judge said, "You too are right." One of the judge's children, six or seven years old, was playing nearby with a toy and hadn't missed a point in the arguments. At that moment, raising his puzzled little face, he exclaimed—but not without authority—"But Father! It can't be that both are right." "You too are right," said the judge to him. Either my friend didn't tell me or I have forgotten, how the tale ended. It is most likely that the judge reconciled in all his answers and told Tizio and Sempronio that if each was partly right, each was also in part wrong. Let us do likewise. This we shall do with the very arguments of the two adversaries. But we shall get conclusions far different from theirs.

We shall say to the first that when you claim that the author of an historical novel must make clear to you the actual from the invented material, you obviously haven't thought about writing one. You prescribe nothing less than the impossible. To convince you, think for a moment how these things must be combined to be part of the same story. For example, to describe historical events with which the author has bound up his conceived action (and surely you approve of historical events entering an historical novel), he must combine real circumstances taken from history or from all kinds of documents; because what could better serve to show these events in their true (and may I say individual) state than likely situations invented by the author? You want him to give you not insignificant and naked history, but something richer and more complete. You want that flesh back on the carcass which is, to some degree, history. Similarly he will have historical characters (and you are perfectly happy to find real historical figures in an historical novel) and say and do things which they did in all truth, when they were real flesh and blood, as well as things imagined by the author as being fitting to their characters; these placed amid the conceived plan of the action, where he thought it suitable to have them occur. And vice versa, he will also place invented descriptions as well as descriptions drawn from real events amid the facts he contrives about that particular time and place; since what method could be more natural than to make up actions that might have then occurred? Similarly he will give idealized words and actions to his idealized characters, befitting words and actions performed by the men of that particular time and place. The author is only too happy to make his imaginary ideas more probable by inserting elements proper to the truth. This is sufficient to show you that he cannot make the distinctions you demand, or rather he couldn't do this without having the story disintegrate, not just now and then, but at every moment, on every page and in every sentence: as if he were to say, this is positive truth drawn from bona fide memories and this is my invention, but deduced from actual facts; these words were really spoken by the character to whom I attribute them, but on another occasion and under circumstances outside my novel; these words that I put into the mouth of another imaginary character were actually

said by a real man or they were ideas then current, and so forth. Would
you call such a work a novel? Do you think it would deserve any kind
of name? Who could conceive of such a work! . . .

(Begun 1828, published 1845)

(Translated by Caroline D. Banks and H. E. Hugo)

NATHANIEL HAWTHORNE (1804-1864)
The Preface to *The House of the Seven Gables*

WHEN A writer calls his work a Romance, it need hardly be
observed that he wishes to claim a certain latitude, both as
to its fashions and material, which he would not have felt
himself entitled to assume had he professed to be writing a Novel.
The latter form of composition is presumed to aim at a very minute
fidelity, not merely to the possible, but to the probable and ordinary
course of man's experience. The former—while, as a work of art, it
must rigidly subject itself to laws, and while it sins unpardonably so
far as it may swerve aside from the truth of the human heart—has
fairly a right to present that truth under circumstances, to a great
extent, of the writer's own choosing or creation. If he think fit, also,
he may so manage his atmospherical medium as to bring out or mellow
the lights and deepen and enrich the shadows of the picture. He
will be wise, no doubt, to make a very moderate use of the privileges
here stated, and, especially, to mingle the Marvelous rather as a slight,
delicate, and evanescent flavor, than as any portion of the actual substance of the dish offered to the public. He can hardly be said, however, to commit a literary crime even if he disregard this caution.

In the present work, the author has proposed to himself—but
with what success, fortunately, it is not for him to judge—to keep
undeviatingly within his immunities. The point of view in which this
tale comes under the Romantic definition lies in the attempt to connect a bygone time with the very present that is flitting away from us.
It is a legend prolonging itself, from an epoch now gray in the distance, down into our own broad daylight, and bringing along with it
some of its legendary mist, which the reader, according to his pleasure,
may either disregard, or allow it to float almost imperceptibly about
the characters and events for the sake of a picturesque effect. The
narrative, it may be, is woven of so humble a texture as to require this
advantage, and, at the same time, to render it the more difficult of
attainment.

Many writers lay very great stress upon some definite moral purpose, at which they profess to aim their works. Not to be deficient in this particular, the author has provided himself with a moral,—the truth, namely, that the wrong-doing of one generation lives into the successive ones, and divesting itself of every temporary advantage, becomes a pure and uncontrollable mischief; and he would feel it a singular gratification if this romance might effectually convince mankind—or, indeed, any one man—of the folly of tumbling down an avalanche of ill-gotten gold, or real estate, on the heads of an unfortunate posterity, thereby to maim and crush them, until the accumulated mass shall be scattered abroad in its original atoms. In good faith, however, he is not sufficiently imaginative to flatter himself with the slightest hope of this kind. When romances do really teach anything, or produce any effective operation, it is usually through a far more subtle process than the ostensible one. The author has considered it hardly worth his while, therefore, relentlessly to impale the story with its moral as with an iron rod—or, rather, as by sticking a pin through a butterfly,—thus at once depriving it of life, and causing it to stiffen in an ungainly and unnatural attitude. A high truth, indeed, fairly, finely, and skilfully wrought out, brightening at every step, and crowning the final development of a work of fiction, may add an artistic glory, but is never any truer, and seldom any more evident, at the last page than at the first.

The reader may perhaps choose to assign an actual locality to the imaginary events of this narrative. If permitted by the historical connection,—which, though slight, was essential to his plan,—the author would very willingly have avoided anything of this nature. Not to speak of other objections, it exposes the romance to an inflexible and exceedingly dangerous species of criticism, by bringing his fancy-pictures almost into positive contact with the realities of the moment. It has been no part of his object, however, to describe local manners, nor in any way to meddle with the characteristics of a community for whom he cherishes a proper respect and a natural regard. He trusts not to be considered as unpardonably offending by laying out a street that infringes upon nobody's private rights, and appropriating a lot of land which had no visible owner, and building a house of materials long in use for constructing castles in the air. The personages of the tale—though they give themselves out to be of ancient stability and considerable prominence—are really of the author's own making, or, at all events, of his own mixing; their virtues can shed no lustre, nor their defects redound, in the remotest degree, to the discredit of the venerable town of which they profess to be inhabitants. He would be glad,

therefore, if—especially in the quarter to which he alludes—the book
may be read strictly as a Romance, having a great deal more to do with
the clouds overhead than with any portion of the actual soil of the
County of Essex.   (1851)

GUSTAVE FLAUBERT (1821-1880)

From *Correspondence*

[To Louise Colet from Croisset, January 15, 1852]

THERE ARE in me, literarily speaking, two distinct fellows; one
who is smitten with *jaw-noise*, lyricism, huge eagle-like flights,
all the sonorities of the phrase and the crests of an idea;
the other who digs and burrows after the truth as much as he can,
who likes to bring out a humble fact as powerfully as a big fact, who
would like to make you feel almost *physically* the things that he re-
produces. The latter fellow likes to laugh and enjoys the animal side
of man. To my way of thinking *The Sentimental Education* was an
effort to fuze these two tendencies of my mind. It would have been
easier to do something human in one book and something lyrical in
another. I failed. Despite a few retouchings that one night do to this
work (perhaps I shall make them), too many things are missing, and
it is always what is *lacking* that makes a book weak....

What to me seems beautiful, what I would like to do, is a book
about nothing, a book with no exterior link, which would hold itself
together by the internal strength of its style, just as the earth hangs
in the air without support; a book that would have almost no subject
or at least where the subject would be nearly invisible, if such a thing
would be possible. The finest works contain the least material; the
closer that expression comes to thought, the closer the word comes to
cling to it and disappear in it, and the result is finer. I think the future
of art lies in this direction; I see it in proportion as it has grown from
its beginning, becoming as ethereal as it can, from Egyptian pythons
to Gothic lancets, from the twenty-thousand line Hindu poems to
Byron's effusiveness. Form, in becoming more skillful, has become
more attentuated; it departs from any liturgy, rule, or standard; the
epic is abandoned in favor of the novel, verse for prose; form knows
no more orthodoxy and is as free as the will of its creator. This emancipation from matter we meet everywhere, and governments have
undergone it, all the way from oriental despotisms to the socialist
states of the future.

For this reason there are neither noble nor ignoble subjects; and one might almost posit as axiomatic from the standpoint of pure art that these things don't exist, that style itself is an absolute way of looking at things. I'd need a whole book to develop what I have just said. But I'll write about all this in my old age when I have nothing better to scribble about; in the meantime I am working courageously at my novel. . . .

[*To Louise Colet from Croisset, February 1, 1852*]

A BAD WEEK; the work hasn't been going well; I have reached a point in it where I haven't known what to say. It was all nuances and refinements where I couldn't see a speck myself, and it's very hard to clarify through words what is still obscure in one's own thought. I made sketches, wasted a lot of paper, floundered around and fumbled, perhaps now I'll find my way back again. Oh! What a rascal of a thing style is! I think you have no idea of what kind of an old book I am writing. The sloppier I was in my other books, the more in this one I am trying to be neatly-groomed and to follow a straight geometrical line: no lyricism, no commentary, the author's personality absent. It will be sad reading; there will be atrociously miserable and sordid things in it. Bouilhet thinks that the tone is right and hopes the book will be good. God grant it! But as far as time goes, it is taking on formidable proportions. I shall certainly not be through by the beginning of next winter. . . .

[*To Louise Colet from Croisset, September 19, 1852*]

How MY *Bovary* is getting on my nerves! I am beginning to see it through, however, a little. I have never in my life written anything more difficult than what I am now doing, trivial dialogue! This scene at the inn is perhaps going to take me three months; I don't know, there are moments when I want to weep, so much do I feel my incapability. But I would rather die than to push it out of the way. I have to portray simultaneously in the same conversation five or six characters (who are speaking), several others who are spoken about, the place where they are, the whole countryside, giving physical descriptions of people and objects, and in the middle of all this a man and a woman who are beginning (through sympathetic tastes) to fall in love with each other. If only I had more space! But it all must be swift without being dry, and well worked out without being sticky, all the time while I hold in reserve details which would be very striking here. I am going to do the whole thing very quickly and then proceed by successive revisions of the whole thing; by dint of beginning again perhaps I can pull it all together. The language in itself is most painful for me. I have to make my utterly commonplace characters talk in a literary style, and politeness of language takes away so much that is picturesque in any speech! ...

[*To Mlle. Leroyer de Chatepie from Paris, March 18, 1857*]

I HASTEN to thank you; I have received everything you sent me. Thank you for your letter, for the books, and above all for your portrait. I am touched by this delicate attention.

I am going to read your three volumes slowly, attentively; that is to say, in a way that they deserve, I am sure of that in advance.

But I am stopped from doing so for the moment, because before I return to the country, I am very busy with some archeological work about one of antiquity's least-known periods, a job which is the preparation for still another. I am going to write a novel whose action takes place three centuries before Christ, because I feel the need to take leave of the modern world where my pen has been too long steeped, and which moreover tires me as much to reproduce as it disgusts me to look at it.

With a reader like you, Madame, one so understanding, frankness is a duty. Thus I am going to answer your questions: *Madame Bovary* has nothing true in it. It is a *totally fictitious* story; I put nothing in it of my own feelings or of my own life. The illusion (if there is one) stems, on the contrary, from the *impersonality* of the book. This is one of my principles: you must not *write of yourself*. The artist must be within his work like God within the Creation; invisible and all-powerful; we feel him throughout, but we do not see him.

And furthermore art should rise above personal emotions and nervous susceptibilities! It is time that we give it, through a pitiless methodology, the precision of the physical sciences! The prime difficulty for me remains the style, the form, and the indefinable beauty *resulting from the conception itself* which is, as Plato said, the splendor of truth.

(Translated by H. E. Hugo)

CHARLES BAUDELAIRE (1821-1867)

From *"Madame Bovary" by Gustave Flaubert*

HE FINAL years under Louis-Philippe had seen the last outbursts of an attitude still capable of being excited by the play of the imagination; but the new novelist found himself facing an absolutely worn-out society—worse than worn out—brutalized and gluttonous, having only a horror of fiction and love for possession.

Under such conditions, a healthy mind, enthusiastic about beauty but also used to a good fight, assessing the best and the worst of the situation, had to tell himself: "What is the surest way to shake up these old people? In all truth, they don't really know what they love; they only know that they are positively disgusted with greatness; passions that are strong and pure, along with poetic abandon, make them blush and hurts their feelings. So be vulgar when you choose your subject, because the nineteenth-century reader is insulted by too grand a subject. Be icily cool when you tell about how the vulgar show their ardor in their passions and adventures; be, as the academicians say, objective and impersonal."

"Also, since lately our ears have been filled with puerile academic babbling, even as we have heard talk of a certain literary procedure called *realism*—a disgusting insult thrown at the face of every analyst, which means for the vulgar not a new method of creating but rather a minute description of small details—we shall profit from the confusion of opinion and the general ignorance. We shall spread out a nervous, picturesque, subtle and exact style on a commonplace canvas. We shall enclose the hottest, most boiling-over feelings within the most trivial tale. The most solemn, most serious words will be uttered by the most ridiculous mouths."

"What area is the most foolish, what environment most stupid, richest in absurdities, filled with the most intolerant imbeciles?"

"The provinces."

"Who are the most unbearable actors living there?"

"The little people who get excited by their little jobs whose practise makes their ideas all wrong."

"What is the most worn-out theme, most prostituted, most exhausted example of Barbarism?"

"Adultery."

Then the poet says to himself: "I don't need my *heroine* to be a heroine. She only has to be pretty enough; have nerves, ambition, a frantic aspiration toward a better world, and she will be interesting enough. Moreover, my feat of skill will be nobler, and our sinner will at least have this comparatively rare virtue of being different from all those ostentatious babblers belonging to the period just behind us."

"I don't need to worry about style, picturesque details, and describing backgrounds; these I already have superabundantly. I shall go along depending on analysis and logic, thus proving that all subjects are equally good or bad depending on the way that they are handled, and the vulgarest can be the best one."

From that moment, *Madame Bovary*—a wager, a real gamble like every work of art—was born. . . .

Several critics have commented that this book, beautiful as it is in the minuteness and liveliness of its descriptions, contains not one single character who represents morality and who represents the conscience of the author. Where is he, that proverbial and legendary character responsible for explaining the story and directing the intelligence of the reader?

Nonsense! This is an eternal and incorrigible confusion of functions and genres. A real work of art has no need for an indictment. The logic of the work suffices for all ethical prerequisites, and it is up to the reader to draw his own conclusions from the conclusion....

(1857)

(Translated by H. E. Hugo)

FYODOR M. DOSTOIEVSKY (1821-1881)
From *The Diary of a Writer*

A Few Words about George Sand

EORGE Sand's debut in literature coincided with the years of my early youth, and now I am very glad this happened so long ago because at present—over thirty years since—I can speak almost quite candidly. It should be observed that in those days this—that is, fiction—was the only thing permitted, whereas the rest, virtually every thought, especially coming from France, was strictly forbidden. Oh, it stands to reason that very often we did not know how to behold things, and, indeed, where could we have learned this? —Even Metternich did not know how to behold things, not to speak of our imitators. Therefore, "dreadful things" used to slip through (for example, all Bielinsky slipped through). To avoid any possible mistake, especially at the very end of that period, almost everything began to be interdicted, so that, as is known, it came to the point that one had to read between the lines. Nevertheless, novels were permitted —in the beginning, in the middle and at the very end of that period. And right here, specifically in the case of George Sand, the guardians committed a grave error. Do you remember the verses:

> Tomes by Thiers and by Rabeau—
> Those he memorizes,
> And, like raging Mirabeau,
> Liberty he eulogizes.

These are exceptionally talented verses; they will survive forever, because they are historical verses; but they are all the more precious as they were written by Denys Davydov, a poet, a littérateur and a most honest Russian. And even if Denys Davydov, in those days, considered —whom of all men?—Thiers (of course, for his *History of the Revolution*) dangerous and placed him in that verse side by side with some fellow Rabeau (there must have been, then, such a man, too; however, I know nothing about him)—officially, then, too little could have been permitted. And what was the result?—That which in those days burst into Russia in the form of novels not only did in like manner serve the cause, but even so, perhaps, proved the most "dangerous" form, as things stood in those days, since there would have been but few lovers of Rabeau, whereas there came forth thousands of lovers of George Sand. At this point it may be remarked that notwithstanding all the Magnitzkys and Liprandis, ever since the Eighteenth Century, every intellectual movement in Europe invariably became promptly known in Russia, and it used to be forthwith transmitted from the upper strata of our intellectuals to the rank and file of the thinking, or even slightly interested, people. Exactly the same took place in the case of the European movement of the Thirties. Very soon, at the very beginning of the Thirties, we took cognizance of that immense European literary movement. The names of many newly appearing orators, historians, tribunes and professors were already known. Though partly and only superficially, it became known whither this movement tended. And most passionately it has revealed itself in art, in fiction, and principally—in George Sand. True, Senkovsky and Bulgarin had warned the public against George Sand even before Russian translations of her novels had appeared. They scared the Russian ladies particularly by the fact that she wore trousers; it was sought to frighten them with the idea of depravity and to ridicule her. Senkovsky himself, who had been planning to translate George Sand in his magazine *Library for Reading*, began to call her in print Mrs. Egor Sand, and it seems that he was earnestly pleased with his wit. Later, in 1848, Bulgarin, in his *Northern Bee*, printed accounts to the effect that day after day she had been attending drinking bouts in company with Pierre Leroux somewhere near the town gates, and that she took part in "Athenian parties" at the Ministry of the Interior, sponsored by the robber and Minister of the Interior Ledru-Rollin. This I have read myself, and I remember it well. But then, in 1848, George Sand was known by virtually all the reading public in Russia, and no one gave credence to Bulgarin. For the first time, she appeared in Russian translation about the middle

The selection from *The Diary of a Writer*, F. M. Dostoievsky, Volume I, pp. 344-350, translated and annotated by Boris Brasol (Copyright 1949, Charles Scribner's Sons) is reprinted by permission of Charles Scribner's Sons.

of the Thirties. It is a pity that I do not remember and do not know
when and which of her works were translated in Russia. But all the
more startling must have been the impression. I imagine that much as
I, then a young lad, everybody in those days was impressed with the
chaste, sublime purity of the characters and of the ideals, and the
modest charm of the austere, reserved tone of the narrative—and such
a woman wears trousers and engages in debauch! I must have been
about sixteen years old when I first read her novel *Uskok*, one of the
most delightful of her early works. I recall that I was in a state of
fever all night.

I believe I do not err when I say that George Sand—judging at
least by my personal recollections—promptly assumed in Russia
virtually the first place among a whole Pléiad of new writers who at
that period suddenly rose to fame and won renown all over Europe.
Even Dickens, who appeared in Russia about the same time as she,
was, perhaps, less popular with our public. I am not even speaking of
Balzac who came earlier than she and who, however, in the Thirties,
produced such works as *Eugénie Grandet* and *Père Goriot* (to whom
Bielinsky was so unjust, having completely missed his significance in
French literature). However, I am telling all this not from the standpoint of any critical evaluation, but I am simply recalling the tastes of
the rank and file of the Russian readers and of the impression directly
produced on them. The main thing is that the reader managed to
extract even from novels everything against which he was being
guarded. At least, in the middle of the Forties, the rank and file Russian
reader knew, even though partly, that George Sand was one of the
most brilliant, stern and just representatives of that category of the
contemporaneous Western new men who, when they appeared, started
with a direct negation of those "positive" acquisitions which brought
to a close the activities of the bloody French—more correctly, European—revolution of the end of the past century. After it had come
to an end, after Napoleon I, it was sought to express the new longings
and the new ideals. Progressive minds had only too well grasped the
fact that despotism had merely assumed a new guise; that nothing
but "*ôte-toi de là, que je m'y mette*" had taken place; that the new
world conquerors (the bourgeois) proved, perhaps, even worse than
the former despots (the nobility); that "*Liberté, Egalité, Fraternité*"
is but a high-sounding phrase, and nothing but a phrase. Moreover,
there came into being certain doctrines, in which such lofty phrases
had been converted into impossible phrases. The conquerors would
be scoffingly uttering—rather recalling—these three sacramental words.
Even science, in the persons of its brilliant representatives (econo-
mists), then came, as it were, with its new word, to the assistance of

mockery and in condemnation of the Utopian meaning of these three words for which so much blood had been shed. Thus, side by side with the triumphant conquerors, despondent and sad faces, frightening the triumphers, began to appear. It was precisely at that epoch that suddenly a new word had been uttered and new hopes had arisen: men came who boldly proclaimed that the cause had been interrupted in vain and unjustly; that nothing had been accomplished by the political shift of the conquerors; that the cause had still to be pursued; that the renovation of humanity must be radical and social. Why, of course, along with these mottoes, a great many of the ugliest and most noxious inferences were drawn; yet, the cardinal point was that once more hope began to gleam and faith began to be regenerated. The history of this movement is known; it still continues, and it would seem that it does not intend to come to a stop at all. I do not wish to speak here either for or against the movement: I merely meant to indicate George Sand's true place in it. Her place must be sought at its very inception. At that time people in Europe were saying that she preached a new status for woman and she prophesied "the rights of free wifehood" (this is Senkovsky's expression about her). But this was not quite so, since her sermons were by no means confined to woman alone; nor did she ever invent the term "free wifehood." George Sand belonged to the whole movement, and not to the mere sermons on women's rights. True, being a woman herself, she naturally preferred to portray *heroines* rather than heroes, and, of course, women of the whole world should not don mourning garb in her memory, because one of their loftiest and most beautiful representatives has passed away, and, in addition, an almost unprecedented woman by reason of the power of her mind and talent—a name which has become historical and which is destined not to be forgotten by, or to disappear from, European humanity.

As for her heroines, I reiterate, I was astonished from the very start—ever since the age of sixteen—by the strangeness of the contradiction between what people had been writing and saying about her, and what in reality I personally perceived. In fact, many—at least, several—of her heroines represented a type of such elevated moral purity that it could not have been conceived without an immense ethical quest in the soul of the poetess herself; without the confession of most complete duty; without the comprehension and admission of most sublime beauty and mercy, patience and justice. True, side by side with mercy, patience and the acknowledgment of the obligations of duty, there was the extraordinary pride of the quest and of the protest; yet it was precisely that pride which was so precious because it sprang from the most sublime truth, without which mankind could never have retained its place on so lofty a moral height. This pride is not rancour *quand même*, based upon the idea that I am better than you, and you are worse than me; nay, this is merely a feeling of the most chaste impossibility of compromise with untruth and vice, although—I repeat—this feeling precludes neither all-forgiveness nor mercy. Moreover, commensurately with this pride, an enormous duty was to be assumed. These heroines of hers thirsted for sacrifices and heroic deeds. I was then particularly fond of several girl characters in her early works, which were portrayed, for example, in the then so-called Venetian novels (to which *Uskok* and *Aldini* belonged also) —types which culminated in the romance *Jeanne*, an altogether ingenious work setting forth a serene and, perhaps, an incontestable solution of the historical question of Joan of Arc. In a contemporary peasant girl she suddenly resurrects before the reader the image of the historical Joan of Arc, and graphically justifies the actual possibility of that majestic and miraculous event. This is a typically George-sandesque task, since no one but she among contemporary poets bore in the soul so pure an ideal of an innocent girl—pure and so potent by reason of its innocence. These girl characters, to which I am referring, reiterate in several successive works one and the same problem, one and the same theme (not only girls, however: this theme was later reiterated in the magnificent novel *La Marquise*, also one of her early works). A straightforward, honest, but inexperienced, character of a young feminine creature is pictured, one possessing that proud chastity which is neither afraid of, nor can even be contaminated by, contact with vice—even if that creature should accidentally find herself in the very den of vice. The want of magnanimous sacrifice (supposedly specifically expected from her) startles the youthful girl's heart, and unhesitatingly, without sparing herself, disinterestedly, self-sacrificingly and fearlessly, she suddenly takes the most perilous and fatal step. That which she sees and encounters does not in the least confuse or intimidate her; on the contrary, it forthwith increases courage in the youthful heart which, at this juncture, for the first time, realizes the full measure of its strength—the strength of innocence, honesty and purity; it doubles the energy, reveals new paths and new horizons to a mind which up to that time had not known itself, a vigorous and fresh mind not yet soiled with the compromise of life. Added to this is the most perfect and delightful form of the poem. George Sand was particularly fond of winding up her poems *happily*—with the triumph of innocence, sincerity and youthful, fearless naïveté. Could these images disturb society or arouse doubts and fear?—On the contrary, the severest fathers and mothers began to permit in their families the reading of George Sand, and they merely kept wondering:

"Why did everybody say such things about her?" But right here, at this point, warning voices began to sound: "Precisely in this pride of woman's quest; in this irreconcilability of chastity with vice; in this rejection of any compromises with evil; in this fearlessness with which innocence rises to the struggle and looks brightly into the eyes of the offense—therein precisely is the venom, the future poison of woman's protest, of woman's emancipation."

Well, perhaps, they were correct about that poison; poison did actually come into being. But what was it seeking to destroy, what was to perish and what was to survive as a result of its action?—Such were the questions which immediately arose and which for a long time remained unsolved.

In our day all these questions have long been settled (so it seems). In passing, it may be remarked that by the middle of the Forties George Sand's fame, and the faith in the power of her genius, stood so high that we all, her contemporaries, had been expecting from her something incomparably greater in the future—some new, yet unheard-of word, even something finitively decisive. These hopes did not materialize: it developed that by that time—by the end of the Forties—she had already said everything which she was destined and predestined to express, and now over her fresh grave the last word about her can be said.

George Sand was not a thinker but she was one of the most clairvoyant foreseers (if this flourishing term be permitted) of a happy future awaiting mankind, in the realization of whose ideals she had confidently and magnanimously believed all her life—this because she herself was able to conceive this ideal in her soul. The preservation of this faith to the end is usually the lot of all lofty souls, of all genuine friends of humanity. George Sand died a *déiste*, with a staunch belief in God and in her immortal life. But this does not fully cover the ground: in addition, she was, perhaps, the most Christian among all persons of her age—French writers—even though she did not confess Christ (as does a Roman Catholic). Of course, being a Frenchwoman, in accord with the conceptions of her compatriots, George Sand could not consciously adhere to the idea "that in the whole universe there is no name other than His through which one may be saved"—the fundamental idea of Orthodoxy—yet, despite this seeming and formal contradiction, George Sand, I repeat, was perhaps, without knowing it herself, one of the staunchest confessors of Christ. She based her socialism, her convictions, her hopes and her ideals upon the moral feeling of man, upon the spiritual thirst of mankind and its longing for perfection and purity, and not upon "ant-necessity." All her life she believed absolutely in human personality (to the point of its

immortality), elevating and broadening this concept in each one of
her works; and thereby she concurred in thought and feeling with one
of the basic ideas of Christianity, *i.e.*, the recognition of human personality and its freedom (consequently, also of its responsibility).
Hence, the recognition of duty and the austere moral quests, and the
complete acknowledgment of man's responsibility. And, perhaps, in
the France of her time there was no thinker and no writer who understood as clearly as she that "man shall not live by bread alone." As
to the pride of her quests and of her protest—I repeat—this pride
never precluded mercy, forgiveness of offense, or even boundless
patience based upon compassion for the offender himself. On the
contrary, time and again, in her works George Sand has been captivated
by the beauty of these truths and on more than one occasion she has
portrayed characters of the most sincere forgiveness and love. It is said
that she died an excellent mother, working to the last days of her
life as a friend of neighboring peasants, boundlessly beloved by her
friends. It seems that she was partly inclined to value the aristocracy
of her extraction (on her mother's side she descended from the Royal
House of Saxony), but, of course, it may be positively asserted that
if she did value aristocracy in people, she must have based it on the
perfection of the human soul: she could not help but love the great,
she could not reconcile herself with the base or cede an idea—and
in this particular sense she may have been excessively haughty. True,
she did not like to depict in her novels humble people, righteous but
yielding, religious fanatics and downtrodden folks, such as appear in
almost every novel of the great Christian—Dickens. She, on the contrary, haughtily placed her heroines on a pedestal as true queens. This
she loved to do, and this peculiarity should be noted, since it is
rather typical.   (1876)

GEORGE ELIOT (Mary Ann Evans, 1819-1880)

From "Leaves from a Notebook" in
The Impressions of Theophrastus Such

STORY TELLING. What is the best way of telling a story?
Since the standard must be the interest of the audience,
there must be several or many good ways rather than
one best. For we get interested in the stories life presents to us
through divers orders and modes of presentation. Very commonly
our first awakening to a desire of knowing a man's past or future comes
from our seeing him as a stranger in some unusual or pathetic or
humorous situation, or manifesting some remarkable characteristics.

We make inquiries in consequence, or we become observant and attentive whenever opportunities of knowing more may happen to present themselves without our search. You have been a refined face among the prisoners picking tow in jail; you afterward see the same unforgetable face in a pulpit: he must be of dull fibre who would not care to know more about a life which showed such contrasts, though he might gather his knowledge in a fragmentary and unchronological way.

Again, we have heard much, or at least something not quite common, about a man whom we have never seen, and hence we look round with curiosity when we are told that he is present; whatever he says or does before us is charged with a meaning due to our previous hearsay knowledge about him, gathered either from dialogue of which he was expressly and emphatically the subject, or from incidental remark, or from general report either in or out of print.

These indirect ways of arriving at knowledge are always the most stirring even in relation to impersonal subjects. To see a chemical experiment gives an attractiveness to a definition of chemistry, and fills it with a significance which it would never have had without the pleasant shock of an unusual sequence such as the transformation of a solid into gas, and *vice versa*. To see a word for the first time either as substantive or adjective in a connection where we care about knowing its complete meaning, is the way to vivify its meaning in our recollection. Curiosity becomes the more eager from the incompleteness of the first information. Moreover, it is in this way that memory works in its incidental revival of events: some salient experience appears in inward vision, and in consequence the antecedent facts are retraced from what is regarded as the beginning of the episode in which that experience made a more or less strikingly memorable part. "Ah! I remember addressing the mob from the hustings at Westminster—you wouldn't have thought that I could ever have been in such a position. Well, how I came there was in this way——"; and then follows a retrospective narration.

The modes of telling a story founded on these processes of outward and inward life derive their effectiveness from the superior mastery of images and pictures in grasping the attention—or, one might say with more fundamental accuracy, from the fact that our earliest, strongest impressions, our most intimate convictions, are simply images added to more or less of sensation. These are the primitive instruments of thought. Hence it is not surprising that early poetry took this way—telling a daring deed, a glorious achievement, without caring for what went before. The desire for orderly narration is a later, more reflective birth. The presence of the Jack in the box

affects every child: it is the more reflective lad, the miniature philosopher, who wants to know how he got there.

The only stories life presents to us in an orderly way are those
of our autobiography, or the career of our companions from our childhood upward, or perhaps of our own children. But it is a great art to
make a connected strictly relevant narrative of such careers as we can
recount from the beginning. In these cases the sequence of associations
is almost sure to overmaster the sense of proportion. Such narratives
ab ovo are summer's-day stories for happy loungers; not the cup of
self-forgetting excitement to the busy who can snatch an hour of
entertainment.

But the simple opening of a story with a date and necessary
account of places and people, passing on quietly toward the more
rousing elements of narrative and dramatic presentation, without need
of retrospect, has its advantages which have to be measured by the
nature of the story. Spirited narrative, without more than a touch of
dialogue here and there, may be made eminently interesting, and is
suited to the novelette. Examples of its charm are seen in the short
tales in which the French have a mastery never reached by the English,
who usually demand coarser flavors than are given by that delightful
gayety which is well described by La Fontaine[1] as not anything that
provokes fits of laughter, but a certain charm, an agreeable mode of
handling which lends attractiveness to all subjects even the most
serious. And it is this sort of gayety which plays around the best
French novelettes. But the opening chapters of the "Vicar of Wakefield" are as fine as anything that can be done in this way.

Why should a story not be told in the most irregular fashion
that an author's idiosyncrasy may prompt, provided that he gives us
what we can enjoy? The objections to Sterne's wild way of telling
"Tristram Shandy" lie more solidly in the quality of the interrupting
matter than in the fact of interruption. The dear public would do
well to reflect that they are often bored from the want of flexibility
in their own minds. They are like the topers of "one liquor."

Historic Imagination. The exercise of a veracious imagination
in historical picturing seems to be capable of a development that might
help the judgment greatly with regard to present and future events.
By veracious imagination, I mean the working out in detail of the
various steps by which political or a social change was reached, using
all extant evidence and supplying deficiencies by careful analogical

[1] Je n'appelle pas gayeté ce qui excite le rire, mais un certain charme, un
air agréable qu'on peut donner à toutes sortes de sujets, mesme les plus
sérieux."—Preface to Fables.

creation. How triumphant opinions originally spread—how institutions arose—what were the conditions of great inventions, discoveries, or theoretic conceptions—what circumstances affecting individual lots are attendant on the decay of long-established systems,—all these grand elements of history require the illumination of special imaginative treatment. But effective truth in this application of art requires freedom from the vulgar coercion of conventional plot, which is become hardly of higher influence on imaginative representation than a detailed "order" for a picture sent by a rich grocer to an eminent painter—allotting a certain portion of the canvas to a rural scene, another to a fashionable group, with a request for a murder in the middle distance, and a little comedy to relieve it. A slight approximation to the veracious glimpses of history artistically presented, which I am indicating, but applied only to an incident of contemporary life, is "Un paquet de lettres" by Gustave Droz. For want of such real, minute vision of how changes come about in the past, we fall into ridiculously inconsistent estimates of actual movements, condemning in the present what we belaud in the past, and pronouncing impossible processes that have been repeated again and again in the historical preparation of the very system under which we live. A false kind of idealization dulls our perception of the meaning in words when they relate to past events which have had a glorious issue: for lack of comparison no warning image rises to check scorn of the very phrases which in other associations are consecrated.

Utopian pictures help the reception of ideas as to constructive results, but hardly so much as a vivid presentation of how results have been actually brought about, especially in religious and social change. And there is the pathos, the heroism often accompanying the decay and final struggle of old systems, which has not had its share of tragic commemoration. What really took place in and around Constantine before, upon, and immediately after his declared conversion? Could a momentary flash be thrown on Eusebius in his sayings and doings as an ordinary man in bishop's garments? Or on Julian and Libanius? There has been abundant writing on such great turning-points, but not such as serves to instruct the imagination in true comparison. I want something different from the abstract treatment which belongs to grave history from a doctrinal point of view, and something different from the schemed picturesqueness of ordinary historical fiction. I want brief, severely conscientious reproductions, in their concrete incidents, of pregnant movements in the past. . . . (1879)

ÉMILE ZOLA (1840-1902)

From *The Experimental Novel*

N MY literary studies, I have often spoken about the experimental method applied to the novel and to the drama. The return to nature, the naturalistic evolution that marks the century, little by little is guiding all manifestations of human intelligence down the same scientific avenue. Alone the idea of a literature determined by sciences has remained astonishing, owing to its not being made precise and understandable. Thus it seems to me useful to state clearly what must be meant by the experimental novel.

I merely have here to undertake a task of adaptation, because the experimental method has been established with marvellous force and clarity by Claude Bernard in his *Introduction to the Study of Experimental Medicine*. This book by a scholar whose authority is decisive serves me as a solid base. I find there all the questions that must be treated; and I shall limit myself, as irrefutable arguments, to giving citations from it which are necessary for me. Thus it will be little more than a compilation of texts; for I count on entrenching myself on all points behind Claude Bernard. Most of the time it will suffice me to replace the word "doctor" by the word "novelist" to make my ideas clear and bring to them the rigor of scientific truth. . . .

To return to the novel, we note that the novelist similarly is composed of observer and experimenter. The observer in him states the facts as he has seen them, posits the point of departure, establishes the solid ground on which the characters are made to move and the phenomena to develop. Then the experimenter enters and institutes experience, that is to say makes the characters act within a particular story, in order to show that the succession of actions will be such as are required by the determinism of the phenomena to be studied. Here it is almost always an experience of "seeing," as Claude Bernard puts it. The novelist sets about in his research after truth. I shall take for an example the figure of Baron Hulot, in Balzac's *Cousin Betty*. The general fact observed by Balzac is the destruction that a man's amorous temperament brings about for himself, his family, and society. As soon as Balzac had chosen his subject, he was committed to observed facts; then he instituted the experience by submitting Hulot to a series of experiments, by making him move through various environments, in order to show the functioning of the mechanism of his passion. Thus it is evident that not only observation was present, but that experimentation was there; since Balzac does not limit himself strictly to photographic facts which he collected, and he intervenes in a discreet fashion in order to place his character under conditions of which he remains the master. The problem is to know how such a passion, acting in a certain environment and under certain circumstances, will occur from the point of view of the individual and of society; and an experimental novel like *Cousin Betty*, for example, is merely the official report of the proceedings of the experience, which the novelist repeats before the eyes of the public. . . .

Doubtlessly here we are far from the certainties of chemistry and even of physiology. We still do not know the reagents which decompose the passions and which allow them to be analyzed. I shall remind you frequently throughout this study that the experimental novel is younger than experimental medicine, which itself has just been born. But I do not mean to report on results that have been attained. I simply desire clearly to outline a method. If the experimental novelist still works gropingly in the most obscure and the most complex of the sciences, this is no denial that this science does not exist. Undeniably the naturalist novel, such as we conceive it to be at this time, is the faithful record of experimentation that the novelist makes about mankind, by dint of observation. . . . Again I quote Claude Bernard's remark which has struck me: "The experimenter is nature's examining magistrate." We novelists are the examining magistrates of men and their passions.

Yet note what clarity bursts forth as soon as we adjust ourselves to the point of view of the experimental method as applied to the novel, with all the scientific rigor that is sustained by today's material! A foolish reproach made against us, the naturalist writers, is that our sole wish is to be photographers. We state in vain that we accept the fact of temperament and personal expression. They continue to answer us with imbecilic arguments about the impossibility of being strictly truthful, and about the necessity to arrange the facts in order to reconstitute any kind of work of art. So be it! With the application of the experimental method to the novel, the fighting stops. The idea of experimentation carries with it the idea of modification. We take our point of departure from real facts, which forms our indestructible basis. But in order to show the mechanism of these facts, we must produce and direct phenomena. This is our share of the invention; here lies the genius in the work. Thus without taking recourse to questions of form, style, which I shall later examine, I assert that even now we have to modify nature—without departing from nature—when we employ the experimental method in our novels. If we can go back to this definition: "Observation indicates, experience teaches," we can from now on even claim this great experimental lesson for our books.

Far from being minimized, the writer here becomes singularly greater. An experiment, even the simplest, is always based upon an idea, which itself is born from an observation. As Claude Bernard says: "The experimental idea is neither imaginary nor purely arbitrary; it must always have a purchase on observed reality, that is to say on nature." On this idea and on questioning he bases the entire method. "The appearance of the experimental idea," he says further on, "is completely spontaneous, and of a completely individual nature. It is a particular sentiment, a *quid proprium*, that constitutes the originality, the invention, or the genius of each individual." Finally he makes doubt to be the great scientific lever. "The doubter is the real wise man; he only questions himself and his interpretations, but he believes in science. In the experimental sciences he even admits a criterion or an absolute principle, the determinism of phenomena, which is as absolute for the phenomena of living organisms as it is for inorganic matter." Thus instead of enclosing the novelist within narrow confines, the experimental method leaves him with all his intelligence as a thinker and all his genius as a creator. He has to see, understand, invent. A fact observed should cause to flash forth the idea of instituting an experiment, to write the novel in order to arrive at some complete comprehension of the truth. Then when he shall have discussed and drawn up a plan of this experiment, he will at the same time judge its results with the freedom of mind of a man who accepts the sole facts consonant with the determined phenomena. He takes his point of departure from questioning to arrive at absolute knowledge. He only ceases to doubt when the mechanism of the passion, which he takes apart and puts back together again, functions according to the laws fixed by nature. No greater or freer task exists for the human mind. Later we shall observe the defeats of scholastic and systematic thinkers and those theorists about the ideal, when they are ranked alongside the triumph of the experimenters. . . .

. . . In the last century, a more exact application of the experimental method created chemistry and physics, which separated themselves from the irrational and the supernatural. Thanks to analysis we have discovered that there are fixed laws; we have been making ourselves masters of phenomena. Thus a new path has been opened. Living organisms, for which the vitalists still admit some mysterious influence, have in their turn been brought back and reduced to the general mechanism of nature. Science has proved that the conditions for existence for every phenomenon are identical for live creatures as well as for inanimate bodies. From here on, little by little, physiology has been acquiring the certainties of chemistry and physics. But should we stop here? Evidently not. When it is proved that man's body is a machine that some day might be taken apart and put together again at the pleasure of the experimenter, then we certainly shall have to pass on to mankind's emotional and intellectual activity. From thence we shall enter a domain which hitherto has belonged to philosophy and to literature. Here will be science's decisive conquest over the hypotheses of philosophers and writers. We have experimental chemistry and physics; we will have experimental physiology; still later we shall have the experimental novel. Here is a progression that is self-manifest and whose last term is simple to predict from the present situation. Everything is related. We had to start from determinism for inorganic matter to get to a determinism for living bodies; and since scientists like Claude Bernard today demonstrate how fixed laws govern the human body, we can proclaim without fear of being in error the hour when the laws governing thought and the emotions will be formulated. The same determinism controls cobblestones and the brain of man. . . .

. . . From now on, science enters our novelists' domain, who are at this very moment the analysts of mankind in its social and individual activity. Through our observations and experiments we are carrying on the task of the physiologist, who in turn is continuing that of the physicist and the chemist. We are creating a kind of scientific psychology in order to fill out scientific physiology; and to complete the evolution, we only need to bring to bear the decisive implement of the experimental method on our studies of man and nature. In a word, we must work on characters, on passions, on human and social facts, the way the chemist and physicist work on inanimate matter and the way the physiologist works on living beings. Determinism rules everything. Scientific investigation, experimental reasoning battle the hypotheses of the idealists one by one; and this replaces novels of pure imagination by novels of observation and experimentation. . . .

Without daring to formulate laws, I would estimate that the question of heredity has a great influence on man's intellectual and sensual qualities. I also give considerable importance to environment. Here I should discuss Darwin's theories; but since this is only a general study of the experimental method applied to the novel, I would go too far astray if I went into details. I shall say only one word about environment. We have just seen the conclusive importance Claude Bernard gives to the study of the intra-organic environment, with which we must reckon if we wish to find the deterministic phenomena among living creatures. Very well! In the study of a family, of any group of living creatures, I believe that the social environment has equally first-rate importance. Some day physiology will doubtlessly explain the mechanism of thought and the passions; we shall know how the individual man-machine functions, how he thinks, how he loves, how he progresses from reason to passion to madness; but these phenomena, these facts about the mechanism of organs acting under the influence of the interior environment, are not produced in isolation and in some void. Man is not alone; he lives in society, within a social environment; and from now on this social environment, for us novelists, modifies all phenomena endlessly. Indeed, our great task lies there, in the reciprocal working of society on the individual and the individual on society. . . .

Henceforth the doctor will be the master of all diseases; he will infallibly cure, he will work on living bodies for their happiness and for the vigor of the race. We shall enter into a century where all-powerful man shall have enslaved nature and used its laws to make flourish the greatest sum-total of justice and liberty possible upon this earth. There is no nobler and loftier goal. Here is our role as intelligent human beings: to penetrate the *how* of things, to become superior to things and reduce them to a state of obedient clockwork.

Fine! This dream of the physiologist and the experimental doctor is also the novelist's who applies the experimental method to the natural and social study of mankind. Our goal is their's: we too wish to be the masters of intellectual and personal phenomena is order to direct them. In a word, we are experimental moralists, showing through experimentation the way a passion behaves in a social environment. The day we grasp the mechanism of this passion, we can handle it, subdue it, or at least make it the least possibly offensive. And there lies the practical usefulness and the lofty ethics of our naturalistic works. They experiment on men, take apart and put back together the human machinery to make it operate under the influence of environments. When we have progressed, when we shall have discovered laws, we will only have to work on individuals and the environments if we want to attain better social conditions. Hence we are making practical sociology, and our job helps political and economic science. I do not know, I repeat, any nobler task or greater assiduousness, to have mastery over good and evil, to control life, to resolve in the long run all the problems of socialism; above all put justice on a solid footing by dealing with problems of criminality through experimentation. Are we not here the most useful of human toilers and is not our work the most ethical? . . .

The experimental method can alone elevate the novel from the lies and mistakes amid which it has been crawling along. All my literary life has been directed by this conviction. I am deaf to the voices of critics who ask me to formulate laws about heredity and the influence of environment on characters; those who raise negative and discouraging objections and address them to me out of sheer laziness of mind, out of stubborn, traditional obstinacy, through some more or less conscious attachment to a religious or a philosophical belief. The experimental direction that the novel today takes is conclusive. In all truth, this is not at all the ephemeral influence of any kind of private system; it is the result of scientific evolution, of the study of man himself. These are my convictions in this regard, and I seek to make them penetrate into the minds of the young writers who read me; for I feel that above all we must inspire them with the scientific spirit and initiate them into the notions and tendencies of modern science. . . .

Up to now I have neglected the question of form and the naturalist writer, and it is form precisely that is special to literature. Not only does genius, for the writer, exist in the feeling and in the *a priori* idea, but it also resides in the form and the style. But the question of method and the question of rhetoric are distinctly separate. And naturalism, I say again, consists uniquely in the experimental method, in observation and experimentation applied to literature. Rhetoric, for the moment, is not relevant. Let us establish the method, which must be common to all; then let us accept for literature all the rhetorics which arise; let us regard them as expressions of the literary temperament of the writers.

If you want my real opinion, I think today an exaggerated preponderance is given to form. I could have a great deal to say on this subject, but that would exceed the limits of this study. Basically, I suggest that the method itself establishes the form; that a language is only a logic, a natural and scientific construct. The best writer will not be the one who gallops madly amid hypotheses, but rather the one who marches squarely to the middle of the truth. Actually we are rotten with lyricism; we think quite wrongly that the grand style is composed of startling sublimity, ever close to tumbling over into lunacy. The grand style is composed of logic and clarity. . . .   (1880)

(Translated by H. E. Hugo)

ANTHONY TROLLOPE (1815-1882)

From An Autobiography

On Novels and the Art of Writing Them

IT IS NEARLY twenty years since I proposed to myself to write a history of English prose fiction. I shall never do it now, but the subject is so good a one that I recommend it heartily to some man of letters, who shall at the same time be indefatigable and light-handed. I acknowledge that I broke down in the task, because I could not endure the labour in addition to the other labours of my life. Though the book might be charming, the work was very much the reverse. It came to have a terrible aspect to me, as did that proposition that I should sit out all the May meetings of a season. According to my plan of such a history it would be necessary to read an infinity of novels, and not only to read them, but so to read them as to point out the excellences of those which are most excellent, and to explain the defects of those which, though defective, had still reached sufficient reputation to make them worthy of notice. I did read many after this fashion,—and here and there I have the criticisms which I wrote. In regard to many, they were written on some blank page within the book. I have not, however, even a list of the books so criticised. I think that the *Arcadia* was the first, and *Ivanhoe* the last. My plan, as I settled it at last, had been to begin with *Robinson Crusoe*, which is the earliest really popular novel which we have in our language, and to continue the review so as to include the works of all English novelists of reputation, except those who might still be living when my task should be completed. But when Dickens and Bulwer died, my spirit flagged, and that which I had already found to be very difficult had become almost impossible to me at my then period of life.

I began my own studies on the subject with works much earlier than *Robinson Crusoe*, and made my way through a variety of novels which were necessary for my purpose, but which in the reading gave me no pleasure whatever. I never worked harder than at the *Arcadia*, or read more detestable trash than the stories written by Mrs. Aphra Behn; but these two were necessary to my purpose, which was not only to give an estimate of the novels as I found them, but to describe how it had come to pass that the English novels of the present day have become what they are, to point out the effects which they have produced, and to inquire whether their great popularity has on the whole done good or evil to the people who read them. I still think that the book is one well worthy to be written.

I intended to write that book to vindicate my own profession as a novelist, and also to vindicate that public taste in literature which has created and nourished the profession which I follow. And I was stirred up to make such an attempt by a conviction that there still exists among us Englishmen a prejudice in respect to novels which might, perhaps, be lessened by such a work. This prejudice is not against the reading of novels, as is proved by their general acceptance among us. But it exists strongly in reference to the appreciation in which they are professed to be held; and it robs them of much of that high character which they may claim to have earned by their grace, their honesty, and good teaching.

No man can work long at any trade without being brought to consider much whether that which he is daily doing tends to evil or to good. I have written many novels, and have known many writers of novels, and I can assert that such thoughts have been strong with them and with myself. But in acknowledging that these writers have received from the public a full measure of credit for such genius, ingenuity, or perseverance as each may have displayed, I feel that there is still wanting to them a just appreciation of the excellence of their calling, and a general understanding of the high nature of the work which they perform.

By the common consent of all mankind who have read, poetry takes the highest place in literature. That nobility of expression, and all but divine grace of words, which she is bound to attain before she can make her footing good, is not compatible with prose. Indeed it is that which turns prose into poetry. When that has been in truth achieved, the reader knows that the writer has soared above the earth, and can teach his lessons somewhat as a god might teach. He who sits down to write his tale in prose makes no such attempt, nor does he dream that the poet's honour is within his reach;—but his teaching is of the same nature, and his lessons all tend to the same end. By either, false sentiments may be fostered; false notions of humanity may be engendered; false honour, false love, false worship may be created; by either, vice instead of virtue may be taught. But by each, equally, may true honour, true love, true worship, and true humanity be inculcated; and that will be the greatest teacher who will spread such truth the widest. But at present, much as novels, as novels, are brought and read, there exists still an idea, a feeling which is very prevalent, that novels at their best are but innocent. Young men and women,— and old men and women too,—read more of them than of poetry, because such reading is easier than the reading of poetry; but they read them,—as men eat pastry after dinner,—not without some inward conviction that the taste is vain if not vicious. I take upon myself to say that it is neither vicious nor vain.

But all writers of fiction who have desired to think well of their own work, will probably have had doubts on their minds before they have arrived at this conclusion. Thinking much of my own daily labour and of its nature, I felt myself at first to be much afflicted and then to be deeply grieved by the opinion expressed by wise and thinking men as to the work done by novelists. But when, by degrees, I dared to examine and sift the sayings of such men, I found them to be sometimes silly and often arrogant. I began to inquire what had been the nature of English novels since they first became common in our own language, and to be desirous of ascertaining whether they had done harm or good. I could well remember that, in my own young days, they had not taken that undisputed possession of drawing-rooms which they now hold. Fifty years ago, when George IV. was king, they were not indeed treated as Lydia had been forced to treat them in the preceding reign, when, on the approach of elders, *Peregrine Pickle* was hidden beneath the bolster, and *Lord Ainsworth* put away under the sofa. But the families in which an unrestricted permission was given for the reading of novels were very few, and from many they were altogether banished. The high poetic genius and correct morality of Walter Scott had not altogether succeeded in making men and women understand that lessons which were good in poetry could not be bad in prose. I remember that in those days an embargo was laid upon novel-reading as a pursuit, which was to the novelist a much heavier tax than that want of full appreciation of which I now complain.

There is, we all know, no such embargo now. May we not say that people of an age to read have got too much power into their own hands to endure any very complete embargo? Novels are read right and left, above stairs and below, in town houses and in country parsonages, by young countesses and by farmer's daughters, by old lawyers and by young students. It has not only come to pass that a special provision of them has to be made for the godly, but that the provision so made must now include books which a few years since the godly would have thought to be profane. It was this necessity which, a few years since, induced the editor of *Good Words* to apply to me for a novel,—which, indeed, when supplied was rejected, but which now, probably, owing to further change in the same direction, would have been accepted.

If such be the case—if the extension of novel-reading be so wide as I have described it—then very much good or harm must be done by novels. The amusement of the time can hardly be the only result of any book that is read, and certainly not so with a novel, which appeals especially to the imagination, and solicits the sympathy of the young. A vast proportion of the teaching of the day,—greater probably than many of us have acknowledged to ourselves,—comes from these books, which are in the hands of all readers. It is from them that girls learn what is expected from them, and what they are to expect when lovers come; and also from them that young men unconsciously learn what are, or should be, or may be, the charms of love,—though I fancy that few young men will think so little of their natural instincts and powers as to believe that I am right in saying so. Many other lessons also are taught. In these times, when the desire to be honest is pressed so hard, is so violently assaulted by the ambition to be great; in which riches are the easiest road to greatness; when the temptations to which men are subjected dulls their eyes to the perfected iniquities of others; when it is so hard for a man to decide vigorously that the pitch, which so many are handling, will defile him if it be touched;—men's conduct will be actuated much by that which is from day to day depicted to them as leading to glorious or inglorious results. The woman who is described as having obtained all that the world holds to be precious, by lavishing her charms and her caresses unworthily and heartlessly, will induce other women to do the same with theirs,—as will she who is made interesting by exhibitions of bold passion teach others to be spuriously passionate. The young man who in a novel becomes a hero, perhaps a Member of Parliament, and almost a Prime Minister, by trickery, falsehood, and flash cleverness, will have many followers, whose attempts to rise in the world ought to lie heavily on the conscience of the novelists who create fictitious Cagliostros. There are Jack Sheppards other than those who break into houses and out of prisons,—Macheaths, who deserve the gallows more than Gay's hero.

Thinking of all this, as a novelist surely must do,—as I certainly have done through my whole career,—it becomes to him a matter of deep conscience how he shall handle those characters by whose words and doings he hopes to interest his readers. It will very frequently be the case that he will be tempted to sacrifice something for effect, to say a word or two here, or to draw a picture there, for which he feels that he has the power, and which when spoken or drawn would be alluring. The regions of absolute vice are foul and odious. The savour of them, till custom has hardened the palate and the nose, is disgusting. In these he will hardly tread. But there are outskirts on these regions, on which sweet-smelling flowers seem to grow, and grass to be green. It is in these border-lands that the danger lies. The novelist may not be dull. If he commit that fault he can do neither harm nor good.

He must please, and the flowers and the grass in these neutral terri-
tories sometimes seem to give him so easy an opportunity of pleasing!

The writer of stories must please, or he will be nothing. And he
must teach whether he wish to teach or no. How shall he teach lessons
of virtue and at the same time make himself a delight to his readers?
That sermons are not in themselves often thought to be agreeable we
all know. Nor are disquisitions on moral philosophy supposed to be
pleasant reading for our idle hours. But the novelist, if he have a conscience, must preach his sermons with the same purpose as the clergyman, and must have his own system of ethics. If he can do this efficiently, if he can make virtue alluring and vice ugly, while he charms
his readers instead of wearying them, then I think Mr. Carlyle need
not call him distressed, nor talk of that long ear of fiction, nor question
whether he be or not the most foolish of existing mortals.

I think that many have done so; so many that we English novelists
may boast as a class that such has been the general result of our own
work. Looking back to the past generation, I may say with certainty
that such was the operation of the novels of Miss Edgeworth, Miss
Austen, and Walter Scott. Coming down to my own times, I find
such to have been the teaching of Thackeray, of Dickens, and of George
Eliot. Speaking, as I shall speak to any who may read these words, with
that absence of self-personality which the dead may claim, I will boast
that such has been the result of my own writing. Can any one by
search through the works of the six great English novelists I have
named, find a scene, a passage, or a word that would teach a girl to be
immodest, or a man to be dishonest? When men in their pages have
been described as dishonest and women as immodest, have they not
ever been punished? It is not for the novelist to say, badly and simply:
"Because you lied here, or were heartless there, because you Lydia Ben-
net forgot the lessons of your honest home, or you Earl Leicester were
false through your ambition, or you Beatrix loved too well the glitter
of the world, therefore you shall be scourged with scourges either in
this world or in the next;" but it is for him to show, as he carries on
his tale, that his Lydia, or his Leicester, or his Beatrix, will be dis-
honoured in the estimation of all readers by his or her vices. Let a
woman be drawn clever, beautiful, attractive,—so as to make men love
her, and women almost envy her,—and let her be made also heartless,
unfeminine, and ambitious of evil grandeur, as was Beatrix, what a
danger is there not in such a character! To the novelist who shall handle
it, what peril of doing harm! But if at last it have been so handled
that every girl who reads of Beatrix shall say: "Oh! not like that;—
let me not be like that!" and that every youth shall say: "Let me not
have such a one as that to press my bosom, anything rather than that!"

—then will not the novelist have preached his sermon as perhaps no clergyman can preach it?

Very much of a novelist's work must appertain to the intercourse between young men and young women. It is admitted that a novel can hardly be made interesting or successful without love. Some few might be named, but even in those the attempt breaks down, and the softness of love is found to be necessary to complete the story. *Pickwick* has been named as an exception to the rule, but even in *Pickwick* there are three or four sets of lovers, whose little amatory longings give a softness to the work. I tried it once with *Miss Mackenzie*, but I had to make her fall in love at last. In this frequent allusion to the passion which most stirs the imagination of the young, there must be danger. Of that the writer of fiction is probably well aware. Then the question has to be asked, whether the danger may not be so averted that good may be the result,—and to be answered.

In one respect the necessity of dealing with love is advantageous, —advantageous from the very circumstance which has made love necessary to all novelists. It is necessary because the passion is one which interests or has interested all. Every one feels it, has felt it, or expects to feel it,—or else rejects it with an eagerness which still perpetuates the interest. If the novelist, therefore, can so handle the subject as to do good by his handling, as to teach wholesome lessons in regard to love, the good which he does will be very wide. If I can teach politicians that they can do their business better by truth than by falsehood, I do a great service; but it is done to a limited number of persons. But if I can make young men and women believe that truth in love will make them happy, then, if my writings be popular, I shall have a very large class of pupils. No doubt the cause for that fear which did exist as to novels arose from an idea that the matter of love would be treated in an inflammatory and generally unwholesome manner. "Madam," says Sir Anthony in the play, "a circulating library in a town is an evergreen tree of diabolical knowledge. It blossoms through the year; and depend on it, Mrs. Malaprop, that they who are so fond of handling the leaves will long for the fruit at last." Sir Anthony was no doubt right. But he takes it for granted that the longing for the fruit is an evil. The novelist who writes of love thinks differently, and thinks that the honest love of an honest man is a treasure which a good girl may fairly hope to win,—and that if she can be taught to wish only for that, she will have been taught to entertain only wholesome wishes.

I can easily believe that a girl should be taught to wish to love by reading how Laura Bell loved Pendennis. Pendennis was not in truth a very worthy man, nor did he make a very good husband; but the girl's love was so beautiful, and the wife's love when she became a wife so womanlike, and at the same time so sweet, so unselfish, so wifely, so worshipful,—in the sense in which wives are told that they ought to worship their husbands,—that I cannot believe that any girl can be injured, or even not benefited, by reading of Laura's love.

There once used to be many who thought, and probably there still are some, even here in England, who think that a girl should hear nothing of love till the time come in which she is to be married. That, no doubt, was the opinion of Sir Anthony Absolute and of Mrs Malaprop. But I am hardly disposed to believe that the old system was more favourable than ours to the purity of manners. Lydia Languish, though she was constrained by fear of her aunt to hide the book, yet had *Peregrine Pickle* in her collection. While human nature talks of love so forcibly it can hardly serve our turn to be silent on the subject. "Naturam expellas furcâ, tamen usque recurret." There are countries in which it has been in accordance with the manners of the upper classes that the girl should be brought to marry the man almost out of the nursery—or rather perhaps out of the convent—without having enjoyed that freedom of thought which the reading of novels and of poetry will certainly produce; but I do not know that the marriages so made have been thought to be happier than our own.

Among English novels of the present day, and among English novelists, a great division is made. There are sensational novels and anti-sensational, sensational novelists and anti-sensational, sensational readers and anti-sensational. The novelists who are considered to be anti-sensational are generally called realistic. I am realistic. My friend Wilkie Collins is generally supposed to be sensational. The readers who prefer the one are supposed to take delight in the elucidation of character. Those who hold by the other are charmed by the continuation and gradual development of a plot. All this is, I think, a mistake,—which mistake arises from the inability of the imperfect artist to be at the same time realistic and sensational. A good novel should be both, and both in the highest degree. If a novel fail in either, there is a failure in art. Let those readers who believe that they do not like sensational scenes in novels think of some of those passages from our great novelists which have charmed them most:—of Rebecca in the castle with Ivanhoe; of Burley in the cave with Morton; of the mad lady tearing the veil of the expectant bride, in *Jane Eyre*; of Lady Castlewood as, in her indignation, she explains to the Duke of Hamilton Henry Esmond's right to be present at the marriage of his Grace with Beatrix;—may I add, of Lady Mason, as she makes her confession at the feet of Sir Peregrine Orme? Will any one say that the authors of these passages have sinned in being over-sensational? No doubt, a string of horrible incidents, bound together without truth in detail, and told as affecting personages without character,—wooden blocks, who cannot make themselves known to the reader as men and women, —does not instruct or amuse, or even fill the mind with awe. Horrors heaped upon horrors, and which are horrors only in themselves, and not as touching any recognised and known person, are not tragic, and soon cease even to horrify. And such would-be tragic elements of a story may be increased without end, and without difficulty. I may tell you of a woman murdered,—murdered in the same street with you, in the next house,—that she was a wife murdered by her husband,—a bride not yet a week a wife. I may add to it for ever. I may say that the murderer roasted her alive. There is no end to it. I may declare that a former wife was treated with equal barbarity; and may assert that, as the murderer was led away to execution, he declared his only sorrow, his only regret to be, that he could not live to treat a third wife after the same fashion. There is nothing so easy as the creation and the cumulation of fearful incidents after this fashion. If such creation and cumulation be the beginning and the end of the novelist's work,—and novels have been written which seem to be without other attractions,—nothing can be more dull or more useless. But not on that account are we averse to tragedy in prose fiction. As in poetry, so in prose, he who can deal adequately with tragic elements is a greater artist and reaches a higher aim than the writer whose efforts never carry him above the mild walks of everyday life. The *Bride of Lammermoor* is a tragedy throughout, in spite of its comic elements. The life of Lady Castlewood, of whom I have spoken, is a tragedy. Rochester's wretched thraldom to his mad wife, in *Jane Eyre*, is a tragedy. But these stories charm us not simply because they are tragic, but because we feel that men and women with flesh and blood, creatures with whom we can sympathise, are struggling amidst their woes. It all lies in that. No novel is anything, for the purposes either of comedy or tragedy, unless the reader can sympathise with the characters whose names he finds upon the pages. Let an author so tell his tale as to touch his reader's heart and draw his tears, and he has, so far, done his work well. Truth let there be,—truth of description, truth of character, human truth as to men and women. If there be such truth, I do not know that a novel can be too sensational. . . . (1876, published 1883)

HENRY JAMES (1843-1916)

The Art of Fiction

 SHOULD not have fixed so comprehensive a title to these few remarks, necessarily wanting in any completeness upon a subject the full consideration of which would carry us far, did I not seem to discover a pretext for my temerity in the interesting pamphlet lately published under this name by Mr. Walter Besant. Mr. Besant's lecture at the Royal Institution—the original form of his pamphlet—appears to indicate that many persons are interested in the art of fiction, and are not indifferent to such remarks as those who practice it may attempt to make about it. I am therefore anxious not to lose the benefit of this favorable association, and to edge in a few words under cover of the attention which Mr. Besant is sure to have excited. There is something very encouraging in his having put into form certain of his ideas on the mystery of story-telling.

It is a proof of life and curiosity—curosity on the part of the brotherhood of novelists as well as on the part of their readers. Only a short time ago it might have been supposed that the English novel was not what the French call *discutable*. It had no air of having a theory, a conviction, a consciousness of itself behind it—of being the expression of an artistic faith, the result of choice and comparison. I do not say it was necessarily the worse for that: it would take much more courage than I possess to intimate that the form of the novel as Dickens and Thackeray (for instance) saw it had any taint of incompleteness. It was, however, *naïf* (if I may help myself out with another French word); and evidently if it be destined to suffer in any way for having lost its *naïveté* it has now an idea of making sure of the corresponding advantages. During the period I have alluded to there was a comfortable good-humored feeling abroad that a novel is a novel, as a pudding is a pudding, and that our only business with it could be to swallow it. But within a year or two, for some reason or other, there have been signs of returning animation—the era of discussion would appear to have been to a certain extent opened. Art lives upon discussion, upon experiment, upon curiosity, upon variety of attempt, upon the exchange of views and the comparison of standpoints; and there is a presumption that those times when no one has anything particular to say about it, and has no reason to give for practice or preference, though they may be times of honor, are not times of development—are times, possibly, even a little of dullness. The successful application of any art is a delightful spectacle, but the theory too is interesting; and though there is a great deal of the latter without the former I suspect there has never been a genuine success that has not had a latent core of conviction. Discussion, suggestion, formulation, these things are fertilizing when they are frank and sincere. Mr. Besant has set an excellent example in saying what he thinks, for his part, about the way in which fiction should be written, as well as about the way in which it should be published; for his view of the "art," carried on into an appendix, covers that too. Other laborers in the same field will doubtless take up the argument, they will give it the light of their experience, and the effect will surely be to make our interest in the novel a little more what it had for some time threatened to fail to be—a serious, active, inquiring interest, under protection of which this delightful study may, in moments of confidence, venture to say a little more what it thinks of itself.

It must take itself seriously for the public to take it so. The old superstition about fiction being "wicked" has doubtless died out in England; but the spirit of it lingers in a certain oblique regard directed toward any story which does not more or less admit that it is only a joke. Even the most jocular novel feels in some degree the weight of the proscription that was formerly directed against literary levity: the jocularity does not always succeed in passing for orthodoxy. It is still expected, though perhaps people are ashamed to say it, that a production which is after all only a "make-believe" (for what else is a "story"?) shall be in some degree apologetic—shall renounce the pretension of attempting really to represent life. This, of course, any sensible, wide-awake story declines to do, for it quickly perceives that the tolerance granted to it on such a condition is only an attempt to stifle it disguised in the form of generosity. The old evangelical hostility to the novel, which was as explicit as it was narrow, and which regarded it as little less favorable to our immortal part than a stage-play, was in reality far less insulting. The only reason for the existence of a novel is that it does attempt to represent life. When it relinquishes this attempt, the same attempt that we see on the canvas of the painter, it will have arrived at a very strange pass. It is not expected of the picture that it will make itself humble in order to be forgiven; and the analogy between the art of the painter and the art of the novelist is, so far as I am able to see, complete. Their inspiration is the same, their process (allowing for the different quality of the vehicle) is the same, their success is the same. They may learn from each other, they may explain and sustain each other. Their cause is the same, and the honor of one is the honor of another. The Mahometans think a picture an unholy thing, but it is a long time since any Christian did, and it is therefore the more odd that in the Christian mind the traces (dissimulated though they may be) of a suspicion of the sister art should

linger to this day. The only effectual way to lay it to rest is to empha-
size the analogy to which I just alluded—to insist on the fact that as
the picture is reality, so the novel is history. That is the only general
description (which does it justice) that we may give of the novel.
But history also is allowed to represent life; it is not, any more than
painting, expected to apologize. The subject-matter of fiction is stored
up likewise in documents and records, and if it will not give itself away,
as they say in California, it must speak with assurance, with the tone
of the historian. Certain accomplished novelists have a habit of giving
themselves away which must often bring tears to the eyes of people
who take their fiction seriously. I was lately struck, in reading over
many pages of Anthony Trollope, with his want of discretion in this
particular. In a digression, a parenthesis or an aside, he concedes to the
reader that he and this trusting friend are only "making believe." He
admits that the events he narrates have not really happened, and that he
can give his narrative any turn the reader may like best. Such a betrayal
of a sacred office seems to me, I confess, a terrible crime; it is what I
mean by the attitude of apology, and it shocks me every whit as much
in Trollope as it would have shocked me in Gibbon or Macaulay. It
implies that the novelist is less occupied in looking for the truth (the
truth, of course I mean, that he assumes, the premises that we must
grant him, whatever they may be) than the historian, and in doing so
it deprives him at a stroke of all his standing-room. To represent and
illustrate the past, the actions of men, is the task of either writer, and
the only difference that I can see is, in proportion as he succeeds, to
the honor of the novelist, consisting as it does in his having more difficulty in collecting his evidence, which is so far from being purely
literary. It seems to me to give him a great character, the fact that he
has at once so much in common with the philosopher and the painter;
this double analogy is a magnificent heritage.

It is of all this evidently that Mr. Besant is full when he insists
upon the fact that fiction is one of the *fine* arts, deserving in its turn
of all the honors and emoluments that have hitherto been reserved for
the successful profession of music, poetry, painting, architecture. It is
impossible to insist too much on so important a truth, and the place
that Mr. Besant demands for the work of the novelist may be represented, a trifle less abstractly, by saying that he demands not only
that it shall be reputed artistic, but that it shall be reputed very artistic
indeed. It is excellent that he should have struck this note, for his
doing so indicates that there was need of it, that his proposition may
be to many people a novelty. One rubs one's eyes at the thought; but
the rest of Mr. Besant's essay confirms the revelation. I suspect in truth
that it would be possible to confirm it still further, and that one would

not be far wrong in saying that in addition to the people to whom it has never occurred that a novel ought to be artistic, there are a great many others who, if this principle were urged upon them, would be filled with an indefinable mistrust. They would find it difficult to explain their repugnance, but it would operate strongly to put them on their guard. "Art," in our Protestant communities, where so many things have got so strangely twisted about, is supposed in certain circles to have some vague injurious effect upon those who make it an important consideration, who let it weigh in the balance. It is assumed to be opposed in some mysterious manner to morality, to amusement, to instruction. When it is embodied in the work of the painter (the sculptor is another affair!) you know what it is: it stands there before you, in the honesty of pink and green and a gilt frame; you can see the worst of it at a glance, and you can be on your guard. But when it is introduced into literature it becomes more insidious—there is danger of its hurting you before you know it. Literature should be either instructive or amusing, and there is in many minds an impression that these artistic preoccupations, the search for form, contribute to neither end, interfere indeed with both. They are too frivolous to be edifying, and too serious to be diverting; and they are moreover priggish and paradoxical and superfluous. That, I think, represents the manner in which the latent thought of many people who read novels as an exercise in skipping would explain itself if it were to become articulate. They would argue, of course, that a novel ought to be "good," but they would interpret this term in a fashion of their own, which indeed would vary considerably from one critic to another. One would say that being good means representing virtuous and aspiring characters placed in prominent positions; another would say that it depends on a "happy ending," on a distribution at the last of prizes, pensions, husbands, wives, babies, millions, appended paragraphs, and cheerful remarks. Another still would say that it means being full of incident and movement, so that we shall wish to jump ahead, to see who was the mysterious stranger, and if the stolen will was ever found, and shall not be distracted from this pleasure by any tiresome analysis or "description." But they would all agree that the "artistic" idea would spoil some of their fun. One would hold it accountable for all the description, another would see it revealed in the absence of sympathy. Its hostility to a happy ending would be evident, and it might even in some cases render any ending at all impossible. The "ending" of a novel is, for many persons, like that of a good dinner, a course of dessert and ices, and the artist in fiction is regarded as a sort of meddlesome doctor who forbids agreeable aftertastes. It is therefore true that this conception of Mr. Besant's of the novel as a superior form encounters not only a negative but a positive indifference. It matters little that as a work of art it should really be as little or as much of its essence to supply happy endings, sympathetic characters, and an objective tone, as if it were a work of mechanics: the association of ideas, however incongruous, might easily be too much for it if an eloquent voice were not sometimes raised to call attention to the fact that it is at once as free and as serious a branch of literature as any other.

Certainly this might sometimes be doubted in presence of the enormous number of works of fiction that appeal to the credulity of our generation, for it might easily seem that there could be no great character in a commodity so quickly and easily produced. It must be admitted that good novels are much compromised by bad ones, and that the field at large suffers discredit from overcrowding. I think, however, that this injury is only superficial, and that the superabundance of written fiction proves nothing against the principle itself. It has been vulgarized, like all other kinds of literature, like everything else today, and it has proved more than some kinds accessible to vulgarization. But there is as much difference as there ever was between a good novel and a bad one: the bad is swept with all the daubed canvases and spoiled marble into some unvisited limbo, or infinite rubbish-yard beneath the back-windows of the world, and the good subsists and emits its light and stimulates our desire for perfection. As I shall take the liberty of making but a single criticism of Mr. Besant, whose tone is so full of love of his art, I may as well have done with it at once. He seems to me to mistake, in attempting to say so definitely beforehand, what sort of an affair the good novel will be. To indicate the danger of such an error as that has been the purpose of these few pages; to suggest that certain traditions on the subject, applied *a priori*, have already had much to answer for, and that the good health of an art which undertakes so immediately to reproduce life must demand that it be perfectly free. It lives upon exercise, and the very meaning of exercise is freedom. The only obligation to which in advance we may hold a novel, without incurring the accusation of being arbitrary, is that it be interesting. That general responsibility rests upon it, but it is the only one I can think of. The ways in which it is at liberty to accomplish this result (of interesting us) strike me as innumerable, and such as can only suffer from being marked out or fenced in by prescription. They are as various as the temperament of man, and they are successful in proportion as they reveal a particular mind, different from others. A novel is in its broadest definition a personal, a direct impression of life: that, to begin with, constitutes its value, which is greater or less according to the intensity of the impression. But there will be no intensity at all, and therefore no value, unless there is freedom to feel and say. The tracing of a line to be followed, of a tone to be taken, of a form to be filled out, is a limitation of that freedom and a suppression of the very thing that we are most curious about. The form, it seems to me, is to be appreciated after the fact: then the author's choice has been made, his standard has been indicated; then we can follow lines and directions and compare tones and resemblances. Then in a word we can enjoy one of the most charming of pleasures, we can estimate quality, we can apply the test of execution. The execution belongs to the author alone; it is what is most personal to him, and we measure him by that. The advantage, the luxury, as well as the torment and responsibility of the novelist, is that there is no limit to what he may attempt as an executant—no limit to his possible experiments, efforts, discoveries, successes. Here it is especially that he works, step by step, like his brother of the brush, of whom we may always say that he has painted his picture in a manner best known to himself. His manner is his secret, not necessarily a jealous one. He cannot disclose it as a general thing if he would; he would be at a loss to teach it to others. I say this with a due recollection of having insisted on the community of method of the artist who paints a picture and the artist who writes a novel. The painter *is* able to teach the rudiments of his practice, and it is possible, from the study of good work (granted the aptitude), both to learn how to paint and to learn how to write. Yet it remains true, without injury to the *rapprochement*, that the literary artist would be obliged to say to his pupil much more than the other, "Ah, well, you must do it as you can!" It is a question of degree, a matter of delicacy. If there are exact sciences, there are also exact arts, and the grammar of painting is so much more definite that it makes the difference.

I ought to add, however, that if Mr. Besant says at the beginning of his essay that the "laws of fiction may be laid down and taught with as much precision and exactness as the laws of harmony, perspective, and proportion" he mitigates what might appear to be an extravagance by applying his remark to "general" laws, and by expressing most of these rules in a manner with which it would certainly be unaccommodating to disagree. That the novelist must write from his experience, that his "characters must be real and such as might be met with in actual life"; that "a young lady brought up in a quiet country village should avoid descriptions of garrison life," and "a writer whose friends and personal experiences belong to the lower middle-class should carefully avoid introducing his characters into society"; that one should enter one's notes in a common-place book; that one's figures should be clear in outline; that making them clear by some trick of speech or of carriage is a bad method, and "describing them at length" is a worse one; that English Fiction should have a "conscious moral purpose"; that "it is almost impossible to estimate too highly the value of careful workmanship—that is, of style"; that "the most important point of all is the story," that "the story is everything": these are principles with most of which it is surely impossible not to sympathize. That remark about the lower middle-class writer and his knowing his place is perhaps rather chilling; but for the rest I should find it difficult to dissent from any one of these recommendations. At the same time, I should find it difficult positively to assent to them, with the exception, perhaps, of the injunction as to entering one's notes in a commonplace book. They scarcely seem to me to have the quality that Mr. Besant attributes to the rules of the novelist—the "precision and exactness" of "the laws of harmony, perspective, and proportion." They are suggestive, they are even inspiring, but they are not exact, though they are doubtless as much so as the case admits of: which is a proof of that liberty of interpretation for which I just contended. For the value of these different injunctions—so beautiful and so vague—is wholly in the meaning one attaches to them. The characters, the situation, which strike one as real will be those that touch and interest one most, but the measure of reality is very difficult to fix. The reality of Don Quixote or of Mr. Micawber is a very delicate shade; it is a reality so colored by the author's vision that, vivid as it may be, one would hesitate to propose it as a model: one would expose one's self to some very embarrassing questions on the part of a pupil. It goes without saying that you will not write a good novel unless you possess the sense of reality; but it will be difficult to give you a recipe for calling that sense into being. Humanity is immense, and reality has a myriad forms; the most one can affirm is that some of the flowers of fiction have the odor of it, and others have not; as for telling you in advance how your nosegay should be composed, that is another affair. It is equally excellent and inconclusive to say that one must write from experience; to our suppositious aspirant such a declaration might savor of mockery. What kind of experience is intended, and where does it begin and end? Experience is never limited, and it is never complete; it is an immense sensibility, a kind of huge spider-web of the finest silken threads suspended in the chamber of consciousness, and catching every air-borne particle in its tissue. It is the very atmosphere of the mind; and when the mind is imaginative—much more when it happens to be that of a man of genius—it takes to itself the faintest hints of life, it converts the very pulses of the air into revelations. The young lady living in a village has only to be a damsel upon whom nothing is lost to make it quite unfair (as it seems to me) to declare to her that she shall have nothing to say about the military. Greater miracles have been seen than that, imagination assisting, she should speak the truth about some of these gentlemen. I remember an English novelist, a woman of genius, telling me that she was much commended for the impression she had managed to give in one of her tales of the nature and way of life of the French Protestant youth. She had been asked where she learned so much about this recondite being, she had been congratulated on her peculiar opportunities. These opportunities consisted in her having once, in Paris, as she ascended a staircase, passed an open door where, in the household of a *pasteur*, some of the young Protestants were seated at table round a finished meal. The glimpse made a picture; it lasted only a moment, but that moment was experience. She had got her direct personal impression, and she turned out her type. She knew what youth was, and what Protestantism; she also had the advantage of having seen what it was to be French, so that she converted these ideas into a concrete image and produced a reality. Above all, however, she was blessed with the faculty which when you give it an inch takes an ell, and which for the artist is a much greater source of strength than any accident of residence or of place in the social scale. The power to guess the unseen from the seen, to trace the implication of things, to judge the whole piece by the pattern, the condition of feeling life in general so completely that you are well on your way to knowing any particular corner of it—this cluster of gifts may almost be said to constitute experience, and they occur in country and in town, and in the most differing stages of education. If experience consists of impressions, it may be said that impressions *are* experience, just as (have we not seen it?) they are the very air we breathe. Therefore, if I should certainly say to a novice, "Write from experience and from experience only," I should feel that this was rather a tantalizing monition if I were not careful immediately to add, "Try to be one of the people on whom nothing is lost!"

I am far from intending by this to minimize the importance of exactness—of truth of detail. One can speak best from one's own taste, and I may therefore venture to say that the air of reality (solidity of specification) seems to me to be the supreme virtue of a novel—the merit on which all its other merits (including that conscious moral purpose of which Mr. Besant speaks) helplessly and submissively depend. If it be not there they are all as nothing, and if these be there, they owe their effect to the success with which the author has produced the illusion of life. The cultivation of this success, the study of this exquisite process, form, to my taste, the beginning and the end of the art of the novelist. They are his inspiration, his despair, his reward, his torment, his delight. It is here in very truth that he competes with life; it is here that he competes with his brother the painter in *his* attempts to render the look of things, the look that conveys their meaning, to catch the color, the relief, the expression, the surface, the substance of the human spectacle. It is in regard to this that Mr. Besant is well inspired when he bids him take notes. He cannot possibly take too many, he cannot possibly take enough. All life solicits him, and to "render" the simplest surface, to produce the most momentary illusion, is a very complicated business. His case would be easier, and the rule would be more exact, if Mr. Besant had been able to tell him what notes to take. But this, I fear, he can never learn in any manual; it is the business of his life. He has to take a great many in order to select a few, he has to work them up as he can, and even the guides and philosophers who might have most to say to him must leave him alone when it comes to the application of precepts, as we leave the painter in communion with his palette. That his characters "must be clear in outline" as Mr. Besant says—he feels that down to his boots; but how he shall make them so is a secret between his good angel and himself. It would be absurdly simple if he could be taught that a great deal of "description" would make them so, or that on the contrary the absence of description and the cultivation of dialogue, or the absence of dialogue and the multiplication of "incident," would rescue him from his difficulties. Nothing, for instance, is more possible than that he be of a turn of mind for which this odd, literal opposition of description and dialogue, incident and description, has little meaning and light. People often talk of these things as if they had a kind of internecine distinctness, instead of melting into each other at every breath, and being intimately associated parts of one general effort of expression. I cannot imagine composition existing in a series of blocks, nor conceive, in any novel worth discussing at all, of a passage of description that is not in its intention narrative, a passage of dialogue that is not in its intention descriptive, a touch of truth of any sort that does not partake of the nature of incident, or an incident that derives its interest from any other source than the general and only source of the success of a work of art—that of being illustrative. A novel is a living thing, all one and continuous, like any other organism, and in proportion as it lives will it be found, I think, that in each of the parts there is something of each of the other parts. The critic who over the close texture of a finished work shall pretend to trace a geography of items will mark some frontiers as artificial, I fear, as any that have been known to history. There is an old-fashioned distinction between the novel of character and the novel of incident which must have cost many a smile to the intending fabulist who was keen about his work. It appears to me as little to the point as the equally celebrated distinction between the novel and the romance—to answer as little to any reality. There are bad novels and good novels, as here are bad pictures and good pictures; but that is the only distinction in which I see any meaning, and I can as little imagine speaking of a novel of character as I can imagine speaking of a picture of character. When one says picture one says of character, when one says novel one says of incident, and the terms may be transposed at will. What is character but the determination of incident? What is incident but the illustration of character? What is either a picture or a novel that is *not* of character? What else do we seek in it and find in it? It is an incident for a woman to stand up with her hand resting on a table and look at you in a certain way; or if it be not an incident I think it will be hard to say what is. At the same time it is an expression of character. If you say you don't see it (character in *that—allons donc!*), this is exactly what the artist who has reasons of his own for thinking he *does* see it undertakes to show you. When a young man makes up his mind that he has not faith enough after all to enter the Church as he intended, that is an incident, though you may not hurry to the end of the chapter to see whether perhaps he doesn't change once more. I do not say that these are extraordinary or startling incidents. I do not pretend to estimate the degree of interest proceeding from them, for this will depend upon the skill of the painter. It sounds almost puerile to say that some incidents are intrinsically much more important than others, and I need not take this precaution after having professed my sympathy for the major ones in remarking that the only classification of the novel that I can understand is into that which has life and that which has it not.

The novel and the romance, the novel of incident and that of character—these clumsy separations appear to me to have been made by critics and readers for their own convenience, and to help them out of some of their occasional predicaments, but to have little reality or interest for the producer, from whose point of view it is of course that we are attempting to consider the art of fiction. The case is the same with another shadowy category which Mr. Besant apparently is disposed to set up—that of the "modern English novel"; unless indeed it be that in this matter he has fallen into an accidental confusion of standpoints. It is not quite clear whether he intends the remarks in which he alludes to it to be didactic or historical. It is as difficult to suppose a person intending to write a modern English as to suppose him writing an ancient English novel: that is a label which begs the question. One writes the novel, one paints the picture, of one's language and of one's time, and calling it modern English will not, alas! make the difficult task any easier. No more, unfortunately, will calling this or that work of one's fellow-artist a romance—unless it be, of course, simply for the pleasantness of the thing, as for instance when Hawthorne gave this heading to his story of *Blithedale*. The French, who have brought the theory of fiction to remarkable completeness, have but one name for the novel, and have not attempted smaller things in it, that I can see, for that. I can think of no obligation to which the "romancer" would not be held equally with the novelist; the standard of execution is equally high for each. Of course it is of execution that we are talking—that being the only point of a novel that is open to contention. This is perhaps too often lost sight of, only to produce interminable confusions and cross-purposes. We must grant the artist his subject, his idea, his *donnée*: our criticism is applied only to what he makes of it. Naturally I do not mean that we are bound to like it or find it interesting: in case we do not our course is perfectly simple—to let it alone. We may believe that of a certain idea even the most sincere novelist can make nothing at all, and the event may perfectly justify our belief; but the failure will have been a failure to execute, and it is in the execution that the fatal weakness is recorded. If we pretend to respect the artist at all, we must allow him his freedom of choice, in the face, in particular cases, of innumerable presumptions that the choice will not fructify. Art derives a considerable part of its beneficial exercise from flying in the face of presumptions, and some of the most interesting experiments of which it is capable are hidden in the bosom of common things. Gustave Flaubert has written a story about the devotion of a servant-girl to a parrot, and the production, highly finished as it is, cannot on the whole be called a success. We are perfectly free to find it flat, but I think it might have been interesting; and I, for my part, am extremely glad he should have written it; it is a contribution to our knowledge of what can be done—or what cannot. Ivan Turgénieff has written a tale about a deaf and dumb serf and a lap-dog, and the thing is touching, loving, a little masterpiece. He struck the note of life where Gustave Flaubert missed it—he flew in the face of a presumption and achieved a victory.

Nothing, of course, will ever take the place of the good old fashion of "liking" a work of art or not liking it: the most improved criticism will not abolish that primitive, that ultimate test. I mention this to guard myself from the accusation of intimating that the idea, the subject, of a novel or a picture, does not matter. It matters, to my sense, in the highest degree, and if I might put up a prayer it would be that artists should select none but the richest. Some, as I have already hastened to admit, are much more remunerative than others, and it would be a world happily arranged in which persons intending to treat them should be exempt from confusions and mistakes. This fortunate condition will arrive only, I fear, on the same day that critics become purged from error. Meanwhile, I repeat, we do not judge the artist with fairness unless we say to him, "Oh, I grant you your starting-point, because if I did not I should seem to prescribe to you, and heaven forbid I should take that responsibility. If I pretend to tell you what you must not take, you will call upon me to tell you then what you must take; in which case I shall be prettily caught. Moreover, it isn't till I have accepted your data that I can begin to measure you. I have the standard, the pitch; I have no right to tamper with your flute and then criticize your music. Of course I may not care for your idea at all; I may think it silly, or stale, or unclean; in which case I wash my hands of you altogether. I may content myself with believing that you will not have suceeded in being interesting, but I shall, of course, not attempt to demonstrate it, and you will be as indifferent to me as I am to you. I needn't remind you that there are all sorts of tastes: who can know it better? Some people, for excellent reasons, don't like to read about carpenters; others, for reasons even better, don't like to read about courtesans. Many object to Americans. Others (I believe they are mainly editors and publishers) won't look at Italians. Some readers don't like quiet subjects; others don't like bustling ones. Some enjoy a complete illusion, others the consciousness of large concessions. They choose their novels accordingly and if they don't care about your idea they won't, *a fortiori*, care about your treatment."

So that it comes back very quickly, as I have said, to the liking: in spite of M. Zola, who reasons less powerfully than he represents, and who will not reconcile himself to this absoluteness of taste, thinking that there are certain things that people ought to like, and that they can be made to like. I am quite at a loss to imagine anything (at any rate in this matter of fiction) that people *ought* to like or to dislike. Selection will be sure to take care of itself, for it has a constant motive behind it. That motive is simply experience. As people feel life, so they will feel the art that is most closely related to it. This closeness of relation is what we should never forget in talking of the effort of the novel. Many people speak of it as a factitious, artificial form, a product of ingenuity, the business of which it is to alter and arrange the things that surround us, to translate them into conventional, traditional moulds. This, however, is a view of the matter which carries us but a very short way, condemns the art to an eternal repetition of a few familiar *clichés*, cuts short its development, and leads us straight up to a dead wall. Catching the very note and trick, the strange irregular rhythm of life, that is the attempt whose strenuous force keeps Fiction upon her feet. In proportion as in what she offers us we see life *without* rearrangement do we feel that we are touching the truth; in proportion as we see it *with* rearrangement do we feel that we are being put off with a substitute, a compromise and convention. It is not uncommon to hear an extraordinary assurance of remark in regard to this matter of rearranging which is often spoken of as if it were the last word of art. Mr. Besant seems to me in danger of falling into the great error with his rather unguarded talk about "selection." Art is essentially selection, but it is a selection whose main care is to be typical, to be inclusive. For many people art means rose-colored window panes and selection means picking a bouquet for Mrs. Grundy. They will tell you glibly that artistic considerations have nothing to do with the disagreeable, with the ugly; they will rattle off shallow commonplaces about the province of art and the limits of art till you are moved to some wonder in return as to the province and the limits of ignorance. It appears to me that no one can ever have made a seriously artistic attempt without becoming conscious of an immense increase— a kind of revelation—of freedom. One perceives in that case—by the light of a heavenly ray—that the province of art is all life, all feeling, all observation, all vision. As Mr. Besant so justly intimates, it is all experience. That is a sufficient answer to those who maintain that it must not touch the sad things of life, who stick into its divine unconscious bosom little prohibitory inscriptions on the end of sticks, such as we see in public gardens—"It is forbidden to walk on the grass; it is forbidden to touch the flowers; it is not allowed to introduce dogs or to remain after dark; it is requested to keep to the right." The young aspirant in the line of fiction whom we continue to imagine will do nothing without taste, for in that case his freedom would be of little use to him; but the first advantage of his taste will be to reveal to him the absurdity of the little sticks and tickets. If he have taste, I must add, of course he will have ingenuity, and my disrespectful reference to that quality just now was not meant to imply that it is useless in fiction. But it is only a secondary aid; the first is a capacity for receiving straight impressions.

Mr. Besant has some remarks on the question of "the story" which I shall not attempt to criticize, though they seem to me to contain a singular ambiguity, because I do not think I understand them. I cannot see what is meant by talking as if there were a part of a novel which is the story and part of it which for mystical reasons is not— unless indeed the distinction be made in a sense in which it is difficult to suppose that any one should attempt to convey anything. "The story," if it represents anything, represents the subject, the idea, the *donnée* of the novel; and there is surely no "school"—Mr. Besant speaks of a school—which urges that a novel should be all treatment and no subject. There must assuredly be something to treat; every school is intimately conscious of that. This sense of the story being the idea, the starting-point, of the novel, is the only one that I see in which it can be spoken of as something different from its organic whole; and since in proportion as the work is successful the idea permeates and penetrates it, informs and animates it, so that every word and every punctuation-point contribute directly to the expression, in that proportion do we lose our sense of the story being a blade which may be drawn more or less out of its sheath. The story and the novel, the idea and the form, are the needle and thread, and I never heard of a guild of tailors who recommended the use of the thread without the needle, or the needle without the thread. Mr. Besant is not the only critic who may be observed to have spoken as if there were certain things in life which constitute stories, and certain others which do not. I find the same odd implication in an entertaining article in the *Pall Mall Gazette,* devoted, as it happens, to Mr. Besant's lecture. "The story is the thing!" says this graceful writer, as if with a tone of opposition to some other idea. I should think it was, as every painter who, as the time for "sending in" his picture looms in the distance, finds himself still in quest of a subject—as every belated artist not fixed about his theme will heartily agree. There are some subjects which speak to us and others which do not, but he would be a clever man who should undertake to give a rule—an *index expurgatorius*—by which the story and the no-story should be known apart. It is impossible (to me at least) to imagine any such rule which shall not be altogether arbitrary. The writer in the *Pall Mall* opposes the delightful (as I suppose) novel of *Margot la Balafrée* to certain tales in which "Bostonian nymphs" appear to have "rejected English dukes for psychological reasons." I am not acquainted with the romance just designated, and can scarcely forgive the *Pall Mall* critic for not mentioning the name of the author, but the title appears to refer to a lady who may have received a scar in some heroic adventure. I am inconsolable at not being acquainted with this episode, but am utterly at a loss to see why it is a story when the rejection (or acceptance) of a duke is not, and why a reason, psychological or other, is not a subject when a cicatrix is. They are all particles of the multitudinous life with which the novel deals, and surely no dogma which pretends to make it lawful to touch the one and unlawful to touch the other will stand for a moment on its feet. It is the special picture that must stand or fall, according as it seems to possess truth or to lack it. Mr. Besant does not, to my sense, light up the subject by intimating that a story must, under penalty of not being a story, consist of "adventures." Why of adventures more than of green spectacles? He mentions a category of impossible things, and among them he places "fiction without adventure." Why without adventure, more than without matrimony, or celibacy, or parturition, or cholera, or hydropathy, or Jansenism? This seems to me to bring the novel back to the hapless little *rôle* of being an artificial, ingenious thing—bring it down from its large, free character of an immense and exquisite correspondence with life. And what *is* adventure when it comes to that, and by what sign is the listening pupil to recognize it? It is an adventure—an immense one—for me to write this little article; and for a Bostonian nymph to reject an English duke is an adventure only less stirring, I should say, than for an English duke to be rejected by a Bostonian nymph. I see dramas within dramas in that, and innumerable points of view. A psychological reason is, to my imagination, an object adorably pictorial; to catch the tint of its complexion— I feel as if that idea might inspire one to Titianesque efforts. There are few things more exciting to me, in short, than a psychological reason, and yet, I protest, the novel seems to me the most magnificent form of art. I have just been reading, at the same time, the delightful story of *Treasure Island*, by Mr. Robert Louis Stevenson, and, in a manner less consecutive, the last tale from M. Edmond de Goncourt, which is entitled *Chérie*. One of these works treats of murders, mysteries, islands of dreadful renown, hairbreadth escapes, miraculous coincidences, and buried doubloons. The other treats of a little French girl who lived in a fine house in Paris, and died of wounded sensibility because no one would marry her. I call *Treasure Island* delightful, because it appears to me to have succeeded wonderfully in what it attempts; and I venture to bestow no epithet upon *Chérie*, which strikes me as having failed deplorably in what it attempts—that is, in tracing the development of the moral consciousness of a child. But one of these productions strikes me as exactly as much of a novel as the other, and as having a "story" quite as much. The moral consciousness of a child is as much a part of life as the islands of the Spanish Main, and the one sort of geography seems to me to have those "surprises" of which Mr. Besant speaks quite as much as the other. For myself (since it comes back in the last resort, as I say, to the preference of the individual), the picture of the child's experience has the advantage that I can at successive steps (an immense luxury, near to the "sensual pleasure" of which Mr. Besant's critic in the *Pall Mall* speaks) say Yes or No, as it may be, to what the artist puts before me. I have been a child in fact, but I have been on a quest for a buried treasure only in supposition, and it is a simple accident that with M. de Goncourt I should have for the most part to say No. With George Eliot, when she painted that country with a far other intelligence, I always said Yes.

The most interesting part of Mr. Besant's lecture is unfortunately the briefest passage—his very cursory allusion to the "conscious moral purpose" of the novel. Here again it is not very clear whether he be recording a fact or laying down a principle; it is a great pity that in the latter case he should not have developed his idea. This branch of the subject is of immense importance, and Mr. Besant's few words point to considerations of the widest reach, not to be lightly disposed of. He will have treated the art of fiction but superficially who is not prepared to go every inch of the way that these considerations will carry him. It is for this reason that at the beginning of these remarks I was careful to notify the reader that my reflections on so large a theme have no pretension to be exhaustive. Like Mr. Besant, I have left the question of the morality of the novel till the last, and at the last I find I have used up my space. It is a question surrounded with difficulties, as witness the very first that meets us, in the form of a definite question, on the threshold. Vagueness, in such a discussion, is fatal, and what is the meaning of your morality and your conscious moral purpose? Will you not define your terms and explain how (a novel being a picture) a picture can be either moral or immoral? You wish to paint a moral picture or carve a moral statue: will you not tell us how you would set about it? We are discussing the Art of Fiction; questions of art are questions (in the widest sense) of execution; questions of morality are quite another affair, and will you not let us see how it is that you find it so easy to mix them up? These things are so clear to Mr. Besant that he has deduced from them a law which he sees embodied in English Fiction, and which is "a truly admirable thing and a great cause for congratulation." It is a great cause for congratulation indeed when such thorny problems become as smooth as silk. I may add that in so far as Mr. Besant perceives that in point of fact English Fiction has addressed itself preponderantly to these delicate questions he will appear to many people to have made a vain discovery. They will have been positively struck, on the contrary, with the moral timidity of the usual English novelist; with his (or with her) aversion to face the difficulties with which on every side the treatment of reality bristles. He is apt to be extremely shy (whereas the picture that Mr. Besant draws is a picture of boldness), and the sign of his work, for the most part, is a cautious silence on certain subjects. In the English novel (by which of course I mean the American as well), more than in any other, there is a traditional difference between that which people know and that which they agree to admit that they know, that which they see and that which they speak of, that which they feel to be a part of life and that which they allow to enter into literature. There is the great difference, in short, between what they talk of in conversation and what they talk of in print. The essence of moral energy is to survey the whole field, and I should directly reverse Mr. Besant's remark and say not that the English novel has a purpose, but that it has a diffidence. To what degree a purpose in a work of art is a source of corruption I shall not attempt to inquire; the one that seems to me least dangerous is the purpose of making a perfect work. As for our novel, I may say lastly on this score that as we find it in England today it strikes me as addressed in a large degree to "young people," and that this in itself constitutes a presumption that it will be rather shy. There are certain things which it is generally agreed not to discuss, not even to mention, before young people. That is very well, but the absence of discussion is not a symptom of the moral passion. The purpose of the English novel— "a truly admirable thing, and a great cause for congratulation"—strikes me therefore as rather negative.

There is one point at which the moral sense and the artistic sense lie very near together; that is in the light of the very obvious truth that the deepest quality of a work of art will always be the quality of the mind of the producer. In proportion as that intelligence is fine will the novel, the picture, the statue partake of the substance of beauty and truth. To be constituted of such elements is, to my vision, to have purpose enough. No good novel will ever proceed from a superficial mind; that seems to me an axiom which, for the artist in fiction, will cover all needful moral ground: if the youthful aspirant take it to heart it will illuminate for him many of the mysteries of "purpose." There are many other useful things that might be said to him, but I have come to the end of my article, and can only touch them as I pass. The critic in the *Pall Mall Gazette*, whom I have already quoted, draws attention to the danger, in speaking of the art of fiction, of generalizing. The danger that he has in mind is rather, I imagine, that of particularizing, for there are some comprehensive remarks which, in addition to those embodied in Mr. Besant's suggestive lecture, might without fear of misleading him be addressed to the ingenuous student. I should remind him first of the magnificence of the form that is open to him, which offers to sight so few restrictions and such in-numerable opportunities. The other arts, in comparison, appear con-fined and hampered; the various conditions under which they are exercised are so rigid and definite. But the only condition that I can think of attaching to the composition of the novel is, as I have already said, that it be sincere. This freedom is a splendid privilege, and the first lesson of the young novelist is to learn to be worthy of it. "Enjoy it as it deserves," I should say to him; "take possession of it, explore it to its utmost extent, publish it, rejoice in it. All life belongs to you, and do not listen either to those who would shut you up into corners of it and tell you that it is only here and there that art inhabits, or to those who would persuade you that this heavenly messenger wings her way outside of life altogether, breathing a superfine air, and turning away her head from the truth of things. There is no impression of life, no manner of seeing it and feeling it, to which the plan of the novelist may not offer a place; you have only to remember that talents so dissimilar as those of Alexandre Dumas and Jane Austen, Charles Dickens and Gustave Flaubert have worked in this field with equal glory. Do not think too much about optimism and pessimism; try and catch the color of life itself. In France today we see a prodigious effort (that of Emile Zola, to whose solid and serious work no explorer of the capacity of the novel can allude without respect), we see an extraordinary effort, vitiated by a spirit of pessimism on a narrow basis. M. Zola is magnificent, but he strikes an English reader as ignorant; he has an air of working in the dark; if he had as much light as energy, his results would be of the highest value. As for the aberrations of a shallow optimism, the ground (of English fiction especially) is strewn with their brittle particles as with broken glass. If you must indulge in conclusions, let them have the taste of a wide knowledge. Remember that your first duty is to be as complete as possible—to make as perfect a work. Be generous and delicate and pursue the prize."

(1884)

GUY DE MAUPASSANT (1850-1893)

From the Preface to *Pierre et Jean*

 HAVE no intention whatsoever to make a plea here for the little novel that follows. Quite to the contrary, the ideas that I shall try to make understood here would involve rather the criticism of the genre of psychological study I have undertaken in *Pierre et Jean.*

I wish to concern myself with the novel in general.

I am not the only one to whom the same reproach has been made by the same critics, each time a new book appears.

Amid sentences full of praise, I find regularly the following, written by the same pens:

"The greatest defect of this book is that it is not, strictly speaking, a novel."

You might answer by the same argument:

"The greatest defect in the writer who has done me the honor of judging me, is that he is not a critic."

What are, in all truth, the essential characteristics of the critic?

He must understand—without bias, without preconceived opinions, without academic theories, without being allied to any artistic
family—discriminate between and explain all the most contradictory
tendencies, the most diametrically-opposed temperaments, and acknowledge the most varied inquiries into art.

Thus the critic who after reading *Manon Lescaut*, *Paul et
Virginie*, *Don Quixote*, *Les liaisons dangereuses*, *Werther*, *The Elective Affinities*, *Clarissa Harlowe*, *Émile*, *Candide*, *Cinq-Mars*, *René*,
Les Trois Mousquetaires, *Mauprat*, *Père Goriot*, *La Cousine Bette*,
Colomba, *Le Rouge et le Noir*, *Mlle. de Maupin*, *Notre-Dame de
Paris*, *Salambô*, *Madame Bovary*, *Adolphe*, *M. de Camors*, *L'Assommoir*, *Sappho*, etc.—and can dare to write, "This is a novel, and
that is not"—seems to me to be endowed with a perspicacity that
strongly resembles incompetence.

Generally, criticism means by a novel an adventure that is more
or less probable, arranged after the manner of a stage play into three
acts, where the first includes the exposition, the second the action, and
the third the denouement.

This way of composing is absolutely admissible, with the condition that we accept equally all other ways.

Do rules exist for writing a novel, so that a story written without
these be called by some other name?

If *Don Quixote* is a novel, is *Le Rouge et le Noir* also one? If
Monte-Cristo is a novel, is *L'Assommoir*? Can we make a comparison
between Goethe's *Elective Affinities*, Dumas' *Trois Mousquetaires*,
Flaubert's *Mme. Bovary*, M. O. Feuillet's *M. de Camors*, and Zola's
Germinal? Which of these works is a novel? Where are those famous
rules? Where do they come from? Who established them? By virtue of
what principle and by what rationale?

It would seem however that these critics know in a certain in-
dubitable fashion what constitutes a novel and what distinguishes it
from something that isn't one. What this means quite simply is that,
without their being creators, they become regimented into a school;
and they reject, quite like novelists themselves, all works conceived and
written outside of their own aesthetics.

To the contrary, an intelligent critic ought to investigate everything that least resembles novels that have been already written, and
encourage the young men as much as possible to explore new
trails. . . .

Thus, after literary schools that wished to give us a deformed,
superhuman, poetic, tender, charming or superb vision of life, came
the realist or naturalist school which claimed to show us the truth,
nothing but the truth, and the whole truth.

We must with equal interest acknowledge as true these very different theories of art and judge the works that they have produced, uniquely from the point of view of their artistic value even as we accept *a priori* the general ideas that conceived them.

To contest the right of a writer to create a poetic work or a realistic work, is to wish to compel him to change his temperament, deny his originality, and not allow him to make use of the eyes and the intelligence that nature has given him.

To reproach him for seeing things as beautiful or ugly, small or epic, gracious or sinister, is to reproach him for conforming to such-and-such an attitude and not having a vision consonant with our own.

Let him be free to understand, observe, and to conceive as he sees fit, as long as he is an artist. Let us become poetically exalted when we judge an idealist and prove to him that his dream is mediocre, banal, not crazy or magnificent enough. But if we judge a naturalist, show him how the truth in life differs from the truth in his book. . . .

In short, if yesterday's novelist chose and told about the crises of life, the acute conditions of the soul and of the heart, today's novelist writes the history of the heart, the soul, and the intelligence as they exist in a normal state. In order to produce the effect he seeks— that is to say the emotion contained within simple reality—and to extract the artistic lesson he wishes to take from it, that is to say the revealing of what in his eyes is really contemporary man, he only has to use facts about unimpeachable and unvarying truth.

But putting ourselves at the point of view of these realistic artists, we must discuss and dispute their theory which seems to be summed up in these words: "Nothing but the truth and the whole truth."

Since their aim is to extract philosophy from certain constant and everyday facts, they often should correct events to the benefit of probability and to the detriment of the truth, because

Often the truth is sometimes not probable.

If he is an artist, the realist will seek not to give us a banal photograph of life, but rather to give us the most complete, impressive, and convincing vision of life—more than reality itself is.

To relate everything would be impossible, because you would have to have at least a volume for each day in order to ennumerate the mass of insignificant incidents that fill up our lives.

A choice therefore obtrudes itself—which is the first blow struck against a theory about "the whole truth."

Life, furthermore, is made up of the most different things, the most unexpected, contrary, and disparate: it is brutal, without coherence

and connection, full of inexplicable, illogical and contradictory catastrophes which must be classed under the heading of *miscellaneous
facts.*

This is why the artist, having chosen his theme, only picks out
details that are characteristic and of value for his subject, out of this
life so burdened with chance and futility; and he rejects all the re-
mainder and puts it to one side. . . .   (1887)

(Translated by H. E. Hugo)

EUGÈNE MARIE MELCHIOR DE VOGÜÉ (1848-1910)

From the Introduction to *The Russian Novel*

URGENEV came among us like some missionary of the Russian
genius; he proved by his example the high artistic value of
this same genius; but the Western public remained skeptical.
Our opinions about the Russians have been determined by one of those
facile formulae that the French love so well, and with which they
wipe out a country as if it were a single individual: "A nation that was
rotten before it was ripe," we say, and that answers for everything.
And the Russians bear us no grudge for this; a considerable number
of them have employed this judgment against themselves. Let me
cite a few brief statements. Do you know that Mirabeau explained
away the Prussian monarchy in identical terms? He wrote in his
Secret History: "Rottenness before maturity: I am very afraid this
may be the motto behind Prussian power." Subsequent events have
proved these fears to have been ill-founded. In the same way J.-J.
Rousseau speaking of Russia in his *Social Contract,* did not miss an
occasion to utter a paradox: "The Russian Empire wants to subjugate
Europe and will itself be subjugated. Its subjects and neighbors, the
Tartars, shall become Russia's master and ours. To me this revolution
seems inevitable." Ségur, better informed through his personal experience, said more aptly: "The Russians still are what people have made
them; one day, when they are freer, they shall be themselves."

That day, which has been slow to appear in other connections,
has at last dawned for literature. Around 1840—well before Europe
deigned to acknowledge the fact—a school that called itself *the
natural school* (or *naturalist,* since the Russian word may be translated
in these two ways) absorbed all the literary energy of the country.
It devoted itself to the novel and immediately produced remarkable
works. This school reminded one much of the English school and
owed much to Dickens, rather little to Balzac, whose fame had not

yet placed him in the fore. It preceded our realism, the kind that Flaubert was later to establish. A few of these Russians from the start achieved conceptions of desolation and crudities of expression which we have just recently attained, by dint of hard work. If there is any merit in this, it is important that we admit their priority. But other writers stripped realism of its excesses, and like the English they communicated a higher form of beauty via realism, owing to a similar moral inspiration—a compassion from which all impure elements have been filtered, and which a spirit of evangelicalism has raised to sublimity.

They lack the intellectual solidity and the virile strength of the Anglo-Saxons, that confident granite-like race that masters itself the same way it rules the sea. The flowing Russian soul is derived from traversing every philosophy and every error; it has stopped off at nihilism and pessimism, and a superficial reader may often confuse Tolstoy with Flaubert. Yet this nihilism is never accepted without revolt, and the soul is never impenitent. You hear it groaning and searching. At last it finds itself to be redeemed by love: a more or less active love with Turgenev or Tolstoy, with Dostoevsky a love unbridled to the point of becoming a painful passion. The Russians are blown by the wind of every doctrine that comes to them from the outside: skepticism, fatalism, positivism. But unknown to them, in the most intimate recesses of their hearts they always remain the type of Christian about which an eloquent voice once said: "They have never stopped being sympathetic to that universal weeping by which mankind and things, tributaries of time, nourish the inexhaustible sea." If you read through their strangest books, you will detect a controlling work in their vicinity toward which they all gravitate. This is the venerable volume we see in the place of honor in the Imperial Library at St. Petersburg, the *Gospel* by Ostromir of Novgorod (1056). This work symbolizes the inspiration and the spirit of these recent manifestations of a national literature. . . .

I am convinced that the influence of these great Russian writers will have a salutary influence on our worn-out art: it will enable us to be off again, to observe reality better at the same time that we look further; and above all to enable us to discover the emotions again. Already we have seen some of these things injected into certain novels, works that show a completely new set of moral values. I have trouble understanding those persons who are afraid of these foreign influences, and who seem to fear for the integrity of French genius. Aren't they forgetting our entire literary history? Like everything that lives, literature is an organism that subsists on nutriment: it must continually absorb foreign elements in order to transmute them into its own substance. If a stomach is healthy such an assimilation holds no dangers; if it is too worn-out, you have only the choice between dying for want of food or from indigestion. If this is the case for us, one Russian broth more or less is not going to weaken our keeping death at bay.

When the great century started, literature was at the point of death with the affectations of the Hôtel de Rambouillet. Corneille went to Spain to find his victuals and Molière did the same thing in Italy. We then enjoyed marvellous health, and we have been living two-hundred years on our capital investment. The nineteenth-century meant that other needs arose, and once again our national economy was meager. At that time we borrowed from England and Germany; and literature, again flourishing, experienced the fine rebirth we all know about. But now a time of famine and anemia has struck it. The Russians have arrived in the nick of time; and if we are still capable of digesting, we shall invigorate our blood at their expense. To those who blush for owing something to "barbarians," may I recall that the intellectual world is a huge society made up of mutual aid and charity. The Koran has a rather lovely anecdote: "How will we know when the end of the world has come?" asks the Prophet. "It shall be the day when one soul can no longer do anything for another soul." Thank Heaven that the Russian soul can do a great deal for ours!

At the moment when I have been studying this Russian soul through its literature, I have almost solely spoken about French letters, and I do not apologize for this. During the years I spent in Russia overhearing foreign ideas, listening to this vague and musical language —a flexible garment for new ideas—I dreamed endlessly about what one might take back to enrich our thought, our old language created out of the labor and acquisitions of our ancestors. They demanded contributions from the world in order to bedeck their queen; they knew that everything was permitted in her service; that you might hold passers-by for ransom, arm pirates, scour the seas and lie in wait for wrecks.

Let us imitate them. Certain scholars claim that French thought need only roam about the universe, and that it is enough for it to look at itself in its Parisian looking-glass. Others say that the language henceforth should speak with an impersonal and impassive voice, that we must work it like those mosaics of hard and cold stones that Raphael's grandchildren manufacture for Americans in Florence. Poor language! I thought that the ages had melted it in the fire, smeltered it in the furnace—this bell that emits its mighty peals to the world. To make it stronger and more superb, how all of them, those crude workers—Rabelais, Pascal, Saint-Simon, Mirabeau, Chateaubriand, Michelet—threw their laughter, their rage, their loves, their sorrows, their entire souls, into the vat! . . . Language and thought: every epoch has to recast them without respite. Now after those evil days when they have wavered, the task has come to us. Let us rework them after the fashion of that Corinthian metal which emerged out of defeat and conflagration rich in all the earth's treasures, all the nation's relics; rich with its ruins and unhappiness—that magnificent and sonorous metal, so excellent for forging jewels and swords. (1888)

(Translated by H. E. Hugo)

LEO TOLSTOI (1828-1910)
From the Introduction to
The Works of Guy de Maupassant

T WAS, I think, in 1881 that Turgénev while visiting me took out of his portmanteau a small French book entitled *La Maison Tellier*, and gave it to me.

"Read it some time," said he in an off-hand way just as, a year before, he had given me a number of *Russian Wealth* that contained an article by Gárshin, who was then only beginning to write. Evidently on this occasion, as in Gárshin's case, he was afraid of influencing me one way or the other, and wished to know my own unbiassed opinion.

"It is by a young French writer," said he. "Have a look at it. It isn't bad. He knows you and esteems you highly," he added, as if wishing to propitiate me. "As a man he reminds me of Druzhínin. He is, like Druzhínin, an excellent son, an admirable friend, *un homme d'un commerce sûr,*[1] and besides that he associates with the working people, guides them, and helps them. Even in his relations with women he reminds me of Druzhínin." And Turgénev told me something astonishing, incredible, of Maupassant's conduct in that respect.

That time (1881) was for me a period of most ardent inner reconstruction of my whole outlook on life, and in this reconstruction the activity called the fine arts, to which I had formerly devoted all my powers, had not only lost the importance I formerly attributed to it, but had become simply obnoxious to me on account of the un-

What is Art? translated by Alymer Maude (Oxford Press: World's Classics, 1930-1938) and reprinted with permission of the publishers.

[1] A reliable man.

natural position it had hitherto occupied in my life, as it generally does in the estimation of the people of the well-to-do classes.

And therefore such works as the one Turgénev was recommending to me did not then interest me in the least. But to please him I read the book he had handed me.

From the first story, *La Maison Tellier*, despite the indecency and insignificance of the subject, I could not help recognizing that the author had what is called talent.

He possessed that particular gift called talent, which consists in the capacity to direct intense concentrated attention, according to the author's tastes, on this or that subject, in consequence of which the man endowed with this capacity sees in the things to which he directs his attention some new aspect which others have overlooked; and this gift of seeing what others have not seen Maupassant evidently possessed. But judging by the little volume I read, he unfortunately lacked the chief of the three conditions, besides talent, essential to a true work of art. These are: (1) a correct, that is, a moral relation of the author to his subject; (2) clearness of expression, or beauty of form, —the two are identical; and (3) sincerity, that is, a sincere feeling of love or hatred of what the artist depicts. Of these three, Maupassant possessed only the two last and was quite lacking in the first. He had not a correct, that is a moral, relation to the subjects depicted.

Judging by what I read I was convinced that Maupassant possessed talent, that is to say, the gift of attention revealing in the objects and facts of life with which he deals qualities others have not perceived. He was also master of a beautiful style, expressing what he wanted to say clearly, simply, and with charm. He was also master of that condition of true artistic production without which a work of art does not produce its effect, namely, sincerity; that is, he did not pretend that he loved or hated, but really loved or hated what he described. But unfortunately, lacking the first and perhaps the chief condition of good artistic production, a correct moral relation to what he described —that is to say, a knowledge of the difference between good and evil— he loved and described things that should not have have been loved and described. Thus in this little volume, the author described with great detail and fondness how women seduce men, and men women; and in *La femme de Paul* he even describes certain obscenities difficult to understand. And he presents the country labouring folk not merely with indifference but even with contempt, as though they were animals.

This unconsciousness of the difference between good and evil is particularly striking in the story, *Une partie de campagne*, in which is given, as a very pleasant and amusing joke, a detailed description of how two men rowing with bare arms in a boat, tempt and afterwards seduce at the same time, one of them an elderly mother and the other a young girl, her daughter.

The sympathy of the author is evidently all the time so much on the side of these two wretches that he not merely ignores, but simply does not see, what must have been felt by the seduced mother and the maid (her daughter), by the father, and by a young man who is evidently engaged to the daughter; and therefore not merely is an objectionable description of a revolting crime presented in the form of an amusing jest, but the occurrence itself is described falsely, for what is given is only one side, and that the most insignificant—namely, the pleasure received by the rascals.

In that same little volume there is a story, *Histoire d'une fille de ferme*, which Turgénev particularly recommended to me and which particularly displeased me, again by this incorrect relation of the author to his subject. He evidently sees in all the working folk he describes mere animals, who rise to nothing more than sexual and maternal love, so that his descriptions give one an incomplete and artificial impression.

Lack of understanding of the life and interests of working people and the presentation of them as semi-brutes moved only by sensuality, spite, and greed, is one of the chief and most important defects of most recent French writers, including Maupassant, who not only in this but in all his other stories where he refers to the people, always describes them as coarse, dull animals at whom one can only laugh. Of course the French writers should know the nature of their own people better than I do; but despite the fact that I am a Russian and have not lived among the French peasants, I nevertheless affirm that in so representing their people the French authors are wrong, and that the French labourers cannot be such as they represent them to be. If France—such as we know her, with her truly great men and the great contributions those great men have made to science, art, citizenship, and the moral development of mankind—if this France exists, then that working class which has maintained and maintains on its shoulders this France with its great men, must consist not of brutes but of people with great spiritual qualities; and I therefore do not believe what I read in novels such as *La terre* and in Maupassant's stories; just as I should not believe it if I were told of the existence of a beautiful house standing without foundations. It may very well be that these high qualities of the people are not such as are described to us in *La petite Fadette* and *La Mare aux diables*, but I am firmly convinced that these qualities exist, and a writer who portrays the people only as Maupassant does, describing with sympathy only the *hanches* and *gorges* [2] of the Breton servant-girls, and describing with detestation and ridicule the life of the labouring men, commits a great artistic mistake, because he describes his subject only from one, and that the least interesting, physical, side and leaves quite out of sight another, and the most important, spiritual, side wherein the essence of the matter lies.

On the whole, the perusal of the little book handed me by Turgénev left me quite indifferent to the young writer.

So repugnant to me were the stories, *Une partie de campagne*, *La femme de Paul*, *L'historie d'une fille de ferme*, that I did not then notice the beautiful story, *Le papa de simon*, and the story, excellent in its description of the night, *Sur l'eau*.

"Are there not in our time, when so many people want to write, plenty of men of talent who do not know to what to apply this gift or who boldly apply it to what should not, and need not, be described?" thought I. And so I said to Turgénev, and thereupon forgot about Maupassant.

The first thing of his that fell into my hands after that was *Une Vie*, which some one advised me to read. That book at once compelled me to change my opinion of Maupassant, and since then I have read with interest everything signed by him. *Une Vie* is excellent, not only incomparably the best of his novels, but perhaps the best French novel since Hugo's *Les Misérables*. Here, besides remarkable talent—that special strenuous attention applied to the subject, by which the author perceives quite new features in the life he describes—are united in almost equal degree all three qualities of a true work of art: *first, a correct, that is a moral, relation of the author to his subject; secondly, beauty of form; and thirdly, sincerity, that is, love of what the author describes.* Here the meaning of life no longer presents itself to the author as consisting in the adventures of various male and female libertines; here the subject, as the title indicates, is life—the life of a ruined, innocent, amiable woman, predisposed to all that it good, but ruined by precisely the same coarse animal sensuality which in his former stories the author presented as if it were the central feature of life, dominant over all else. And in this book the author's whole sympathy is on the side of what is good.

The form, which was beautiful in the first stories, is here brought to such a pitch of perfection as, in my opinion, has been attained by no other French writer of prose. And above all, the author here really loves and deeply loves, the good family he describes; and he really hates that coarse debauchee who destroys the happiness and peace of

2 Hips and throats.

this charming family and, in particular, ruins the life of the heroine.

That is why all the events and characters of this novel are so life-like and memorable. The weak, kindly, debilitated mother; the upright, weak, attractive father; the daughter, still more attractive in her simplicity, artlessness, and sympathy with all that is good; their mutual relations, their first journey, their servants and neighbours; the calculating grossly sensual, mean, petty, insolent suitor, who as usual deceives the innocent girl by the customary empty idealization of the foulest instincts; the marriage, Corsica with the beautiful descriptions of nature, and then village life, the husband's coarse faithlessness, his seizure of power over the property, his quarrel with his father-in-law, the yielding of the good people and the victory of insolence; the relations with the neighbours—all this is life itself in its complexity and variety. And not only is all this vividly and finely described, but the sincere pathetic tone of it all involuntarily infects the reader. One feels that the author loves this woman, and loves her not for her external form but for her soul, for the goodness there is in her; that he pities her and suffers on her account, and this feeling is involuntarily communicated to the reader. And the questions: Why, for what end, is this fine creature ruined? Ought it indeed to be so? arise of themselves in the reader's soul and compel him to reflect on the meaning of human life. . . .   (1894)

JOSEPH CONRAD (1857-1924)

The Preface to *The Nigger of the Narcissus*

 WORK that aspires, however humbly, to the condition of art should carry its justification in every line. And art itself may be defined as a single-minded attempt to render the highest kind of justice to the visible universe, by bringing to light the truth, manifold and one, underlying its every aspect. It is an attempt to find in its forms, in its colours, in its light, in its shadows, in the aspects of matter, and in the facts of life what of each is fundamental, what is enduring and essential—their one illuminating and convincing quality—the very truth of their existence. The artist, then, like the thinker or the scientist, seeks the truth and makes his appeal. Impressed by the aspect of the world the thinker plunges into ideas, the scientist into facts—whence, presently, emerging they make their appeal to those qualities of our being that fit us best for the hazardous enterprise of living. They speak authoritatively to our common sense, to our intelligence, to our desire of peace, or to our desire of unrest; not seldom to our prejudices, sometimes to our fears, often to our egoism—but always to our credulity. And their words are heard with reverence, for their concern is with weighty matters: with the cultivation of our minds and the proper care of our bodies, with the attainment of our ambitions, with the perfection of the means and the glorification of our precious aims.

It is otherwise with the artist.

Confronted by the same enigmatical spectacle the artist descends within himself, and in that lonely region of stress and strife, if he be deserving and fortunate, he finds the terms of his appeal. His appeal is made to our less obvious capacities: to that part of our nature which, because of the warlike conditions of existence, is necessarily kept out of sight within the more resisting and hard qualities—like the vulnerable body within a steel armour. His appeal is less loud, more profound, less distinct, more stirring—and sooner forgotten. Yet its effect endures for ever. The changing wisdom of successive generations discards ideas, questions facts, demolishes theories. But the artist appeals to that part of our being which is not dependent on wisdom; to that in us which is a gift and not an acquisition—and, therefore, more permanently enduring. He speaks to our capacity for delight and wonder, to the sense of mystery surrounding our lives; to our sense of pity, and beauty, and pain; to the latent feeling of fellowship with all creation—and to the subtle but invincible conviction of solidarity that knits together the loneliness of innumerable hearts, to the solidarity in dreams, in joy, in sorrow, in aspirations, in illusions, in hope, in fear, which binds men to each other, which binds together all humanity—the dead to the living and the living to the unborn.

It is only some such train of thought, or rather of feeling, that can in a measure explain the aim of the attempt, made in the tale which follows, to present an unrestful episode in the obscure lives of a few individuals out of all the disregarded multitude of the bewildered, the simple, and the voiceless. For, if any part of truth dwells in the belief confessed above, it becomes evident that there is not a place of splendour or a dark corner of the earth that does not deserve, if only a passing glance of wonder and pity. The motive then, may be held to justify the matter of the work; but this preface, which is simply an avowal of endeavour, cannot end here—for the avowal is not yet complete.

Fiction—if it at all aspires to be art—appeals to temperament. And in truth it must be, like painting, like music, like all art, the appeal of one temperament to all the other innumerable temperaments whose subtle and resistless power endows passing events with their true meaning, and creates the moral, the emotional atmosphere of the place and time. Such an appeal to be effective must be an impression conveyed through the senses; and, in fact, it cannot be made in any other way, because temperament, whether individual or collective, is not amenable to persuasion. All art, therefore, appeals primarily to the senses, and the artistic aim when expressing itself in written words must also make its appeal through the senses, if its high desire is to reach the secret spring of responsive emotions. It must strenuously aspire to the plasticity of sculpture, to the colour of painting, and to the magic suggestiveness of music—which is the art of arts. And it is only through complete, unswerving devotion to the perfect blending of form and substance; it is only through an unremitting never-discouraged care for the shape and ring of sentences that an approach can be made to plasticity, to colour, and that the light of magic suggestiveness may be brought to play for an evanescent instant over the commonplace surface of words: of the old, old words worn thin, defaced by ages of careless usage.

The sincere endeavour to accomplish that creative task, to go as far on that road as his strength will carry him, to go undeterred by faltering, weariness or reproach, is the only valid justification for the worker in prose. And if his conscience is clear, his answer to those who in the fulness of a wisdom which looks for immediate profit, demand specifically to be edified, consoled, amused; who demand to be promptly improved, or encouraged, or frightened, or shocked, or charmed, must run thus:—My task which I am trying to achieve is, by the power of the written word to make you hear, to make you feel, —it is, before all, to make you *see*. That—and no more, and it is everything. If I succeed, you shall find there according to your deserts: encouragement, consolation, fear, charm—all you demand—and, perhaps, also that glimpse of truth for which you have forgotten to ask.

To snatch in a moment of courage, from the remorseless rush of time, a passing phase of life, is only the beginning of the task. The task approached in tenderness and faith is to hold up unquestioningly, without choice and without fear, the rescued fragment before all eyes in the light of a sincere mood. It is to show its vibration, its colour, its form; and through its movement, its form and its colour, reveal the substance of its truth—disclose its inspired secret: the stress and passion within the core of each convincing moment. In a single-minded attempt of that kind, if one be deserving and fortunate, one may perchance attain to such clearness of sincerity that at last the presented vision of regret or pity, of terror or mirth, shall awaken in the hearts of the beholders that feeling of unavoidable solidarity;

of the solidarity in mysterious origin, in toil, in joy, in hope, in uncertain fate, which binds men to each other and all mankind to the visible world.

It is evident that he who, rightly or wrongly, holds by the convictions expressed above cannot be faithful to any one of the temporary formulas of his craft. The enduring part of them—the truth which each only imperfectly veils—should abide with him as the most precious of his possessions, but they all: Realism, Romanticism, Naturalism, even the unofficial sentimentalism (which, like the poor, is exceedingly difficult to get rid of), all these gods must, after a short period of fellowship, abandon him—even on the very threshold of the temple—to the stammerings of his conscience and to the outspoken consciousness of the difficulties of his work. In that uneasy solitude the supreme cry of Art for Art, itself, loses the exciting ring of its apparent immorality. It sounds far off. It has ceased to be a cry, and is heard only as a whisper, often incomprehensible, but at times and faintly encouraging.

Sometimes, stretched at ease in the shade of a roadside tree, we watch the motions of a labourer in a distant field, and after a time, begin to wonder languidly as to what the fellow may be at. We watch the movements of his body, the waving of his arms, we see him bend down, stand up, hesitate, begin again. It may add to the charm of an idle hour to be told the purpose of his exertions. If we know he is trying to lift a stone, to dig a ditch, to uproot a stump, we look with a more real interest at his efforts; we are disposed to condone the jar of his agitation upon the restfulness of the landscape; and even, if in a brotherly frame of mind, we may bring ourselves to forgive his failure. We understood his object, and, after all, the fellow has tried, and perhaps he had not the strength—and perhaps he had not the knowledge. We forgive, go on our way—and forget.

And so it is with the workman of art. Art is long and life is short, and success is very far off. And thus, doubtful of strength to travel so far, we talk a little about the aim—the aim of art, which, like life itself, is inspiring, difficult—obscured by mists. It is not in the clear logic of a triumphant conclusion; it is not in the unveiling of one of those heartless secrets which are called the Laws of Nature. It is not less great, but only more difficult.

To arrest, for the space of a breath, the hands busy about the work of the earth, and compel men entranced by the sight of distant goals to glance for a moment at the surrounding vision of form and colour, sunshine and shadows; to make them pause for a look, for a sigh, for a smile—such is the aim, difficult and evanescent, and re-

served only for a very few to achieve. But sometimes, by the deserving
and the fortunate, even that task is accomplished. And when it is
accomplished—behold!—all the truth of life is there: a moment of
vision, a sigh, a smile—and the return to an eternal rest.   (1897)

WILLIAM DEAN HOWELLS (1837-1920)
From *My Literary Passions—Criticism and Fiction*

IT USED to be one of the disadvantages of the practice of
romance in America, which Hawthorne more or less whimsi-
cally lamented, that there were so few shadows and inequal-
ities in our broad level of prosperity; and it is one of the reflections
suggested by Dostoievsky's novel, *The Crime and the Punishment*, that
whoever struck a note so profoundly tragic in American fiction would
do a false and mistaken thing—as false and mistaken in its way as
dealing in American fiction with certain nudities which the Latin
peoples seem to find edifying. Whatever their deserts, very few American novelists have been led out to be shot, or finally exiled to the
rigors of a winter at Duluth; and in a land where journeyman carpenters and plumbers strike for four dollars a day the sum of hunger and
cold is comparatively small, and the wrong from class to class has been
almost inappreciable, though all this is changing for the worse. Our
novelists, therefore, concern themselves with the more smiling aspects
of life, which are the more American, and seek the universal in the
individual rather than the social interests. It is worth while, even at
the risk of being called commonplace, to be true to our well-to-do
actualities; the very passions themselves seem to be softened and modified by conditions which formerly at least could not be said to wrong
anyone, to cramp endeavor, or to cross lawful desire. Sin and suffering
and shame there must always be in the world, I suppose, but I believe
that in this new world of ours it is still mainly from one to another
one, and oftener still from one to one's self. We have death, too, in
America, and a great deal of disagreeable and painful disease, which the
multiplicity of our patent medicines does not seem to cure; but this is

From *My Literary Passions—Criticism and Fiction*, published 1910
by Harper & Brothers (New York). Reprinted by permission of the
heirs of William Dean Howells. These selections originally appeared
in *Harper's* Magazine (in 1886 and 1890, respectively). The first was
revised for publication in *My Literary Passions* (1895); the second
was revised for publication in *Criticism and Fiction* (1891). Both
were again revised and published together in the 1910 edition of
My Literary Passions—Criticism and Fiction.

tragedy that comes in the very nature of things, and is not peculiarly American, as the large, cheerful, average of health and success and happy life is. It will not do to boast, but it is well to be true to the facts, and to see that, apart from these purely mortal troubles, the race here has enjoyed conditions in which most of the ills that have darkened its annals might be averted by honest work and unselfish behavior.

Fine artists we have among us, and right-minded as far as they go; and we must not forget this at evil moments when it seems as if all the women had taken to writing hysterical improprieties, and some of the men were trying to be at least as hysterical in despair of being as improper. Other traits are much more characteristic of our life and our fiction. In most American novels, vivid and graphic as the best of them are, the people are segregated if not sequestered, and the scene is sparsely populated. The effect may be in instinctive response to the vacancy of our social life, and I shall not make haste to blame it. There are few places, few occasions among us, in which a novelist can get a large number of polite people, or at least keep them together. Unless he carries a snap-camera his picture of them has no probability; they affect one another like the figures perfunctorily associated in such deadly old engravings as that of "Washington Irving and his Friends." Perhaps it is for this reason that we excel in small pieces with three or four figures, or in studies of rustic communities, where there is propinquity if not society. Our grasp of more urbane life is feeble; most attempts to assemble it in our pictures are failures, possibly because it is too transitory, too intangible in its nature with us, to be truthfully represented as really existent. . . .

. . . In fine, I would have our American novelists be as American as they unconsciously can. Matthew Arnold complained that he found no "distinction" in our life, and I would gladly persuade all artists intending greatness in any kind among us that the recognition of the fact pointed out by Mr. Arnold ought to be a source of inspiration to them, and not discouragement. We have been now some hundred years building up a state on the affirmation of the essential equality of men in their rights and duties, and whether we have been right or been wrong the gods have taken us at our word, and have responded to us with a civilization in which there is no "distinction" perceptible to the eye that loves and values it. Such beauty and such grandeur as we have is common beauty, common grandeur, or the beauty and grandeur in which the quality of solidarity so prevails that neither distinguishes itself to the disadvantage of anything else. It seems to me that these conditions invite the artist to the study and the appreciation of the common, and to the portrayal in every art of those finer and higher aspects which unite rather than sever humanity, if he would thrive in our new order of things. The talent that is robust enough to front the every-day world and catch the charm of its work-worn, care-worn, brave, kindly face, need not fear the encounter, though it seems terrible to the sort nurtured in the superstition of the romantic, the bizarre, the heroic, the distinguished, as the things alone worthy of painting or carving or writing. The arts must become democratic, and then we shall have the expression of America in art; and the reproach which Arnold was half right in making us shall have no justice in it any longer; we shall be "distinguished."

In the meantime it has been said with a superficial justice that our fiction is narrow, though in the same sense I suppose the present English fiction is as narrow as our own; and most modern fiction is narrow in a certain sense. In Italy the best men are writing novels as brief and restricted in range as ours; in Spain the novels are intense and deep, and not spacious; the French school, with the exception of Zola, is narrow; the Norwegians are narrow; the Russians, except Tolstoy, are narrow, and the next greatest after him, Tourguenief, is the narrowest great novelist, as to mere dimensions, that ever lived, dealing nearly always with small groups, isolated and analyzed in the most American fashion. In fact, the charge of narrowness accuses the whole tendency of modern fiction as much as the American school. But I do not by any means allow that this narrowness is a defect, while denying that it is a universal characteristic of our fiction; it is rather, for the present, a virtue. Indeed, I should call the present American work, North and South, thorough rather than narrow. In one sense it is as broad as life, for each man is a microcosm, and the writer who is able to acquaint us intimately with half a dozen people, or the conditions of a neighborhood or a class, has done something which cannot in any bad sense be called narrow; his breadth is vertical instead of lateral, that is all; and this depth is more desirable than horizontal expansion in a civilization like ours, where the differences are not of classes, but of types, and not of types either so much as of characters. A new method was necessary in dealing with the new conditions, and the new method is worldwide, because the whole world is more or less Americanized. Tolstoy is exceptionally voluminous among modern writers, even Russian writers; and it might be said that the forte of Tolstoy himself is not in his breadth sidewise, but in his breadth upward and downward. *The Death of Ivan Ilyitch* leaves as vast an impression on the reader's soul as any episode of *War and Peace*, which, indeed, can be recalled only in episodes, and not as a whole. I think that our writers may be safely counselled to continue their work in the modern

way, because it is the best way yet known. If they make it true, it will
be large, no matter what its superficies are; and it would be the greatest
mistake to try to make it big. . . .   (1910)

VIRGINIA WOOLF (1882-1941)

Modern Fiction

IN MAKING any survey, even the freest and loosest, of modern
fiction it is difficult not to take it for granted that the
modern practice of the art is somehow an improvement
upon the old. With their simple tools and primitive materials, it might
be said, Fielding did well and Jane Austen even better, but compare
their opportunities with ours! Their masterpieces certainly have a
strange air of simplicity. And yet the analogy between literature and
the process, to choose an example, of making motor cars scarcely holds
good beyond the first glance. It is doubtful whether in the course of
the centuries, though we have learnt much about making machines,
we have learnt anything about making literature. We do not come to
write better; all that we can be said to do is to keep moving, now a
little in this direction, now in that, but with a circular tendency
should the whole course of the track be viewed from a sufficiently
lofty pinnacle. It need scarcely be said that we make no claim to
stand, even momentarily, upon that vantage ground. On the flat, in
the crowd, half blind with dust, we look back with envy to those
happier warriors, whose battle is won and whose achievements wear
so serene an air of accomplishment that we can scarcely refrain from
whispering that the fight was not so fierce for them as for us. It is
for the historian of literature to decide; for him to say if we are now
beginning or ending or standing in the middle of a great period of
prose fiction, for down in the plain little is visible. We know that
certain gratitudes and hostilities inspire us; that certain paths seem
to lead to fertile land, others to the dust and the desert; and of this
perhaps it may be worth while to attempt some account.

Our quarrel, then, is not with the classics, and if we speak of
quarreling with Mr. Wells, Mr. Bennett, and Mr. Galsworthy it is
partly that by the mere fact of their existence in the flesh their work
has a living, breathing, every-day imperfection which bids us take
what liberties with it we choose. But it is also true that, while we
thank them for a thousand gifts, we reserve our unconditional gratitude

From *The Common Reader*, First Series, by Virginia Woolf, copyright, 1925, by Harcourt, Brace & World, Inc.; renewed, 1953, by
Leonard Woolf. Reprinted by permission of the publishers.

for Mr. Hardy, for Mr. Conrad, and in a much lesser degree for the Mr. Hudson, of *The Purple Land*, *Green Mansions*, and *Far Away and Long Ago*. Mr. Wells, Mr. Bennett, and Mr. Galsworthy have excited so many hopes and disappointed them so persistently that our gratitude largely takes the form of thanking them for having shown us what they might have done but have not done; what we certainly could not do, but as certainly, perhaps, do not wish to do. No single phrase will sum up the charge or grievance which we have to bring against a mass of work so large in its volume and embodying so many qualities, both admirable and the reverse. If we tried to formulate our meaning in one word we should say that these three writers are materialists. It is because they are concerned not with the spirit but with the body that they have disappointed us, and left us with the feeling that the sooner English fiction turns its back upon them, as politely as may be, and marches, if only into the desert, the better for its soul. Naturally, no single word reaches the centre of three separate targets. In the case of Mr. Wells it falls notably wide of the mark. And yet even with him it indicates to our thinking the fatal alloy in his genius, the great clod of clay that got itself mixed up with the purity of his inspiration. But Mr. Bennett is perhaps the worst culprit of the three, inasmuch as he is by far the best workman. He can make a book so well constructed and solid in its craftsmanship that it is difficult for the most exacting of critics to see through what chink or crevice decay can creep in. There is not so much as a draught between the frames of the windows, or a crack in the boards. And yet—if life should refuse to live there? That is a risk which the creator of *The Old Wives' Tale*, George Cannon, Edwin Clayhanger, and hosts of other figures, may well claim to have surmounted. His characters live abundantly, even unexpectedly, but it remains to ask how do they live, and what do they live for? More and more they seem to us, deserting even the well-built villa in the Five Towns, to spend their time in some softly padded first-class railway carriage, pressing bells and buttons innumerable; and the destiny to which they travel so luxuriously becomes more and more unquestionably an eternity of bliss spent in the very best hotel in Brighton. It can scarcely be said of Mr. Wells that he is a materialist in the sense that he takes too much delight in the solidity of his fabric. His mind is too generous in its sympathies to allow him to spend much time in making things shipshape and substantial. He is a materialist from sheer goodness of heart, taking upon his shoulders the work that ought to have been discharged by Government officials, and in the plethora of his ideas and facts scarcely having leisure to realise, or forgetting to think important, the crudity and coarseness of his human beings. Yet what more

damaging criticism can there be both of his earth and of his Heaven
than that they are to be inhabited here and hereafter by his Joans
and his Peters? Does not the inferiority of their natures tarnish whatever institutions and ideals may be provided for them by the generosity
of their creator? Nor, profoundly though we respect the integrity and
humanity of Mr. Galsworthy, shall we find what we seek in his pages.

If we fasten, then one label on all these books on which is one
word, materialists, we mean by it that they write of unimportant
things; that they spend immense skill and immense industry making
the trivial and the transitory appear the true and the enduring.

We have to admit that we are exacting, and, further, that we
find it difficult to justify our discontent by explaining what it is that
we exact. We frame our question differently at different times. But
it appears most persistently as we drop the finished novel on the crest
of a sigh—Is it worth while? What is the point of it all? Can it be
that owing to one of those little deviations which the human spirit
seems to make from time to time Mr. Bennett has come down with
his magnificent apparatus for catching life just an inch or two on the
wrong side? Life escapes; and perhaps without life nothing else is
worth while. It is a confession of vagueness to have to make use of
such a figure as this, but we scarcely better the matter by speaking,
as critics are prone to do, of reality. Admitting the vagueness which
afflicts all criticism of novels, let us hazard the opinion that for us
at this moment the form of fiction most in vogue more often misses
than secures the thing we seek. Whether we call it life or spirit, truth
or reality, this, the essential thing, has moved off, or on, and refuses
to be contained any longer in such ill-fitting vestments as we provide.
Nevertheless, we go on perseveringly, conscientiously, constructing our
two and thirty chapters after a design which more and more ceases
to resemble the vision in our minds. So much of the enormous labour
of proving the solidity, the likeness to life, of the story is not merely
labour thrown away but labour misplaced to the extent of obscuring
and blotting out the light of the conception. The writer seems constrained, not by his own free will but by some powerful and un-
scrupulous tyrant who has him in thrall to provide a plot, to provide
comedy, tragedy, love, interest, and an air of probability embalming
the whole so impeccable that if all his figures were to come to life they
would find themselves dressed down to the last button of their coats
in the fashion of the hour. The tyrant is obeyed; the novel is done to
a turn. But sometimes, more and more often as time goes by, we
suspect a momentary doubt, a spasm of rebellion, as the pages fill
themselves in the customary way. Is life like this? Must novels be
like this?

Look within and life, it seems, is very far from being "like this."
Examine for a moment an ordinary mind on an ordinary day. The
mind receives a myriad impressions—trivial, fantastic, evanescent, or
engraved with the sharpness of steel. From all sides they come, an
incessant shower of innumerable atoms; and as they fall, as they shape
themselves into the life of Monday or Tuesday, the accent falls differently from of old; the moment of importance came not here but
there; so that if a writer were a free man and not a slave, if he could
write what he chose, not what he must, if he could base his work
upon his own feeling and not upon convention, there would be no
plot, no comedy, no tragedy, no love interest or catastrophe in the
accepted style, and perhaps not a single button sewn on as the Bond
Street tailors would have it. Life is not a series of gig lamps sym-
metrically arranged; but a luminous halo, a semi-transparent envelope
surrounding us from the beginning of consciousness to the end. Is it
not the task of the novelist to convey this varying, this unknown and
uncircumscribed spirit, whatever aberration or complexity it may display, with as little mixture of the alien and external as possible? We
are not pleading merely for courage and sincerity; we are suggesting
that the proper stuff of fiction is a little other than custom would
have us believe it.

It is, at any rate, in some such fashion as this that we seek to
define the quality which distinguishes the work of several young
writers, among whom Mr. James Joyce is the most notable, from that
of their predecessors. They attempt to come closer to life, and to
preserve more sincerely and exacting what interests and moves them,
even if to do so they must discard most of the conventions which are
commonly observed by the novelist. Let us record the atoms as they
fall upon the mind in the order in which they fall, let us trace the
pattern, however disconnected and incoherent in appearance, which
each sight or incident scores upon the consciousness. Let us not take
it for granted that life exists more fully in what is commonly thought
big than in what is commonly thought small. Any one who has read
The Portrait of the Artist as a Young Man or, what promises to be
a far more interesting work, *Ulysses*, now appearing in the *Little
Review*, will have hazarded some theory of this nature as to Mr. Joyce's
intention. On our part, with such a fragment before us, it is hazarded
rather than affirmed; but whatever the intention of the whole there
can be no question but that it is of the utmost sincerity and that the
result, difficult or unpleasant as we may judge it, is undeniably important. In contrast with those whom we have called materialists
Mr. Joyce is spiritual; he is concerned at all costs to reveal the
flickerings of that innermost flame which flashes its messages through

the brain, and in order to preserve it he disregards with complete courage whatever seems to him adventitious, whether it be probability, or coherence or any other of these signposts which for generations have served to support the imagination of a reader when called upon to imagine what he can neither touch nor see. The scene in the cemetery, for instance, with its brilliancy, its sordidity, its incoherence, its sudden lightning flashes of significance, does undoubtedly come so close to the quick of the mind that, on a first reading at any rate, it is difficult not to acclaim a masterpiece. If we want life itself here, surely we have it. Indeed, we find ourselves fumbling rather awkwardly if we try to say what else we wish, and for what reason a work of such originality yet fails to compare, for we must take high examples, with *Youth* or *The Mayor of Casterbridge*. It fails because of the comparative poverty of the writer's mind, we might say simply and have done with it. But it is possible to press a little further and wonder whether we may not refer our sense of being in a bright yet narrow room, confined and shut in, rather than enlarged and set free, to some limitation imposed by the method as well as by the mind. Is it the method that inhibits the creative power? Is it due to the method that we feel neither jovial nor magnanimous, but centred in a self which, in spite of its tremor of susceptibility, never embraces or creates what is outside itself and beyond? Does the emphasis laid, perhaps didactically, upon indecency, contribute to the effect of something angular and isolated? Or is it merely that in any effort of such originality it is much easier, for contemporaries especially, to feel what it lacks than to name what it gives? In any case it is a mistake to stand outside examining "methods." Any method is right, every method is right, that expresses what we wish to express, if we are writers; that brings us closer to the novelist's intention if we are readers. This method has the merit of bringing us closer to what we were prepared to call life itself; did not the reading of *Ulysses* suggest how much of life is excluded or ignored, and did it not come with a shock to open *Tristram Shandy* or even *Pendennis* and be by them convinced that there are not only other aspects of life, but more important ones into the bargain.

However this may be, the problem before the novelist at present, as we suppose it to have been in the past, is to contrive means of being free to set down what he chooses. He has to have the courage to say that what interests him is no longer "this" but "that": out of "that" alone must he construct his work. For the moderns "that," the point of interest, lies very likely in the dark places of psychology. At once, therefore, the accent falls a little differently; the emphasis is upon something hitherto ignored; at once a different outline of form becomes necessary, difficult for us to grasp, incomprehensible to our predecessors. No one but a modern, perhaps no one but a Russian, would have felt the interest of the situation which Tchekov has made into the short story which he calls "Gusev." Some Russian soldiers lie ill on board a ship which is taking them back to Russia. We are given a few scraps of their talk and some of their thoughts; then one of them dies and is carried away; the talk goes on among the others for a time, until Gusev himself dies, and looking "like a carrot or a radish" is thrown overboard. The emphasis is laid upon such unexpected places that at first it seems as if there were no emphasis at all; and then, as the eyes accustom themselves to twilight and discern the shapes of things in a room we see how complete the story is, how profound, and how truly in obedience to his vision Tchekov has chosen this, that, and the other, and placed them together to compose something new. But it is impossible to say "this is comic," or "that is tragic," nor are we certain, since short stories, we have been taught, should be brief and conclusive, whether this, which is vague and inconclusive, should be called a short story at all.

The most elementary remarks upon modern English fiction can hardly avoid some mention of the Russian influence, and if the Russians are mentioned one runs the risk of feeling that to write of any fiction save theirs is waste of time. If we want understanding of the soul and heart where else shall we find it of comparable profundity? If we are sick of our own materialism the least considerable of their novelists has by right of birth a natural reverence for the human spirit. "Learn to make yourself akin to people.... But let this sympathy be not with the mind—for it is easy with the mind—but with the heart, with love towards them." In every great Russian writer we seem to discern the features of a saint, if sympathy for the sufferings of others, love towards them, endeavour to reach some goal worthy of the most exacting demands of the spirit constitute saintliness. It is the saint in them which confounds us with a feeling of our own irreligious triviality, and turns so many of our famous novels to tinsel and trickery. The conclusions of the Russian mind, thus comprehensive and compassionate, are inevitably, perhaps, of the utmost sadness. More accurately indeed we might speak of the inconclusiveness of the Russian mind. It is the sense that there is no answer, that if honestly examined life presents question after question which must be left to sound on and on after the story is over in hopeless interrogation that fills us with a deep, and finally it may be with a resentful, despair. They are right perhaps; unquestionably they see further than we do and without our gross impediments of vision. But perhaps we see something that escapes them, or why should this voice of protest mix itself with our gloom? The voice of protest is the voice of another and an ancient civilization which seems to have bred in us the instinct to enjoy and fight rather than to suffer and understand. English fiction from Sterne to Meredith bears witness to our natural delight in humour and comedy, in the beauty of earth, in the activities of the intellect, and in the splendour of the body. But any deductions that we may draw from the comparison of two fictions so immeasurably far apart are futile save indeed as they flood us with a view of the infinite possibilities of the art and remind us that there is no limit to the horizon, and that nothing—no "method," no experiment, even of the wildest— is forbidden, but only falsity and pretence. "The proper stuff of fiction" does not exist; everything is the proper stuff of fiction, every feeling, every thought; every quality of brain and spirit is drawn upon; no perception comes amiss. And if we can imagine the art of fiction come alive and standing in our midst, she would undoubtedly bid us break her and bully her, as well as honour and love her, for so her youth is renewed and her sovereignty assured.   (1916)

PERCY LUBBOCK (1879-   )

From *Point of View*

THE WHOLE intricate question of method, in the craft of fiction, I take to be governed by the question of the point of view— the question of the relation in which the narrator stands to the story. He tells it as *he* sees it, in the first place; the reader faces the storyteller and listens, and the story may be told so vivaciously that the presence of the minstrel is forgotten, and the scene becomes visible, peopled with the characters of the tale. It may be so, it very often is so for a time. But it is not so always, and the storyteller himself grows conscious of a misgiving. If the spell is weakened at any moment, the listener is recalled from the scene to the mere author before him, and the story rests only upon the author's direct assertion. Is it not possible, then, to introduce another point of view, to set up a fresh narrator to bear the brunt of the reader's scrutiny? If the story-teller is *in* the story himself, the author is dramatized; his assertions gain in weight, for they are backed by the presence of the narrator in the pictured scene. It is advantage scored; the author has shifted his responsibility, and it now falls where the reader can see and measure it; the arbitrary quality which may at any time be detected in the author's voice is disguised in the voice of his spokesman. Nothing is now imported into the story from without; it is self-contained, it has no associations with anyone beyond its circle.

Such is the first step towards dramatization, and in very many a story it may be enough. The spokesman is there, in recognizable relation with his matter; no question of his authority can arise. But now a difficulty may be started by the nature of the tale that he tells. If he has nothing to do but to relate what he has seen, what anyone might have seen in his position, his account will serve very well; there is no need for more. Let him unfold his chronicle as it appears in his memory. But if he is himself the subject of his story, if the story involves a searching exploration of his own consciousness, an account in his own words, after the fact, is not by any means the best imaginable. Far better it would be to see him while his mind is actually at work in the agitation, whatever it may be, which is to make the book. The matter would then be objective and visible to the reader, instead of reaching him in the form of a report at second hand. But how to manage this without falling back upon the author and *his* report, which has already been tried and for good reasons, as it seemed, abandoned? It is managed by a kind of repetition of the same stroke, a further shift of the point of view. The spectator, the listener, the reader, is now himself to be placed at the angle of vision; not an account or a report, more or less convincing, is to be offered him, but a direct sight of the matter itself, while it is passing. Nobody expounds or explains; the story is enacted by its look and behaviour at particular moments. By the first stroke the narrator was brought into the book and set before the reader; but the action appeared only in his narrative. Now the action is there, proceeding while the pages are turned; the narrator is forestalled, he is watched while the story is in the making. Such is the progress of the writer of fiction towards drama; such is his method of evading the drawbacks of a mere reporter and assuming the advantages, as far as possible, of a dramatist. How far he may choose to push the process in his book—that is a matter to be decided by the subject; it entirely depends upon the kind of effect that the theme demands. It may respond to all the dramatization it can get, it may give all that it has to give for less. The subject dictates the method.

And now let the process be reversed, let us start with the purely dramatic subject, the story that will tell itself in perfect rightness, unaided, to the eye of the reader. This story never deviates from a strictly scenic form; one occasion or episode follows another, with no interruption for any reflective summary of events. Necessarily it must be so, for it is only while the episode is proceeding that no question

of a narrator can arise; when the scene closes the play ceases till the
opening of the next. To glance upon the story from a height and to
give a general impression of its course—this is at once to remove the
point of view from the reader and to set up a new one somewhere
else; the method is no longer consistent, no longer purely dramatic.
And the dramatic story is not only scenic, it is also limited to so much
as the ear can hear and the eye see. In rigid drama of this kind there
is naturally no admission of the reader into the private mind of any
of the characters; their thoughts and motives are transmuted into
action. A subject wrought to this pitch of objectivity is no doubt given
weight and compactness and authority in the highest degree; it is like
of piece of modelling, standing in clear space, casting its shadow. It is
the most finished form that fiction can take.

But evidently it is not a form to which fiction can aspire in general. It implies many sacrifices, and these will easily seem to be more
than the subject can usefully make. It is out of the question, of course,
wherever the main burden of the story lies within some particular
consciousness, in the study of a soul, the growth of a character, the
changing history of a temperament; there the subject would be need-
lessly crossed and strangled by dramatization pushed to its limit. It
is out of the question, again, wherever the story is too big, too comprehensive, too widely ranging, to be treated scenically, with no opportunity for general and panoramic survey; it has been discovered, indeed,
that even a story of this kind *may* fall into a long succession of definite
scenes, under some hands, but it has also appeared that in doing so
it incurs unnecessary disabilities, and will likely suffer. These stories,
therefore, which will not naturally accommodate themselves to the
reader's point of view, and the reader's alone, we regard as rather
pictorial than dramatic—meaning that they call for some narrator,
somebody who *knows*, to contemplate the facts and create an impression of them. Whether it is the omniscient author or a man in the
book, he must gather up his experience, compose a vision of it as it
exists in his mind, and lay *that* before the reader. It is the reflection
of an experience; and though there may be all imaginable diversity of
treatment within the limits of the reflection, such is its essential character. In a pictorial book the principle of the structure involves a point
of view which is not the reader's.

It is open to the pictorial book, however, to use a method in its
picture-making that is really no other than the method of drama. It is
somebody's experience, we say, that is to be reported, the general effect
that many things have left upon a certain mind; it is a fusion of
innumerable elements, the deposit of a lapse of time. The straightforward way to render it would be for the narrator—the author or his

selected creature—to view the past retrospectively and discourse upon it, to recall and meditate and summarize. That is picture-making in its natural form, using its own method. But exactly as in drama the subject is distributed among the characters and enacted by them, so in picture the effect may be entrusted to the elements, the reactions of the moment, and *performed* by these. The mind of the narrator becomes the stage, his voice is no longer heard. His voice *is* heard so long as there is narrative of any sort, whether he is speaking in person or is reported obliquely; his voice is heard, because in either case the language and the intonation are his, the direct expression of his experience. In the drama of his mind there is no personal voice, for there is no narrator; the point of view becomes the reader's once more. The shapes of thought in the man's mind tell their own story. And that is the art of picture-making when it uses the dramatic method.

But it cannot always do so. Constantly it must be necessary to offer the reader a summary of facts, an impression of a train of events, that can only be given as somebody's narration. Suppose it were required to render the general effect of a certain year in a man's life, a year that has filled his mind with a swarm of many memories. Looking into his consciousness after the year has gone, we might find much there that would indicate the nature of the year's events without any word on his part; the flickers and flashes of thought from moment to moment might indeed tell us much. But we shall need an account from him too, no doubt; too much has happened in a year to be wholly acted, as I call it, in the movement of the man's thought. He must narrate—he must make, that is to say, a picture of the events as he sees them, glancing back. Now if he speaks in the first person there can, of course, be no uncertainty in the point of view; he has his fixed position, he cannot leave it. His description will represent the face that the facts in their sequence turned towards *him*; the field of vision is defined with perfect distinctness, and his story cannot stray outside it. The reader, then, may be said to watch a reflection of the facts in a mirror of which the edge is nowhere in doubt; it is rounded by the bounds of the narrator's own personal experience.

This limitation may have a convenience and a value in the story, it may contribute to the effect. But it need not be forfeited, it is clear, if the first person is changed to the third. The author may use the man's field of vision and keep as faithfully within it as though the man were speaking for himself. In that case he retains this advantage and adds to it another, one that is likely to be very much greater. For now, while the point of view is still fixed in space, still assigned to the man in the book, it is free in *time*; there no longer stretches, between the narrator and the events of which he speaks, a certain tract of time, across which the past must appear in a more or less distant perspective. All the variety obtainable by a shifting relation to the story in time is thus in the author's hand; the safe serenity of a far retrospect, the promising or threatening urgency of the present, every gradation between the two, can be drawn into the whole effect of the book, and all of it without any change of the seeing eye. It is a liberty that may help the story indefinitely, raising this matter into strong relief, throwing that other back into vaguer shade.

And next, still keeping mainly and ostensibly to the same point of view, the author has the chance of using a much greater latitude than he need appear to use. The seeing eye is with somebody in the book, but its vision is reinforced; the picture contains more, becomes richer and fuller, because it is the author's as well as his creature's, both at once. Nobody notices, but in fact there are now two brains behind that eye; and one of them is the author's, who adopts and shares the *position* of his creature, and at the same time supplements his wit. If you analyse the picture that is now presented, you find that it is not all the work of the personage whose vision the author has adopted. There are touches in it that go beyond any sensation of his, and indicate that some one else is looking over his shoulder—seeing things from the same angle, but seeing more, bringing another mind to bear upon the scene. It is an easy and natural extension of the personage's power of observation. The impression of the scene may be deepened as much as need be; it is not confined to the scope of one mind, and yet there is no blurring of the focus by a double point of view. And thus what I have called the sound of the narrator's voice (it is impossible to avoid this mixture of metaphors) is less insistent in oblique narration, even while it seems to be following the very same argument that it would in direct, because another voice is speedily mixed and blended with it. . . .   (1921)

FORD MADOX FORD (1873-1939)
From *Joseph Conrad: A Personal Remembrance*

IT MIGHT be as well here to put down under separate headings, such as *Construction, Development* and the like, what were the formulæ for the writing of the novel at which Conrad and the writer had arrived, say in 1902 or so, before we finally took up and finished *Romance*. The reader will say that that is to depart from

From *Joseph Conrad: A Personal Remembrance* (London: Duck-worth & Company, 1924). Reprinted by permission of the estate of Ford Madox Ford.

the form of the novel in which form this book pretends to be written. But that is not the case. The novel more or less gradually, more or less deviously lets you into the secrets of the characters of the men with whom it deals. Then, having got them in, it sets them finally to work. Some novels, and still more short stories, will get a character in with a stroke or two as does Maupassant in the celebrated sentence in the *Reine Hortense* which Conrad and the writer were never tired of—quite intentionally—misquoting: "C'était un monsieur à favoris rouges qui entrait toujours le premier. . . ." He was a gentleman with red whiskers who always went first through a doorway. . . . *That* gentleman is so sufficiently got in that you need know no more of him to understand how he will act. He has been 'got in' and can get to work at once. That is called by the official British critics the static method and is, for some reason or other, contemned in England.

Other novels, however, will take much, much longer to develop their characters. Some—and this one is an example—will take almost a whole book to really get their characters in and will then dispose of the 'action' with a chapter, a line, or even a word—or two. The most wonderful instance of all of that is the ending of the most wonderful of all Maupassant's stories, *Champs d'Oliviers* which, if the reader has not read he should read at once. Let us now take a heading. (This method has the advantage that the lay reader who cannot interest himself in literary methods and the Critic-Annalist whose one passion is to cut the cackle and come to the horses can skip the whole chapter, certain that he will miss none of the spicy tit-bits.)

General Effect

We agreed that the general effect of a novel must be the general effect that life makes on mankind. A novel must therefore not be a narration, a report. Life does not say to you: In 1914 my next door neighbour, Mr. Slack, erected a greenhouse and painted it with Cox's green aluminium paint. . . . If you think about the matter you will remember, in various unordered pictures, how one day Mr. Slack appeared in his garden and contemplated the wall of his house. You will then try to remember the year of that occurrence and you will fix it as August 1914 because having had the foresight to bear the municipal stock of the city of Liège you were able to afford a first-class season ticket for the first time in your life. You will remember Mr. Slack—then much thinner because it was before he found out where to buy that cheap Burgundy of which he has since drunk an inordinate quantity though whisky you think would be much better for him! Mr. Slack again came into his garden, this time with a pale, weaselly-faced fellow, who touched his cap from time to time. Mr. Slack will point to his house-wall several times at different points, the weaselly fellow touching his cap at each pointing. Some days after, coming back from business you will have observed against Mr. Slack's wall.... At this point you will remember that you were then the manager of the fresh-fish branch of Messrs. Catlin and Clovis in Fenchurch Street.... What a change since then! Millicent had not yet put her hair up.... You will remember how Millicent's hair looked, rather pale and burnished in plaits. You will remember how it now looks, henna'd: and you will see in one corner of your mind's eye a little picture of Mr. Mills the vicar talking—oh, very kindly—to Millicent after she has come back from Brighton.... But perhaps you had better not risk that. You remember some of the things said by means of which Millicent has made you cringe—and her expression! ... Cox's Aluminium Paint! ... You remember the half empty tin that Mr. Slack showed you—he had a most undignified cold—with the name in a horse-shoe over a blue circle that contained a red lion asleep in front of a real-gold sun....

And, if that is how the building of your neighbour's greenhouse comes back to you, just imagine how it will be with your love-affairs that are so much more complicated....

Impressionism

We accepted without much protest the stigma: "Impressionists" that was thrown at us. In those days Impressionists were still considered to be bad people: Atheists, Reds, wearing red ties with which to frighten householders. But we accepted the name because Life appearing to us much as the building of Mr. Slack's greenhouse comes back to you, we saw that Life did not narrate, but made impressions on our brains. We in turn, if we wished to produce on you an effect of life, must not narrate but render ... impressions.

Selection

We agreed that the whole of Art consists in selection. To render your remembrance of your career as a fish-salesman might enhance the story of Mr. Slack's greenhouse, or it might *not*. A little image of iridescent, blue-striped, black-striped, white fish on a white marble slab with water trickling down to them round a huge mass of orange salmon-roe; a vivid description of a horrible smell caused by a cat having stolen and hidden in the thick of your pelargoniums a cod's head that you had brought back as a perquisite, you having subsequently killed the cat with a hammer, but long, long before you had rediscovered her fishy booty.... Such little impressions might be useful as contributing to illustrate your character—one should not kill a cat with a hammer! They might illustrate your sense of the beautiful— or your fortitude under affliction—or the disagreeableness of Mr. Slack, who had a delicate sense of smell—or the point of view of your only daughter Millicent.

We should then have to consider whether your sense of the beautiful or your fortitude could in our rendering carry the story forward or interest the reader. If it did we should include it; if in our opinion it was not likely to, we should leave it out. Or the story of the cat might in itself seem sufficiently amusing to be inserted as a purposed *longueur*, so as to give the idea of the passage of time. . . . It may be more amusing to read the story of a cat with your missing dinner than to read: "A fortnight elapsed. . . ." Or it might be better after all to write boldly: "Mr. Slack, after a fortnight had elapsed, remarked one day very querulously: 'That smell seems to get worse instead of better.' "

Selection (Speeches)

That last would be compromise, for it would be narration instead of rendering: it would be far *better* to give an idea of the passage of time by picturing a cat with a cod's head, but the length of the story must be considered. Sometimes to render anything at all in a given space will take up too much room—even to render the effect and delivery of a speech. Then just boldly and remorselessly you must relate and *risk* the introduction of yourself as author, with the danger that you may destroy all the illusion of the story.

Conrad and the writer would have agreed that the ideal rendering of Mr. Slack's emotions would be as follows:

"A scrawny, dark-brown neck, with an immense Adam's apple quivering over the blue stripes of a collar erected itself between the sunflower stems above the thin oaken flats of the dividing fence. An unbelievably long, thin gap of a mouth opened itself beneath a black-spotted handkerchief, to say that the unspeakable odour was sufficient to slay all the porters in Covent Garden. Last week it was only bad enough to drive a regiment of dragoons into a faint. The night before the people whom he had had to supper—I wondered who could eat any supper with any appetite under the gaze of those yellow eyes—people, mind you, to whom he had hoped to sell a little bit of property in the neighbourhood. Good people. With more than a little bit in the bank. People whose residence would give the whole neighbourhood a lift. They asked if he liked going out alone at night with so many undiscovered murders about. . . . 'Undiscovered murders!'

he went on repeating as if the words gave him an intimate
sense of relief. He concluded with the phrase: 'I *don't*
think!' "

That would be a very fair *rendering* of part of an episode: it
would have the use of getting quite a lot of Mr. Slack in; but you
might want to get on towards recounting how you had the lucky idea
of purchasing shares in a newspaper against which Mr. Slack had
counselled you. . . . And you might have got Mr. Slack in already!

The rendering in fact of speeches gave Conrad and the writer
more trouble than any other department of the novel whatever. It
introduced at once the whole immense subject of under what convention the novel is to be written. For whether you tell it direct and
as author—which is the more difficult way—or whether you put it
into the mouth of a character—which is easier by far but much more
cumbersome—the question of reporting or rendering speeches has to
be faced. To pretend that any character or any author writing directly
can remember whole speeches with all their words for a matter of
twenty-four hours, let alone twenty-four years, is absurd. The most
that the normal person carries away of a conversation after even a
couple of hours is just a salient or characteristic phrase or two, and
a mannerism of the speaker. Yet, if the reader stops to think at all,
or has any acuteness whatever, to render Mr. Slack's speech directly:
"Thet there odour is enough to do all the porters in Common Gorden
in. Lorst week it wouldn' no more 'n 'v sent a ole squad of tinwiskets
barmy on the crumpet . . ." and so on through an entire monologue
of a page and a half, must set the reader at some point or other wondering, how the author or the narrator can possibly, even if they were
present, have remembered every word of Mr. Slack's long speech. Yet
the object of the novelist is to keep the reader entirely oblivious of the
fact that the author exists—even of the fact that he is reading a book.
This is of course not possible to the bitter end, but a reader *can*
be rendered very engrossed, and the nearer you can come to making
him entirely insensitive to his surroundings, the more you will have
succeeded.

Then again, directly reported speeches in a book do move very
slowly; by the use of indirect locutions, together with the rendering
of the effects of other portions of speech, you can get a great deal more
into a given space. There is a type of reader that likes what is called
conversations—but that type is rather the reader in an undeveloped
state than the reader who has read much. So, wherever practicable,
we used to arrange speeches much as in the paragraph devoted to

Mr. Slack above. But quite often we compromised and gave passages of direct enough speech.

This was one of the matters as to which the writer was more uncompromising than was Conrad. In the novel which he did at last begin on his forty-first birthday there will be found to be hardly any direct speech at all, and probably none that is more than a couple of lines in length. Conrad indeed later arrived at the conclusion that, a novel being in the end a matter of convention—and in the beginning too for the matter of that, since what are type, paper, bindings and all the rest, but matters of agreement and convenience—you might as well stretch convention a little farther, and postulate that your author or your narrator is a person of a prodigious memory for the spoken. He had one minute passion with regard to conversations: he could not bear the repetition of 'he said's and 'she said's, and would spend agitated hours in chasing those locutions out of his or our pages and substituting: 'he replied,' 'she ejaculated,' 'answered Mr. Verloc' and the like. The writer was less moved by this consideration: it seemed to him that you could employ the words 'he said' as often as you like, accepting them as being unnoticeable, like 'a,' 'the' 'his' 'her,' or 'very.'

Conversations

One unalterable rule that we had for the rendering of conversations—for genuine conversations that are an exchange of thought, not interrogatories or statements of fact—was that no speech of one character should ever answer the speech that goes before it. This is almost invariably the case in real life where few people listen, because they are always preparing their own next speeches. When, of a Saturday evening, you are conversing over the fence with your friend Mr. Slack, you hardly notice that he tells you he has seen an incredibly coloured petunia at a market-gardener's, because you are dying to tell him that you have determined to turn author to the extent of writing a letter on local politics to the newspaper of which, against his advice, you have become a large shareholder.

He says: "Right down extraordinary that petunia was—"

You say: "What would you think now of my . . ."

He says: "Diamond-shaped stripes it had, blue-black and salmon. . . ."

You say: "I've always thought I had a bit of a gift. . . ."

Your daughter Millicent interrupts: "Julia Gower has got a pair of snake-skin shoes. She bought them at Wilson and Willocks's."

You miss Mr. Slack's next two speeches in wondering where Millicent got that bangle on her wrist. You will have to tell her more carefully than ever that she must *not* accept presents from Tom, Dick and Harry. By the time you have come out of that reverie Mr. Slack is remarking:

"I said to him use turpentine and sweet oil, three parts to two. What do you think?"

Surprise

We agreed that the one quality that gave interest to Art was the quality of surprise. That is very well illustrated in the snatch of conversation just given. If you reported a long speech of Mr. Slack's to the effect that he was going to enter some of his petunias for the local flower show and those, with his hydrangeas and ornamental sugar-beet, might well give him the Howard Cup for the third time, in which case it would become his property out and out. He would then buy two silver and cut-glass epergnes one to stand on each side of the Cup on his sideboard. He always did think that a touch of silver and cut glass. . . . If, after that you gave a long speech of your own: after, naturally, you had added a few commonplaces as a politeness to Mr. Slack: if you gave a long speech in which with modesty you dwelt on the powers of observation and of the pen that you had always considered yourself to possess, and in which you announced that you certainly meant to write a letter to the paper in which you had shares—on the statuary in the façade of the new town hall which was an offence to public decency. . . . And if in addition to that you added a soliloquy from your daughter Millicent to the effect that she intended to obtain on credit from your bootmakers, charging them to your account, a pair of scarlet morocco shoes with two-inch heels with which to go joy-riding on the Sunday with a young actor who played under the name of Hildebrand Hare and who had had his portrait in your paper. . . . If you gave all these long speeches one after the other you might be aware of a certain dullness when you re-read that *compte rendu*. . . . But if you carefully broke up petunias, statuary, and flower-show motives and put them down in little shreds one contrasting with the other, you would arrive at something much more coloured, animated, life-like and interesting and you would convey a profoundly significant lesson as to the self-engrossment of humanity. Into that live scene you could then drop the piece of news that you wanted to convey and so you would carry the chapter a good many stages forward.

Here, again, compromise must necessarily come in: there must come a point in the dramatic working up of every scene in which the characters do directly answer each other, for a speech or for two or three speeches. It was in this department, as has already been pointed out, that Conrad was matchless and the writer very deficient. Or, again, a point may come in which it is necessary—in which at least it is to take the line of least resistance—to report directly a whole tremendous effort of eloquence as ebullient as an oration by Mr. Lloyd George on the hymns of the Welsh nation. For there are times when the paraphernalia of indirect speech, interruptions and the rest retard your action too much. Then they must go: the sense of reality must stand down before the necessity to get on.

But, on the whole, the indirect, interrupted method of handling interviews is invaluable for giving a sense of the complexity, the tantalisation, the shimmering, the haze, that life is. In the pre-war period the English novel began at the beginning of a hero's life and went straight on to his marriage without pausing to look aside. This was all very well in its way, but the very great objection could be offered against it that such a story was too confined to its characters and, too self-centredly, went on, *in vacuo*. If you are so set on the affair of your daughter Millicent with the young actor that you forget that there *are* flower shows and town halls with nude statuary your intellect will appear a thing much more circumscribed than it should be. Or, to take a larger matter. A great many novelists have treated of the late war in terms solely of the war: in terms of pip-squeaks, trench-coats, wire-aprons, shells, mud, dust, and sending the bayonet home with a grunt. For that reason interest in the late war is said to have died. But, had you taken part actually in those hostilities, you would know how infinitely little part the actual fighting itself took in your mentality. You would be lying on your stomach, in a beast of a funk, with an immense, horrid German barrage going on all over and round you and with hell and all let loose. But, apart from the occasional, petulant question: "When the deuce will our fellows get going and shut 'em up?" your thoughts were really concentrated on something quite distant: on your daughter Millicent's hair, on the fall of the Asquith Ministry, on your financial predicament, on why your regimental ferrets kept on dying, on whether Latin is really necessary to an education, or in what way really *ought* the Authorities to deal with certain diseases. . . . You were there, but great shafts of thought from the outside, distant and unattainable world infinitely for the greater part occupied your mind.

It was that effect then, that Conrad and the writer sought to get into their work, that being Impressionism.

But these two writers were not unaware that there are other methods: they were not rigid in their own methods: they were sensible to the fact that compromise is at all times necessary in the execution of every work of art.

Let us come, then, to the eternally vexed seas of the Literary Ocean.

Style

We agreed on this axiom:

> The first business of Style is to make work interesting: the second business of Style is to make work interesting: the third business of Style is to make work interesting: the fourth business of Style is to make work interesting: the fifth business of Style. . . .

Style, then, has no other business.

A style interests when it carries the reader along: it is then a good style. A style ceases to interest when by reason of disjointed sentences, over-used words, monotonous or jog-trot cadences, it fatigues the reader's mind. *Too* startling words, however apt, *too* just images, too great displays of cleverness are apt in the long run to be as fatiguing as the most over-used words or the most jog-trot cadences. That a face resembles a Dutch clock has been too often said; to say that it resembles a ham is inexact and conveys nothing; to say that it has the mournfulness of an old, squashed-in meat tin, cast away on a waste building lot, would be smart—but too much of that sort of thing would become a nuisance. To say that a face was cramoisy is undesirable: few people nowadays know what the word means. Its employment will make the reader marvel at the user's erudition: in thus marvelling he ceases to consider the story and an impression of vagueness or length is produced on his mind. A succession of impressions of vagueness and length render a book in the end unbearable.

There are, of course, pieces of writing intended to convey the sense of the author's cleverness, knowledge of obsolete words or power of inventing similes: with such exercises Conrad and the writer never concerned themselves.

We used to say: the first lesson that an author has to learn is that of humility. Blessed are the humble because they do not get between the reader's legs. Before everything the author must learn to suppress himself: he must learn that the first thing he has to consider is his story and the last thing that he has to consider is his story, and in between that he will consider his story.

We used to say that a passage of good style began with a fresh, usual word, and continued with fresh, usual words to the end: there was nothing more to it. When we felt that we had really got hold of the reader, with a great deal of caution we would introduce a word not common to a very limited vernacular, but that only very occasionally. Very occasionally indeed: practically never. Yet it is in that way that a language grows and keeps alive. People get tired of hearing the same words over and over again.... It is again a matter for compromise.

Our chief masters in style were Flaubert and Maupassant: Flaubert in the greater degree, Maupassant in the less. In about the proportion of a sensible man's whisky and soda. We stood as it were on those hills and thence regarded the world. We remembered long passages of Flaubert: elaborated long passages in his spirit and with his cadences and then translated them into passages of English as simple as the subject under treatment would bear. We remembered short, staccato passages of Maupassant: invented short staccato passages in his spirit and then translated them into English as simple as the subject would bear. Differing subjects bear differing degrees of simplicity: To apply exactly the same timbre of language to a dreadful interview between a father and a daughter as to the description of a child's bedroom at night is impracticable because it is unnatural. In thinking of the frightful scene with your daughter Millicent which ruined your life, town councillor and parliamentary candidate though you had become, you will find that your mind employs a verbiage quite different from that which occurs when you remember Millicent asleep, her little mouth just slightly opened, her toys beside the shaded night-light.

Our vocabulary, then, was as simple as was practicable. But there are degrees of simplicity. We employed as a rule in writing the language that we employed in talking the one to the other. When we used French in speaking we tried mentally to render in English the least literary equivalent of the phrase. We were, however, apt to employ in our conversation words and periphrases that are not in use by, say, financiers. This was involuntary, we imagining that we talked simply enough. But later a body of younger men with whom the writer spent some years would say, after dinner: "Talk like a book, H.... Do talk like a book!" The writer would utter some speeches in the language that he employed when talking with Conrad: but he never could utter more than a sentence or two at a time. The whole mess would roar with laughter and, for some minutes, would render his voice inaudible.

If you will reflect on the language you then employed—and the writer—you will find that it was something like: "Cheerio, old bean. The beastly Adjutant's Parade is at five ack emma. Will you take my Johnnie's and let me get a real good fug in my downy bug walk? I'm fair blind to the wide to-night." That was the current language then and, in the earlier days of our conversations, some equivalent with which we were unacquainted must normally have prevailed. That we could hardly have used in our books, since within a very short time such languages become incomprehensible. Even to-day the locution 'ack emma' is no longer used and the expression 'blind to the wide' is incomprehensible—the very state is unfamiliar—to more than half the English-speaking populations of the globe.

So we talked and wrote a Middle-High-English of as unaffected a sort as would express our thoughts. And that was all that there really was to our 'style.' Our greatest admiration for a stylist in any language was given to W. H. Hudson of whom Conrad said that his writing was like the grass that the good God made to grow and when it was there you could not tell how it came.

Carefully examined a good—an interesting—style will be found to consist in a constant succession of tiny, unobservable surprises. If you write: "His range of subject was very wide and his conversation very varied and unusual; he could rouse you with his perorations or lull you with his periods; therefore his conversation met with great appreciation and he made several fast friends"—you will not find the world very apt to be engrossed by what you have set down. The results will be different if you put it: "He had the power to charm or frighten rudimentary souls into an aggravated witch-dance; he could also fill the small souls of the pilgrims with bitter misgivings: he had one devoted friend at least, and he had conquered one soul in the world that was neither rudimentary nor tainted with self-seeking."

Or, let us put the matter in another way. The catalogue of an ironmonger's store is uninteresting as literature because things in it are all classified and thus obvious: the catalogue of a farm sale is more interesting because things in it are contrasted. No one would for long read: Nails, drawn wire, ½ inch, per lb. . . . ; nails do., ¾ inch, per lb. . . . ; nails, do., inch, per lb. . . . But it is often not disagreeable to read desultorily "Lot 267. Pair rabbit gins. Lot 268, Antique powder flask. Lot 269, Malay Kris. Lot 270, Set of six sporting prints by Herring. Lot 271, Silver caudle cup . . . for that, as far as it goes, has the quality of surprise.

That is, perhaps, enough about Style. This is not a technical manual, and at about this point we arrive at a region in which the writer's memory is not absolutely clear as to the points on which he and Conrad were agreed. We made in addition an infinite number of experiments, together and separately in points of style and cadence. The writer, as has been said, wrote one immense book entirely in sentences of not more than ten syllables. He read the book over. He found it read immensely long. He went through it all again. He joined short sentences: he introduced relative clauses: he wrote in long sentences that had a gentle sonority and ended with a dying fall. The book read less long. Much less long.

Conrad also made experiments, but not on such a great scale since he could always have the benefit of the writer's performances of that sort. The writer only remembers specifically one instance of an exercise on Conrad's part. He was interested in blank verse at the moment—though he took no interest in English verse as a rule—and the writer happening to observe that whole passages of *Heart of Darkness* were not very far off blank verse Conrad tried for a short time to turn a paragraph into decasyllabic lines. The writer remembers the paragraph quite well. It is the one which begins:

> "She walked with measured steps, draped in striped and fringed cloths, treading the earth proudly with a slight jingle and flash of barbarous ornaments. . . ."

But he cannot remember what Conrad added or took away. There come back vaguely to him a line or two like:

> She carried high her head, her hair was done
> In the shape of a helmet; she had greaves of brass
> To the knee; gauntlets of brass to th' elbow.
> A crimson spot. . . .

That, however, may just as well be the writer's contrivance as Conrad's: it happened too long ago for the memory to be sure. A little later, the writer occupying himself with writing French rhymed *vers libre,* Conrad tried his hand at that too. He produced:

> Riez toujours! La vie n'est pas si gaie,
> Ces tristes jours quand à travers la haie
> Tombe le long rayon
> Dernier
> De mon soleil qui gagne
> Les sommets, la montagne,
> De l'horizon. . . .

There was a line or two more that the writer has forgotten.

That was Conrad's solitary attempt to write verse.

We may as well put the rest of this matter under a separate heading:

Cadence

This was the one subject upon which we never came to any agreement. It was the writer's view that everyone has a natural cadence of his own from which in the end he cannot escape. Conrad held that a habit of good cadence could be acquired by the study of models.

His own he held came to him from constant reading of Flaubert. He did himself probably an injustice.

But questions of cadence and accentuation as of prosody in general we were chary of discussing. They were matters as to which Conrad was very touchy. His ear was singularly faulty for one who was a great writer of elaborated prose to that at times the writer used to wonder how the deuce he *did* produce his effects of polyphonic closings to paragraphs. In speaking English he had practically no idea of accentuation whatever, and indeed no particular habits. He would talk of Mr. Cunninghame Graham's book *Success* alternately as *Suc*cess and Suc*cess*, half a dozen times in the course of a conversation about the works of that very wonderful writer. Over French he was not much better. He became quite enraged when told that if the first line of his verse quoted above was to be regarded as decasyllabic—and it *must* by English people be regarded as decasyllabic—then the word 'vie' must be a monosyllable in spite of its termination in e. He had in the second line quite correctly allowed for '*tristes*' as being two syllables, and '*tombe*' in the third. In the clash of French verse-theories of those days he might be correct or incorrect without committing a solecism, but he could not be incorrect in the first line and formal in the others. Conrad's face would cloud over. He would snatch up a volume of Racine and read half a dozen lines. He would exclaim contemptuously: "Do you mean to say that each of those verses *con*sists of ten syllables?" . . . Yet he would have read the verse impeccably. . . . He would flush up to the eyes. He would cry: "Did you ever hear a Frenchman say vee-yeh when he meant vee? You never did! *Jamais de la vie!*" And with fury he would read his verse aloud, making, with a slight stammer, '*vie*' a monosyllable and, with impetus, two syllables each out of *tristes* and *tombe*. He would begin to gesticulate, his eyes flashing. . . .

One would change the subject of discussion to the unfailing topic of the rottenness of French as a medium for poetry, finding perfect harmony again in the thought that French was as rotten for verse-poetry as was English for any sort of prose. . . .

The curious thing was that when he read his prose aloud his accentuation was absolutely faultless. So that it always seemed to the writer that Conrad's marvellous gift of language was, in the end, dramatic. When he talked his sense of phonetics was dormant, but the moment it came to any kind of performance the excitement would quicken the brain centres that governed his articulation. It was, indeed, the same with his French. When conversing desultorily with the writer, he had much of the accent and the negligence of an aristocratic, meridional lounger of the seventies. . . . But when at

Lamb House, Rye, he addressed compliments to Mr. Henry James, you could imagine, if you closed your eyes, that it was the senior actor of the Théâtre Français, addressing an eulogium to the bust of Molière. . . .

Probably the mere thought of reading aloud subconsciously aroused memories of once-heard orations of Mr. Gladstone or John Bright: so, in writing, even to himself he would accentuate and pronounce his words as had done those now long defunct orators. . . . And it is to be remembered that, during all those years, the writer wrote every word that he wrote, with the idea of reading aloud to Conrad, and that during all those years Conrad wrote that he wrote with the idea of reading it aloud to this writer.

Structure

That gets rid, as far as is necessary in order to give a pretty fair idea of Conrad's methods, of the questions that concern the texture of a book. More official or more learned writers who shall not be novelists shall treat of this author's prose with less lightness—but assuredly too with less love. . . . Questions then of vocabulary, selection of incident, style, cadence and the rest concern themselves with the colour and texture of prose and, since this writer, again, will leave to more suitable pens the profounder appraisements of Conrad's morality, philosophy and the rest, there remains only to say a word or two on the subject of form.

Conrad then, never wrote a true short story, a matter of two or three pages of minutely considered words, ending with a smack . . . with what the French call a *coup de canon.* His stories were always what for lack of a better phrase one has to call 'long-short' stories. For these the form is practically the same as that of the novel. Or, to avoid the implication of saying that there is only one form for the novel, it would be better to put it that the form of long-short stories may vary as much as may the form for novels. The short story of Maupassant, of Tchekhov or even of the late O. Henry is practically stereotyped—the introduction of a character in a word or two, a word or two for atmosphere, a few paragraphs for story, and then, click! a sharp sentence that flashes the illumination of the idea over the whole.

This Conrad—and for the matter of that, the writer—never so much as attempted, either apart or in collaboration. The reason for this lies in all that is behind the mystic word 'justification.' Before everything a story must convey a sense of inevitability: that which happens in it must seem to be the only thing that could have happened. Of course a character may cry: "If I had then acted differently how

different everything would now be." The problem of the author is
to make his then action the only action that character could have
taken. It must be inevitable, because of his character, because of his
ancestry, because of past illness or on account of the gradual coming
together of the thousand small circumstances by which Destiny, who
is inscrutable and august, will push us into one certain predicament.
Let us illustrate:

In the rendering of your long friendship with, and ultimate
bitter hostility towards, your neighbour Mr. Slack who had a greenhouse painted with Cox's aluminium paint you will, if you wish to
get yourself in with the scrupulousness of a Conrad, have to provide
yourself, in the first place, with an ancestry at least as far back as
your grandparents. To account for your own stability of character and
physical robustness you will have to give yourself two dear old grandparents in a lodge at the gates of a great nobleman: if necessary you
will have to give them a brightly polished copper kettle simmering on
a spotless hob, with silhouettes on each side of the mantel: in order
to account for the lamentable procedure of your daughter Millicent
you must provide yourself with an actress- or gipsy-grandmother. Or at
least with a French one. This grandmother will have lived, unfortunately unmarried, with someone of eloquence—possibly with the
great Earl-Prime Minister at whose gates is situated the humble
abode of your other grandparents—at any rate she will have lived
with someone from whom you will have inherited your eloquence.
From her will have descended the artistic gifts to which the reader
will owe your admirable autobiographic novel. If you have any physical
weakness, to counterbalance the robustness of your other grandparents,
you will provide your mother, shortly before your birth, with an
attack of typhoid fever, due to a visit to Venice in company with your
father, who was a gentleman's courier in the family in which your
mother was a lady's maid. Your father, in order to be a courier, will
have had, owing to his illegitimacy, to live abroad in very poor circumstances. The very poor circumstances will illustrate the avarice of
his statesman father—an avarice which will have descended to you
in the shape of that carefulness in money matters that, reacting on
the detrimental tendencies inherited by Millicent from her actress-
grandmother, so lamentably influences your daughter's destiny.

And of course there will have to be a great deal more than that,
always supposing you to be as scrupulous as was Conrad in this matter
of justification. For Conrad—and for the matter of that the writer—
was never satisfied that he had really and sufficiently got his characters
in: he was never convinced that he had convinced the reader, this
accounting for the great lengths of some of his books. He never

introduced a character, however subsidiary, without providing that character with ancestry and hereditary characteristics, or at least with home surroundings—always supposing that character had any influence on the inevitability of the story. Any policeman who arrested any character must be 'justified' because the manner in which he effected the arrest, his mannerisms, his vocabulary and his voice, might have a permanent effect on the psychology of the prisoner. The writer remembers Conrad using almost those very words during the discussion of the plot of the *Secret Agent*.

This method, unless it is very carefully handled, is apt to have the grave defect of holding a story back very considerably. You must as a rule bring the biography of a character in only after you have introduced the character: yet, if you introduce a policeman to make an arrest the rendering of his biography might well retard the action of an exciting point in the story. . . . It becomes then your job to arrange that the very arresting of the action is an incitement of interest in the reader, just as, if you serialise a novel, you take care to let the words *"to be continued in our next"* come in at as harrowing a moment as you can contrive.

And of course the introducing of the biography of a character may have the great use of giving contrast to the tone of the rest of the book. . . . Supposing that in your history of your affair with Mr. Slack you think that the note of your orderly middle-class home is growing a little monotonous, it would be very handy if you could discover that Mr. Slack had a secret, dipso-maniacal wife, confined in a country cottage under the care of a rather criminal old couple: with a few pages of biography of that old couple you could give a very pleasant relief to the sameness of your narrative. In that way the sense of reality is procured. . . . (1924)

E. M. FORSTER (1879-   )

The Plot

HARACTER," says Aristotle, "gives us qualities, but it is in actions—what we do—that we are happy or the reverse." We have already decided that Aristotle is wrong and now we must face the consequences of disagreeing with him. "All human happiness and misery," says Aristotle, "take the form of action." We know better. We believe that happiness and misery exist in the secret life, which each of us leads privately and to which (in his characters) the novelist has access. And by the secret life we mean the life for which there is no external evidence, not, as is vulgarly supposed, that which is revealed by a chance word or a sigh. A chance word or sigh are just as much evidence as a speech or a murder: the life they reveal ceases to be secret and enters the realm of action.

There is, however, no occasion to be hard on Aristotle. He had read few novels and no modern ones—the *Odyssey* but not *Ulysses*— he was by temperament apathetic to secrecy, and indeed regarded the human mind as a sort of tub from which everything can finally be extracted; and when he wrote the words quoted above he had in view the drama, where, no doubt they hold true. In the drama all human happiness and misery does and must take the form of action. Otherwise its existence remains unknown, and this is the great difference between the drama and the novel.

The speciality of the novel is that the writer can talk about his characters as well as through them or can arrange for us to listen when they talk to themselves. He has access to self-communings, and from that level he can descend even deeper and peer into the subconscious. A man does not talk to himself quite truly—not even to himself; the happiness or misery that he secretly feels proceed from causes that he cannot quite explain, because as soon as he raises them to the level of the explicable they lose their native quality. The novelist has a real pull here. He can show the subconscious short-circuiting straight into action (the dramatist can do this too); he can also show it in its relation to soliloquy. He commands all the secret life, and he must not be robbed of this privilege. "How did the writer know that?" it is sometimes said. "What's his standpoint? He is not being consistent, he's shifting his point of view from the limited to the omniscient, and now he's edging back again." Questions like these have too much atmosphere of the law courts about them. All that matters to the reader is whether the shifting of attitude and the secret life are convincing, whether it is $\pi\iota\theta\alpha\nu\delta\nu$ [1] in fact, and with his favourite word ringing in his ears Aristotle may retire.

However, he leaves us in some confusion, for what, with this enlargement of human nature, is going to become of the plot? In most literary works there are two elements: human individuals, whom we have recently discussed, and the element vaguely called art. Art we have also dallied with, but with a very low form of it: the story: the chopped-off length of the tapeworm of time. Now we arrive at a much higher aspect: the plot, and the plot, instead of finding human

[1] ["Plausible."]

beings more or less cut to its requirements, as they are in the drama, finds them enormous, shadowy and intractable, and three-quarters hidden like an iceberg. In vain it points out to these unwieldy creatures the advantages of the triple process of complication, crisis, and solution so persuasively expounded by Aristotle. A few of them rise and comply, and a novel which ought to have been a play is the result. But there is no general response. They want to sit apart and brood or something, and the plot (whom I here visualize as a sort of higher government official) is concerned at their lack of public spirit: "This will not do," it seems to say. "Individualism is a most valuable quality; indeed my own position depends upon individuals; I have always admitted as much freely. Nevertheless there are certain limits, and those limits are being overstepped. Characters must not brood too long, they must not waste time running up and down ladders in their own insides, they must contribute, or higher interests will be jeopardised." How well one knows that phrase, "a contribution to the plot"! It is accorded, and of necessity, by the people in a drama: how necessary is it in a novel?

Let us define a plot. We have defined a story as a narrative of events arranged in their time-sequence. A plot is also a narrative of events, the emphasis falling on causality. "The king died and then the queen died," is a story. "The king died, and then the queen died of grief" is a plot. The time-sequence is preserved, but the sense of causality overshadows it. Or again: "The queen died, no one knew why, until it was discovered that it was through grief at the death of the king." This is a plot with a mystery in it, a form capable of high development. It suspends the time-sequence, it moves as far away from the story as its limitations will allow. Consider the death of the queen. If it is in a story we say "and then?" If it is in a plot we ask "why?" That is the fundamental difference between these two aspects of the novel. A plot cannot be told to a gaping audience of cave men or to a tyrannical sultan or to their modern descendant the movie-public. They can only be kept awake by "and then—and then—" They can only supply curiosity. But a plot demands intelligence and memory also.

Curiosity is one of the lowest of the human faculties. You will have noticed in daily life that when people are inquisitive they nearly always have bad memories and are usually stupid at bottom. The man who begins by asking you how many brothers and sisters you have, is never a sympathetic character, and if you meet him in a year's time he will probably ask you how many brothers and sisters you have, his mouth again sagging open, his eyes still bulging from his head. It is difficult to be friends with such a man, and for two inquisitive people

to be friends must be impossible. Curiosity by itself takes us a very
little way, nor does it take us far into the novel—only as far as the
story. If we would grasp the plot we must add intelligence and memory.

Intelligence first. The intelligent novel-reader, unlike the inquisitive one who just runs his eye over a new fact, mentally picks it
up. He sees it from two points of view: isolated, and related to the
other facts that he has read on previous pages. Probably he does not
understand it, but he does not expect to do so yet awhile. The facts
in a highly organized novel (like *The Egoist*) are often of the nature
of cross-correspondences and the ideal spectator cannot expect to view
them properly until he is sitting up on a hill at the end. This element
of surprise or mystery—the detective element as it is sometimes rather
emptily called—is of great importance in a plot. It occurs through a
suspension of the time-sequence; a mystery is a pocket in time, and
it occurs crudely, as in "Why did the queen die?" and more subtly
in half-explained gestures and words, the true meaning of which only
dawns pages ahead. Mystery is essential to a plot, and cannot be
appreciated without intelligence. To the curious it is just another
"and then—" To appreciate a mystery, part of the mind must be
left behind, brooding, while the other part goes marching on.

That brings us to our second qualification: memory.

Memory and intelligence are closely connected, for unless we
remember we cannot understand. If by the time the queen dies we
have forgotten the existence of the king we shall never make out
what killed her. The plot-maker expects us to remember, we expect
him to leave no loose ends. Every action or word ought to count; it
ought to be economical and spare; even when complicated it should
be organic and free from dead matter. It may be difficult or easy, it
may and should contain mysteries, but it ought not to mislead. And
over it, as it unfolds, will hover the memory of the reader (that dull
glow of the mind of which intelligence is the bright advancing edge)
and will constantly rearrange and reconsider, seeing new clues, new
chains of cause and effect, and the final sense (if the plot has been
a fine one) will not be of clues or chains, but of something aesthetically
compact, something which might have been shown by the novelist
straight away, only if he had shown it straight away it would never
have become beautiful. We come up against beauty here—for the
first time in our enquiry: beauty at which a novelist should never aim,
though he fails if he does not achieve it. I will conduct beauty to her
proper place later on. Meanwhile please accept her as part of a
completed plot. She looks a little surprised at being there, but beauty
ought to look a little surprised: it is the emotion that best suits her
face, as Botticelli knew when he painted her risen from the waves,

between the winds and the flowers. The beauty who does not look surprised, who accepts her position as her due—she reminds us too much of a prima donna.

But let us get back to the plot, and we will do so via George Meredith.

Meredith is not the great name he was twenty or thirty years ago, when much of the universe and all Cambridge trembled. I remember how depressed I used to be by a line in one of his poems: "We live but to be sword or block." I did not want to be either and I knew that I was not a sword. It seems though that there was no real cause for depression, for Meredith is himself now rather in the trough of a wave, and though fashion will turn and raise him a bit, he will never be the spiritual power he was about the year 1900. His philosophy has not worn well. His heavy attacks on sentimentality —they bore the present generation, which pursues the same quarry but with neater instruments, and is apt to suspect anyone carrying a blunderbuss of being a sentimentalist himself. And his visions of Nature—they do not endure like Hardy's, there is too much Surrey about them, they are fluffy and lush. He could no more write the opening chapter of *The Return of the Native* than Box Hill could visit Salisbury Plain. What is really tragic and enduring in the scenery of England was hidden from him, and so is what is really tragic in life. When he gets serious and noble-minded there is a strident over-tone, a bullying that becomes distressing. I feel indeed that he was like Tennyson in one respect: through not taking himself quietly enough he strained his inside. And his novels: most of the social values are faked. The tailors are not tailors, the cricket matches are not cricket, the railway trains do not even seem to be trains, the county families give the air of having been only just that moment unpacked, scarcely in position before the action starts, the straw still clinging to their beards. It is surely very odd, the social scene in which his characters are set: it is partly due to his fantasy, which is legitimate, but partly a chilly fake, and wrong. What with the faking, what with the preaching, which was never agreeable and is now said to be hollow, and what with the home counties posing as the universe, it is no wonder Meredith now lies in the trough. And yet he is in one way a great novelist. He is the finest contriver that English fiction has produced, and any lecture on plot must do homage to him.

Meredith's plots are not closely knit. We cannot describe the action of *Harry Richmond* in a phrase, as we can that of *Great Expectations*, though both books turn on the mistake made by a young man as to the sources of his fortune. A Meredithian plot is not a temple to the tragic or even to the comic Muse, but rather resembles a series of kiosks most artfully placed among wooded slopes, which his people reach by their own impetus, and from which they emerge with altered aspect. Incident springs out of character, and having occurred it alters that character. People and events are closely connected, and he does it by means of these contrivances. They are often delightful, sometimes touching, always unexpected. This shock, followed by the feeling, "Oh, that's all right," is a sign that all is well with the plot: characters, to be real, ought to run smoothly, but a plot ought to cause surprise. The horse-whipping of Dr. Shrapnel in *Beauchamp's Career* is a surprise. We know that Everard Romfrey must dislike Shrapnel, must hate and misunderstand his radicalism, and be jealous of his influence over Beauchamp: we watch too the growth of the misunderstanding over Rosamund, we watch the intrigues of Cecil Baskelett. As far as characters go, Meredith plays with his cards on the table, but when the incident comes what a shock it gives us and the characters too! The tragicomic business of one old man whipping another from the highest motives—it reacts upon all their world, and transforms all the personages of the book. It is not the centre of *Beauchamp's Career*, which indeed has no centre. It is essentially a contrivance, a door through which the book is made to pass, emerging in an altered form. Towards the close, when Beauchamp is drowned and Shrapnel and Romfrey are reconciled over his body, there is an attempt to elevate the plot to Aristotelian symmetry, to turn the novel into a temple wherein dwells interpretation and peace. Meredith fails here: *Beauchamp's Career* remains a series of contrivances (the visit to France is another of them), but contrivances that spring from the characters and react upon them.

And now briefly to illustrate the mystery element in the plot: the formula of "The queen died, it was afterwards discovered through grief." I will take an example, not from Dickens (though *Great Expectations* provides a fine one), nor from Conan Doyle (whom my priggishness prevents me from enjoying), but again from Meredith: an example of a concealed emotion from the admirable plot of *The Egoist*: it occurs in the character of Laetitia Dale.

We are told, at first, all that passes in Laetitia's mind. Sir Willoughby has twice jilted her, she is sad, resigned. Then, for dramatic reasons, her mind is hidden from us, it develops naturally enough, but does not re-emerge until the great midnight scene where he asks her to marry him because he is not sure about Clara, and this time, a changed woman, Laetitia says "No." Meredith has concealed the change. It would have spoiled his high comedy if we had been kept in touch with it throughout. Sir Willoughby has to have a series of crashes, to catch at this and that, and find everything rickety. We should not enjoy the fun, in fact it would be boorish, if we saw the author preparing the booby traps beforehand, so Laetitia's apathy has been hidden from us. This is one of the countless examples in which either plot or character has to suffer, and Meredith with his unerring good sense here lets the plot triumph.

As an example of mistaken triumph, I think of a slip—it is no more than a slip—which Charlotte Brontë makes in *Villette*. She allows Lucy Snowe to conceal from the reader her discovery that Dr. John is the same as her old playmate Graham. When it comes out, we do get a good plot thrill, but too much at the expense of Lucy's character. She has seemed, up to then, the spirit of integrity, and has, as it were, laid herself under a moral obligation to narrate all that she knows. That she stoops to suppress is a little distressing, though the incident is too trivial to do her any permanent harm.

Sometimes a plot triumphs too completely. The characters have to suspend their natures at every turn, or else are so swept away by the course of Fate that our sense of their reality is weakened. We shall find instances of this in a writer who is far greater than Meredith, and yet less successful as a novelist—Thomas Hardy. Hardy seems to me essentially a poet, who conceives of his novels from an enormous height. They are to be tragedies or tragicomedies, they are to give out the sound of hammer-strokes as they proceed; in other words Hardy arranges events with emphasis on causality, the ground plan is a plot, and the characters are ordered to acquiesce in its requirements. Except in the person of Tess (who conveys the feeling that she is greater than destiny) this aspect of his work is unsatisfactory. His characters are involved in various snares, they are finally bound hand and foot, there is ceaseless emphasis on fate, and yet, for all the sacrifices made to it, we never see the action as a living thing as we see it in *Antigone* or *Berenice* or *The Cherry Orchard*. The fate above us, not the fate working through us—that is what is eminent and memorable in the Wessex novels. Egdon Heath before Eustacia Vye has set foot upon it. The woods without the Woodlanders. The downs above Budmouth Regis with the royal princesses, still asleep, driving across them through the dawn. Hardy's success in *The Dynasts* (where he uses another medium) is complete, there the hammer-strokes are heard, cause and effect enchain the characters despite their struggles, complete contact between the actors and the plot is established. But in the novels, though the same superb and terrible machine works, it never catches humanity in its teeth; there is some vital problem that has not been answered, or even posed, in the misfortunes of Jude the Obscure. In other words the characters have been required to contribute too much to the plot; except in their rustic humours, their vitality has been impoverished, they have gone dry and thin. This, as far as I can make out, is the flaw running through Hardy's novels: he has emphasized causality more strongly than his medium permits. As a poet and prophet and visualizer George Meredith is nothing by his side—just a suburban roarer—but Meredith did know what the novel could stand, where the plot could dun the characters for a contribution, where it must let them function as they liked. And the moral—well, I see no moral, because the work of Hardy is my home and that of Meredith cannot be: still the moral from the point of these lectures is again unfavourable to Aristotle. In the novel, all human happiness and misery does not take the form of action, it seeks means of expression other than through the plot, it must not be rigidly canalized.

In the losing battle that the plot fights with the characters, it often takes a cowardly revenge. Nearly all novels are feeble at the end. This is because the plot requires to be wound up. Why is this necessary. Why is there not a convention which allows a novelist to stop as soon as he feels muddled or bored? Alas, he has to round things off, and usually the characters go dead while he is at work, and our final impression of them is through deadness. *The Vicar of Wakefield* is in this way a typical novel, so clever and fresh in the first half, up to the painting of the family group with Mrs. Primrose as Venus, and then so wooden and imbecile. Incidents and people that occurred at first for their own sake now have to contribute to the dénouement. In the end even the author feels he is being a little foolish. "Nor can I go on," he says, "without a reflection on those accidental meetings which though they happen every day, seldom excite our surprise but upon some extraordinary occasion." Goldsmith is of course a lightweight, but most novels do fail here—there is this disastrous standstill while logic takes over the command from flesh and blood. If it was not for death and marriage I do not know how the average novelist would conclude. Death and marriage are almost his only connection between his characters and his plot, and the reader is more ready to meet him here, and take a bookish view of them, provided they occur later on in the book: the writer, poor fellow, must be allowed to finish up somehow, he has his living to get like any one else, so no wonder that nothing is heard but hammering and screwing.

This—as far as one can generalize—is the inherent defect of novels: they go off at the end: and there are two explanations of it: firstly, failure of pep, which threatens the novelist like all workers:

and secondly, the difficulty which we have been discussing. The characters have been getting out of hand, laying foundations and declining to build on them afterwards, and now the novelist has to labour personally, in order that the job may be done to time. He pretends that the characters are acting for him. He keeps mentioning their names and using inverted commas. But the characters are gone or dead.

The plot, then, is the novel in its logical intellectual aspect: it requires mystery, but the mysteries are solved later on: the reader may be moving about in worlds unrealized, but the novelist has no misgivings. He is competent, poised above his work, throwing a beam of light here, popping on a cap of invisibility there, and (qua plot-maker) continually negotiating with himself qua character-monger as to the best effect to be produced. He plans his book beforehand: or anyhow he stands above it, his interest in cause and effect give him an air of predetermination.

And now we must ask ourselves whether the framework thus produced is the best possible for a novel. After all, why has a novel to be planned? Cannot it grow? Why need it close, as a play closes? Cannot it open out? Instead of standing above his work and controlling it, cannot the novelist throw himself into it and be carried along to some goal that he does not foresee? The plot is exciting and may be beautiful, yet is it not a fetich, borrowed from the drama, from the spatial limitations of the stage? Cannot fiction devise a framework that is not so logical yet more suitable to its genius?

Modern writers say that it can, and we will now examine a recent example—a violent onslaught on the plot as we have defined it: a constructive attempt to put something in the place of the plot.

I have already mentioned the novel in question: *Les Faux-monnayeurs* by André Gide. It contains within its covers both the methods. Gide has also published the diary he kept while he was writing the novel, and there is no reason why he should not publish in the future the impressions he had when rereading both the diary and the novel, and in the future-perfect a still more final synthesis in which the diary, the novel, and his impressions of both will interact. He is indeed a little more solemn than an author should be about the whole caboodle, but regarded as a caboodle it is excessively interesting, and repays careful study by critics.

We have, in the first place, a plot in *Les Faux-monnayeurs* of the logical objective type that we have been considering—a plot, or rather fragments of plots. The main fragment concerns a young man called Olivier—a charming, touching and lovable character, who misses happiness, and then recovers it after an excellently contrived dénoue-

ment; confers it also; this fragment has a wonderful radiance and
"lives," if I may use so coarse a word, it is a successful creation on
familiar lines. But it is by no means the centre of the book. No more
are the other logical fragments—that which concerns Georges, Olivier's
schoolboy brother, who passes false coin, and is instrumental in
driving a fellow-pupil to suicide. (Gide gives us his sources for all
this in his diary, he got the idea of Georges from a boy whom he
caught trying to steal a book off a stall, the gang of coiners were
caught at Roen, and the suicide of children took place at Clermont-
Ferrand, etc.) Neither Olivier, nor Georges, nor Vincent a third
brother, nor Bernard their friend is the centre of the book. We come
nearer to it in Edouard. Edouard is a novelist. He bears the same
relation to Gide as Clissold does to Wells. I dare not be more
precise. Like Gide, he keeps a diary, like Gide he is writing a book
called *Les Faux-monnayeurs,* and like Clissold he is disavowed.
Edouard's diary is printed in full. It begins before the plot-fragments,
continues during them, and forms the bulk of Gide's book. Edouard
is not just a chronicler. He is an actor too; indeed it is he who rescues
Olivier and is rescued by him; we leave those two in happiness.

But that is still not the centre. The nearest to the centre lies in
a discussion about the art of the novel. Edouard is holding forth to
Bernard, his secretary and some friends. He has said (what we all accept
as commonplace) that truth in life and truth in a novel are not identical, and then he goes on to say that he wants to write a book which
shall include both sorts of truth.

> "And what is its subject?" asked Sophroniska.
> "There is none," said Edouard sharply. "My novel has
> no subject. No doubt that sounds foolish. Let us say, if you
> prefer, that it will not have 'a' subject. . . . 'A slice of life,'
> the naturalistic school used to say. The mistake that school
> made was always to cut its slice in the same direction, always
> lengthwise, in the direction of time. Why not cut it up and
> down? Or across? As for me, I don't want to cut it at all.
> You see what I mean. I want to put everything into my novel
> and not snip off my material either here or there. I have been
> working for a year, and there is nothing I haven't put in: all
> I see, all I know, all I can learn from other people's lives
> and my own."
> "My poor man, you will bore your readers to death,"
> cried Laura, unable to restrain her mirth.
> "Not at all. To get my effect, I am inventing, as my
> central character, a novelist, and the subject of my book will
> be the struggle between what reality offers him and what he
> tries to make of the offer."

"Have you planned out this book?" asked Sophroniska, trying to keep grave.

"Of course not."

"Why 'of course'?"

"For a book of this type any plan would be unsuitable. The whole of it would go wrong if I decided any detail ahead. I am waiting for reality to dictate to me."

"But I thought you wanted to get away from reality."

"My novelist wants to get away, but I keep pulling him back. To tell the truth, this is my subject: the struggle between facts as proposed by reality, and the ideal reality."

"Very well. Tell it them, Bernard."

"*Les Faux-monnayeurs*," said Bernard. "And now will you please tell us who these faux monnayeurs are."

"I haven't the least idea."

Bernard and Laura looked at each other and then at Sophroniska. There was the sound of a deep sigh.

The fact was that ideas about money, depreciation, inflation, forgery, etc., had gradually invaded Edouard's book—just as theories of clothing invade *Sartor Resartus* and even assume the functions of characters. "Has any of you ever had hold of a false coin?" he asked after a pause. "Imagine a ten-franc piece, gold, false. It is actually worth a couple of sous, but it will remain worth ten francs until it is found out. Suppose I begin with the idea that—"

"But why begin with an idea?" burst out Bernard, who was by now in a state of exasperation. "Why not begin with a fact? If you introduce the fact properly, the idea will follow of itself. If I was writing your *Faux-monnayeurs* I should begin with a piece of false money, with the ten-franc piece you were speaking of, and here it is!"

So saying, Bernard pulled a ten-franc piece out of his pocket and flung it on the table.

"There," he remarked. "It rings all right. I got it this morning from the grocer. It's worth more than a couple of sous, as it's coated in gold, but it's actually made of glass. It will become quite transparent in time. No—don't rub it— you're going to spoil my false coin."

Edouard had taken it and was examining it with the utmost attention.

"How did the grocer get it?"

"He doesn't know. He passed it on me for a joke, and then enlightened me, being a decent fellow. He let me have it for five francs. I thought that, since you were writing *Les Faux-monnayeurs*, you ought to see what false money is like, so I got it to show you. Now that you have looked at it, give it me back. I am sorry to see that reality has no interest for you."

"Yes," said Edouard: "it interests me, but it puts me out."

"That's a pity," remarked Bernard.[1]

This passage is the centre of the book. It contains the old thesis of truth in life versus truth in art, and illustrates it very neatly by the arrival of an actual false coin. What is new in it is the attempt to combine the two truths, the proposal that writers should mix themselves up in their material and be rolled over and over by it; they should not try to subdue any longer, they should hope to be subdued, to be carried away. As for a plot—to pot with the plot, break it up, boil it down. Let there be those "formidable erosions of contour" of which Nietzsche speaks. All that is prearranged is false.

Another distinguished critic has agreed with Gide—that old lady in the anecdote who was accused by her nieces of being illogical. For some time she could not be brought to understand what logic was, and when she grasped its true nature she was not so much angry as contemptuous. "Logic! Good gracious! What rubbish!" she exclaimed. "How can I tell what I think till I see what I say?" Her nieces, educated young women, thought that she was passée; she was really more up to date than they were.

Those who are in touch with contemporary France, say that the present generation follows the advice of Gide and the old lady and resolutely hurls itself into confusion, and indeed admires English novelists on the ground that they so seldom succeed in what they attempt. Compliments are always delightful, but this particular one is a bit of a backhander. It is like trying to lay an egg and being told you have produced a paraboloid—more curious than gratifying. And what results when you try to lay a paraboloid, I cannot conceive—perhaps the death of the hen. That seems the danger in Gide's position —he sets out to lay a paraboloid; he is not well advised, if he wants to write subconscious novels, to reason so lucidly and patiently about the subconscious; he is introducing mysticism at the wrong stage of the process. However that is his affair. As a critic he is most stimulating, and the various bundles of words he has called *Les Faux-monnayeurs* will be enjoyed by all who cannot tell what they think till they see what they say, or who weary of the tyranny by the plot and of its alternative, tyranny by characters.

There is clearly something else in view, some other aspect or

[1] Paraphrased from *Les Faux-monnayeurs*, pp. 238-246. My version, needless to say, conveys neither the subtlety nor the balance of the original.

aspects which we have yet to examine. We may suspect the claim to be consciously subconscious, nevertheless there is a vague and vast residue into which the subconscious enters. Poetry, religion, passion— we have not placed them yet, and since we are critics—only critics— we must try to place them, to catalogue the rainbow. We have already peeped and botanized upon our mothers' graves.

The numbering of the warp and woof of the rainbow must accordingly be attempted and we must now bring our minds to bear on the subject of fantasy.   (1927)

GRANVILLE HICKS (1901-   )

From *The Great Tradition*

HE PROBLEMS that events force upon the writer's attention as he reads the papers or talks with his friends also rise to trouble him in his work. Whether an author starts with the life of some little village or the life of fashionable New York, whether he is interested in the sexual adjustments of men and women or in the quest for a philosophy of life, in the struggles of youth or the tragedies of age, sooner or later, if he is astute and persistent, he comes to certain elementary bread-and-butter questions. These questions many writers try to evade, maintaining that economic issues are of no importance, that human nature is always the same, regardless of the systems under which men live, that the basic themes of life and death have nothing to do with the ways in which life is supported. But evasion is not easy and it is very dangerous. Some authors, while loudly proclaiming the right of evasion, have, like Archibald MacLeish, practiced what they preached against, and written propaganda against propaganda. Others have half-heartedly attacked the problems they insist are unworthy of concern: Wilder in *Heaven's My Destination*, Elizabeth Madox Roberts in *He Sent For a Raven*, and Ernest Hemingway in such stories as "The Gambler, the Nun, and the Radio." Their half-heartedness condemns them to worse confusion than their former indifference, but at least there is evidence that they, too, feel the pressure that forces so many of their contemporaries to decision.

If evasion becomes more difficult, decision becomes easier and its implications more apparent. The revolutionary writers have proceeded from a belief that capitalism is unsound to a belief that it must be destroyed. Most of them have gone further and recognized that only the working class can destroy capitalism. And many have seen that choosing the side of the proletariat in the class struggle means working with it, becoming identified with it, and they have joined or given their aid to militant working-class organizations. A majority of these support the Communist Party.

The large measure of agreement on fundamental political questions distinguishes the revolutionary movement in literature today from any radical movement that preceded it. The muckrakers were for the most part middle-class reformers, agreeing only partly in their analyses of the evils of capitalism and not at all in their remedies. The literary radicalism of the pre-war period, centering in the *Masses*, was a phase of the revolt against nineteenth-century bourgeois standards, particularly standards of sexual conduct. Made possible by the contrast between village surveillance and urban anonymity, it constantly lapsed into Bohemian freakishness. It was an emancipating force, valuably destructive, but it had no deep roots. It was an escape from the middle class, and yet not an identification with the working class. It left the important decision to the future.

Post-war disillusionment and Coolidge prosperity ended the careers of most of the *Masses* radicals. There were a few who, after wandering in strange places, were to return at the end of the decade. And there were a very few who continued to march under the revolutionary banner. Of these the most influential was Michael Gold, author of the first revolutionary novel to receive widespread attention, one of the founders of the New Playwrights Theatre, editor of the *New Masses*, which resumed in 1926 the *Masses-Liberator* tradition, and when the depression dispelled the dreams of the prosperous twenties, leader, by virtue both of his steadfast record and his eloquent challenges, of the new revolutionary movement. *Jews Without Money*, portions of which had appeared in the *Liberator* and the *New Masses* long before it was published as a book, was a reminder, surprisingly necessary in the twenties, that poverty had not been miraculously abolished and that the dreams and sufferings of the poor were a worthy theme for any author. Endowed with Gold's passionate romanticism, the book achieved its effect by a robust power of evocation rather than by what today we think of as revolutionary insight. Novelist, poet, dramatist, critic, columnist, Gold has been the movement's great amateur, but he has been an amateur with something close to genius. He has been the important link between the radicalism of the war period and the revolutionary movement of the present. That he remained steadfast in an era of apostasy and that he triumphed over the emotional, anarchic Bohemianism of the *Masses* group can be attributed to the depth of his roots in the working class. If he is still rather undisciplined, spending his talents at times in ways that are unproductive, it is quite clear to anyone who reads the first impassioned protests of his individualism that he has acquired a measure of discipline, and acquired it because loyalty to the working class demanded it. Otherwise his fine imaginative powers would have been wasted as so many rich talents were in the rank morasses of the twenties.

Once Gold stood almost alone, so that now, young as he is, he seems almost the dean of revolutionary literature. The writers of today have come, by easier paths than his, to his position. Though not many revolutionary writers are members of the Communist Party, most of them give it their allegiance, and all are deeply influenced by its existence. Acceptance of the logic of revolution demands participation in the struggle of the working class, and the Communist Party is the principal means for joining in the fight. When Josephine Herbst takes part in the farmer's struggles, it is in an organization that communists help to guide. When Erskine Caldwell studies conditions in Detroit, it is for the communist *Daily Worker* that he writes his reports. When Jack Conroy, Nelson Algren, and Emmet Gowan make a trip into the South, they seek to test a law that principally affects communists, and they are treated as communist by the authorities. Most of the strikes that have been portrayed in revolutionary novels have been strikes that communists led. It is in this way, and certainly not through any attempt to impose its discipline upon writers, that the Communist Party has become the unifying force in the revolutionary literary movement. Insofar as the Communist Party makes good its claim to be the only party of the militant working class, and insofar as it adheres to the theories of Marxism, it commands the allegiance of the revolutionary writers.

It should be understood that, apart from this fundamental unity, with all it entails, there is no lack of diversity. First of all, no one imagines that mere adherence to a set of political principles, or even the complete mastery of a world philosophy, is any guarantee of literary talent. . . . We have taken for granted a certain minimum qualification, so to speak, and have been principally concerned with what each writer did with the capabilities he had. This is not to say, however, that a discerning eye and a quick ear, the power of penetrating below the surface and the willingness to work for perfect expression, are unimportant. The quality that we call imagination, the ability to rearrange the elements of experience into patterns that are new and different and yet true to experience, is significant, wherever it may be found. We have tried to discover under what conditions imagination ripens into literature, and even now our chief aim is to determine whether the revolutionary movement provides such conditions, but, as we examine a group of writers who share a certain attitude towards life, we cannot ignore kinds and degrees of talent.

There are other and more subtle differences. There are writers who do not adhere to the Communist Party and yet write from the point of view of a class-conscious worker, and there are writers who are very close to the Communist Party and yet differ only slightly from their bourgeois contemporaries. B. Traven, for example, though he has respect for some communists, is contemptuous of party discipline, but he belongs to the working class, and there are no novels that speak more effectively for that class than *The Death Ship* and *The Treasure of the Sierra Madre*. Erskine Caldwell, on the other hand, or Nathan Asch, or Waldo Frank, for all their loyalty to communism, are closer to such writers as Faulkner, Joyce, and Lawrence than they are to Traven. The problem is, indeed, even more complicated, for one often finds the same writer varying from what is revolutionary to what obviously is not. Such inconsistencies, arguing of course, imperfect integration, are not unnatural in the infancy of revolutionary literature. In some degree in fact, though often less conspicuously than in the novelists mentioned, they are to be found in every revolutionary writer.

Finally, there are the most important differences of all, the differences that are inherent in the nature of revolutionary literature. If all bourgeois survivals could be miraculously obliterated, and if the same high talent everywhere prevailed, monotony would by no means be the result. Potentially revolutionary literature, far from being committed to the narrowness about which some of its critics pretend to worry, has a broader field than any literature the world has known. To the themes the writers of the past have adopted the revolutionary artist adds a multitude of themes that they could not or would not use. It is bourgeois literature today that is narrow, with its few patterns of success and failure in love, business and the quest for a philosophy. It is revolutionary literature that is finding new themes and new ways of treating old ones.

If, then, we insist on the unity of the revolutionary literary movement, it is not to be supposed that there is any lack of variety in the novels, poems, and plays that compose it. But it is, nevertheless, a movement, held together by certain conceptions of the relation of literature to life and of the direction that life is taking. It is not a movement in any organizational sense; there is no one who can say, except as an individual opinion, what is revolutionary in literature and what is not; there is no one who can impose themes or dictate treatment. It derives its unity from an historical process, the transition from

private exploitation to social organization. It deserves the name proletarian as well as the name revolutionary, for it speaks for the class
that is making the revolution. At the moment it is only imperfectly
and embryonically the expression of that class, for the proletariat is
only imperfectly conscious of its destiny; but as the workers are forced
by the further collapse of capitalism to a full realization of their power
and opportunity, revolutionary literature will draw its strength from the
proletariat and be, as it cannot be today, truly and fully proletarian. . . .

(1933, revised 1935)

FRANÇOIS MAURIAC (1885-   )

From Chapter V, *God and Mammon*

F THERE is one dogma which has gained the support of the
majority of writers in this century and the last, it is the
dogma of the absolute independence of the artist. It seems
to be agreed, once and for all, that a work of art has no object outside
itself. It only counts in so far as it is gratuitous or useless: anything
written to prove a point or to be of use is disqualified from the realm
of art. Gide says that "the moral issue for the artist is not that he
should present an idea that is useful but that he should present an
idea well."

But we can be sure that this would not have to be said so persistently and so often by some writers if it were not vigorously con-
tradicted by others. In fact, from the other end of the literary world
comes a ceaseless protest against the pretension to absolute independence on the part of the artist. For example, when Ernest Psichari
proclaims that one must write with fear and trembling under the eye
of the Trinity, he is being the mouthpiece of all those who believe in
the immortality of each individual soul, and therefore believe in the
extreme importance of their writings as effecting each immortal destiny.

Then, between these two opposing camps, there is the huge crowd
of novelists who fluctuate and hesitate. On the one hand they admit
that their work is valuable only inasmuch as it apprehends living men
in their completeness, in their heights and in their depths—the human
creature as he is. They feel that any intervention in the unfolding of
their characters—even to prove the truth of what they believe—is an
abuse. They feel a sincere revulsion against falsifying life. On the other
hand, they know that they are treading on dangerous ground, and that

From *God and Mammon*, translated by Christopher Lawson and
Bernard Wall (London: Sheed & Ward, 1936), and reprinted with
permission of the publishers.

their intense desire to depict human emotions and passions may have an incalculable and permanent effect on the lives of many people.

Every novelist worthy of the name and every playwright who is a born Christian suffers from the torment of this dilemma. In French literature there is a famous example. Once in my holidays I followed the fashion of the time and wrote a life of Jean Racine. Racine is typical of the divided and hesitating writer who plays first into the hands of one camp and then into the hands of the other. The ultimate fate of a writer like him depends on the final decision. Everyone knows what agonizing fluxes Racine went through before he reached that decision. At the age of twenty he escaped from Port-Royal because his young genius revolted against the unbearable restraints imposed upon him there. Then, when Nicole, in his letter on *Les Imaginaires* made a violent attack on novelists and playwrights, Racine burned with rage. Nicole had written that "the qualities of the novelist and the playwright, which anyway are not very honourable in the judgment of decent people, are horrible when considered in the light of the principles of the Christian religion and the rules of the Gospel. Novelists and dramatic poets are public poisoners, not only of the bodies, but the souls of the faithful, and they ought to hold themselves guilty of a multitude of spiritual murders." Racine replied to this hard hitting with unparalleled verve and bitterness and venom in two letters which are not enough known. In our desire to excuse Racine for being unable to endure such inflexible doctrines without an outcry, we must be careful not to blame it on the inhuman rigour of the Jansenists. Nicole was only developing a doctrine of St. Augustine; and Bossuet showed himself equally uncompromising in his letter to Père Caffaro on the subject of the play and the novel. Bossuet maintained that the success of plays and novels was due to the fact that people find in them substitutes for love and beauty and for their own feelings; and what answer can be made to that? The real reason why Racine was so furious with Nicole was because he was hurt to the quick. During the following years we can trace the struggle that he had with himself until finally, at the age of thirty-eight, he gave in and renounced for ever the depicting of human passions and personalities.

It is a renunciation that very few writers are capable of making, and Racine's renunciation was certainly not so easy as some people think. Is a man who is capable of writing and who has a masterpiece inside him at liberty not to give it to the world? An author who gives up writing may do it because his belly is empty, as the saying goes, and he would only be able to repeat himself and copy himself. Self-repetition, in fact, is the occupation of most writers on the decline; even when they have given over everything that was expected of them and delivered their message to the world they go on regularly laying eggs because it is their job, and, after all, a man must live.

No human power, however, could reduce a man to silence during his period of fertility; there would have to be a supernatural power. We do not know whether Grace has ever been able to triumph over a writer who has writing-sickness. The conversion of a literary man is usually marked by redoubled activity and effort on his part. He wants the greatest possible number of people to read about the example that he gives to the world. We are still awaiting the miracle of a writer who is reduced to silence by God.

Actually, all the best writers are tugging at one rope. At one end of the rope there are those who are convinced that their work will be valuable only if it is disinterested and does not tamper with reality for reasons of modesty or edification, and at the other end there are those who have a feeling of responsibility towards their readers, of whom, in spite of their scruples, they want as large a number as possible. At one end there is the certainty that there cannot be a work in novel-form which has value outside absolute submission to its object —the human heart: there must be progress in knowledge of mankind, but whatever depths are found there must be no dizziness or disgust or horror. This is a certainty. At the other end there is only a senti-ment, a feeling—at any rate for those who do not belong to a religious faith. For a Christian, eternity hangs in the balance if one soul is troubled or in danger of being lost. But while non-Christians are unable to stop themselves feeling a responsibility, in a dim way they have no difficulty at all in inventing sophisms to persuade themselves that their fear of scandalising others has no connection with reality. I should like to assure them, at this point, that their nebulous feeling corre-sponds with a very deep reality. We can say this: that although the whole matter seems more serious for writers with the faith, it certainly does interest the sceptics—and this, precisely because they only believe in man and know no reality in the world other than human reality.

A few years ago a review posed the question: "Why do you write?" to the literary world. The majority of answerers merely tried to be witty; Paul Morand, for instance, said: "To be rich and esteemed." He was making fun of the whole thing by confusing immediate motives with deep motives.

The deep motive seems to me to lie in the instinct which urges us not to be alone. A writer is essentially a man who will not be re-signed to solitude. Each of us is like a desert, and a literary work is like a cry from the desert, or like a pigeon let loose with a message in its claws, or like a bottle thrown into the sea. The point is: to be heard— even if by one single person. And the point is that our thoughts and, if we are novelists, our characters should be understood and loved and welcomed by other intelligences and other hearts. An author who assures you that he writes for himself alone and that he does not care whether he is heard or not is a boaster and is deceiving either himself or you. Every man suffers if he is alone, and the artist is the man for whom and in whom this suffering takes a physical form. Baudelaire was right when he called artists *lighthouses*. They light a great fire in the darkness, and they set light to themselves so as to attract the greatest number of their fellow-beings to them.

Artists, and particularly writers, are the most squeamish people in the world, and at the same time the most hungry for praise. Indeed it is impossible for writers to be sated with compliments—and they must not be despised for this because, as often as not, their great need of praise is due to a lack of confidence in themselves, and their longing for reassurance is due to a feeling that their work is worthless.

Of all the compliments that can be paid to a writer, there is one especially that will make him glow with pleasure, namely: "You are admired so much among the younger generation." Then his head positively swells, for though he may seem to be detached, what he wants above all things is to get the attention of the younger generation, and if he does not do this he considers he has failed in his mission. Nothing matters to him except that. He has got to reach others, and particularly he has got to reach those who are still capable of being influenced and dominated, the young mentalities which are hesitating and unformed. He wants to leave his mark on this living wax and imprint all that is best in him on those who are going to survive him. It is not enough for the writer who writes so as not to be alone merely to reach other people: he wants to make them replicas of himself: he wants his own image and likeness to be resurrected in them when he himself is in the grave. . . .   (1936)

KLÉBER HAEDENS (1913-   )
From *Paradox about the Novel*

OST CRITICS agree in saying that the novel is first of all an imaginary story. Thus the novelist is a writer who has the gift of arranging plots and telling stories that are good for exciting the curiosity of his readers. He is a kind of magician who helps to pass an evening's time around the fire.

Thus we think that the novelist maintains a direct relationship

Marseilles: Sagittaire, 1941. Reprinted with permission of the publishers.

with the public. There are a certain number of persons whom this sort of genre amuses: the novelist writes for them. This is not the case, for example, of the poet. The poet has us listen to an intimate song, often very strange or very obscure. He has the right to be independent; he can dwell between heaven and earth. But the novelist is accountable to his readers. When he lets the word "novel" be printed on the jacket of his book, he takes upon himself the job of entertaining. If he doesn't pursue this, if he merely incites thinking or dreaming, he is a philosopher and poet, but not a novelist. M. Pierre Benoît once protested against those writers who baptize as "novels" those books that really are not so. He accused them of acting with mercenary motives and knowingly fooling the readers by offering them "merchandise" which was not that "of which the client had the intention of making himself the owner." For M. Pierre Benoît, the question is therefore clear. A novel is a book bought by people who want to be amused.

This is how the novel has been degraded in the public mind, and how little by little it has been cut off from literature. The middle class, always careful how it spends its money, has come to prefer historical tales and fictionalized biography. The story often has more imagination in it than the first novelist who happens to come along; and at the same time that he is enjoying himself, the reader of private lives has the feeling that he is learning something. All the more gained.

Readers and critics consider the story as the true essence of the novel. To be sure, it would be hard to write a novel without supporting it by a story, or at least by the semblance of a story. We do know however some of the most remarkable of contemporary novels, where the anecdotal elements have a pretextual role—*Suzanne and the Pacific*, for instance. In Virginia Woolf's *The Waves*, the plot is reduced to its most simple expression, and it disappears under a flood of feelings and imagery. The same is true for Kafka's novels.

In principle, the story in the novel should make us recognize a chain of events which are like those in real life. Outside of these accessory events, it should assess the value, within the life of one man or a group of human beings, of a series of facts bound to each other by the logic of everyday existence, with a beginning, a middle, and an end. It is evident that this logic is purely a convention, and that the story in the novel—despite all our efforts—can never succeed in giving an exact picture of life. M. Jules Romains has freed many of these conventions: the ease with which characters meet each other, no matter what the time or place, in the middle of a crowd, etc. . . ; characters obsessed by a single concern, and regulating their whole existence by a single desire, thought, preoccupation. It was precisely to destroy these conventions and to render a faithful representation of life that M. Jules Romains conceived the gigantic story of the *Men of Good Will*, where certain characters are unacquainted with each other, never meet, and have no single concern in common. On the other hand, this pretention is surprising. Everybody knows that art is made up of these conventions which experience, in lieu of reason and good sense, serves to inflict. And precisely because the novel is a form of convention in art, the same as tragedy or the epic, we don't understand why novelists seek to tie themselves up with so many chains to what they call life.

The story has a usurped place in the novel. They have made the novelist think that his first duty is to invent a progression of facts that must offer increasing interest to one's curiosity, from the first page to the last. The mission of these facts is to startle and to reassure the reader: startle him by their exceptional quality or their brilliance, reassure him by having him recognize in romantic [*novelish; i.e., romanesque*] adventures, as we have said, adventures similar to those in his own life. These adventures form a whole, a perfectly clear entirety and one well-defined. Arriving at the final page, the reader ought not to have one single doubt about the problem that has been posed him. Will Madame Dupont betray her husband? If this unhappy event occurs, you have to say why, how, and what ensues from it. Once the business is brought to its conclusion, the cause is understood and the novel is finished. In principle, the writer capable of applying these methods is worthy of creating if not a good, at least a real, novel.

This is excessive. One of the first tasks that arises is to put back the story to the secondary position to which it belongs. In most great works, the story has no importance in itself. It is obvious that we aren't going to listen to *Britannicus* to learn whether Nero succeeds in seducing Junia or whether he poisons his brother in the fifth act. The classical authors had no scruples in borrowing their plots from mythology, history, authors of antiquity, or even from their contemporaries, because the fact of inventing a story seemed to them stripped of all value, and vanity itself.

Thus it is for the novel. The plots of many famous novels are familiar to an entire public who has never read them. Before reading *The Dangerous Liaisons*, I knew that Madame de Tourvel gave in to Valmont, I had been told all the wiles and tricks of the Marquise de Merteuil; yet nevertheless once I opened the book, I moved from surprise to surprise. This was because the facts themselves of the story were obliterated in the demoniac atmosphere. An entire world surged forth, with its own laws and legends. Nothing remained of a concrete representation of life; a society vanished away before this most piercing gaze, and an entire unknown universe rose up in cruel, animated, evil light. . . .

"A novelist doesn't have to write well." This is a naïve formula that delights many novelists whom we know. Why? It is the story of the invisible man. The novelist who "writes well" shows himself in every word, a fine sentence stops the reader, turns his attention away from the characters' actions or the peripeties of the story. And this is what must be avoided at any price. Therefore the best style is one without color and without life. Neither too beautiful nor too ugly. If Proust, Gide, Giraudoux, Montherlant do not go down as real novelists for the theorists, this is in part because of their love of their language. However, novels that seem to have been written by gifted school-boys receive all of criticism's care and attention. Gibberish, platitudes, nonsense, triumph comfortably in the modern novel. No one gets angry, and the accursed scribblers depart in peace. Criticism itself obligingly even moves to give distinction to their practise. On the one hand, great writers; on the other hand, great novelists. For they are not the same, and the novelist has the right to treat his language with a scorn that makes you recoil in horror. From the moment that his characters "live," he has everything in order as far as opinion is concerned. . . . (1941)

(Translated by H. E. Hugo)

ANDRÉ GIDE (1869-1951)

From *Imaginary Interviews*

Number 8

HAVE brought you a Paris weekly," he said. "It has a piece about you by your friend Léautaud."

I.—You frighten me.

HE.—There's nothing to be disturbed about. It's just that Léautaud is surprised because, when you were asked by an American magazine to name the twelve books you would take along to a desert island, your list included nothing but novels.

I.—Léautaud is mistaken. It was a French, not an American, magazine that asked the question, and my choice was strictly limited. I was to name the twelve French novels I preferred; or rather the twelve I regarded as landmarks in the history of our literature. I answered with comments to explain my choice, and these were perhaps reprinted in the United States; at any rate, they were included in one of my critical volumes. If I were forced by some disaster to save only twelve books out of my library, there would not be a single novel among those that remained. Still, I might keep *War and Peace*, for the subtle reason that in spite of many efforts, I never found pleasure or even took real interest in that great work, and I don't want to stop trying.

He.—At least you have read it.

I.—From cover to cover, when I was young. At present I am talking about books to reread. Tolstoy has an incomparable power of evocation; but this succession of historical panoramas (I am thinking only of *War and Peace*) where everything is equally lighted; where there are no shadows, no relief, no chiaroscuro, no art, soon plunges me into a state of lassitude. It is a confession I am making, a somewhat hesitant confession; but although it may be the wisest policy, in one's youth, to strain one's power of admiration without being too much worried about one's personal tastes; to learn to enjoy what deserves to be enjoyed, and perhaps wouldn't be liked at all if the reader followed his natural bent; still it can't be a mistake, when one has reached my age, to be perfectly candid with oneself and others by saying: "No, with everything considered and reconsidered, that isn't my type of book"—then try to explain the reasons why.

He.—It is a way of justifying one's early tastes, which had begun by being quite spontaneous.

I.—No; or at least it is more than that. The early tastes, by patient study and comparison, have been strengthened, broadened, clarified; and it is not unlikely that they have changed. I am a Stendhal enthusiast today; but at first I had to make an effort to like him. He used to seem dry to me; I was wrong. But if I had to make my choice among Stendhal's works, I am convinced that I should abandon his novels sooner than leave behind his *Memoirs of an Egotist*, his correspondence, or his *Life of Henri Brulard*. The stories he tells in *The Charterhouse of Parma* and *The Red and the Black* interest me less than his fashion of telling them, less than the author himself. The more he reveals himself, the better I like him. For the same reasons, I should choose Flaubert's letters rather than his novels.

He.—In short, you regard the novel as of secondary importance?

I.—Not at all. And Flaubert's letters would interest me much less if Flaubert weren't the author of *Sentimental Education* and *Salammbô*. But I am something of a botanist and look at the plant to find the explanation of the flower. I have a tendency (perhaps it is a fault) to be more interested in the producer than in the product, just as Valéry is more interested in the "recipe" that the artist followed.

HE.—Would you have the same feeling about Racine's letters to Boileau as compared with his tragedies?

I.—Perhaps, if the letters were more numerous and less reserved; if he used them as an opportunity for discussing his work and his technical problems, like Flaubert, instead of bowing and scraping like the courtiers of his time. . . . But on second thought, no, not even then. Not even for the privilege of penetrating into the secrets of his art, of understanding how, why, and after overcoming what difficulties he was able to achieve perfection in his tragedies, would I sacrifice the pure joy I feel each time I reread them.

HE.—So Racine's dramatic works would be among the twelve books you would keep?

I.—Most certainly. I never grow tired of them, whereas I should soon grow tired of a novel, even if it were the one perfect novel in the world.

HE.—Did you mean to say "perfect novel"?

I.—It was a slip of the tongue and you were right to catch me up. The word "perfect" is particularly inappropriate when applied to a novel. Logically it cannot be applied except to an object or work of art that must obey definite laws. The novel is a form with such vague outlines that it cannot aspire to perfection.

HE.—You would then agree that what Kléber Haedens says in his *Paradox on the Novel* is essentially correct?

I.—Correct and well expressed, but not very important. The artificial rules against which he protests have hardly been a great burden to the novelists of our own time. Haedens is right to say that conforming to the rules doesn't make a second-rate novelist any better. On the other hand, it wouldn't be hard to demonstrate that many of the great novelists paid no attention to the rules, which have ceased to exist or which survive only in the backward minds of certain critics.

HE.—But I remember that when Edmond Jaloux, the least backward of the critics, presented *Madame Bovary* as a model and pattern, he gave us to understand that Flaubert had subjected himself to what he regarded as the laws of the novel.

I.—But the laws weren't pre-established; it was Flaubert who created them and imposed them on himself while composing his book; and he was ready to defy them when writing *The Temptation of St. Anthony* or *Bouvard and Pécuchet*. Goethe likewise, without ever formulating them precisely, confined himself to strict rules for each of his important works; but those rules were inherent in the work itself and varied according to its nature, each work being the answer to a particular and special summons of his genius. *Götz von Berlichingen* is a finished work in its own medium; so too are *Torquato Tasso*, *Iphigenia*, *The Elective Affinities*, and the first *Faust*, in their very different mediums. As for *Wilhelm Meister* and the second *Faust*, if the word "finished" seems inappropriate when applied to them, it is because these two works are in a medium that admits of an infinite fluctuation.

HE.—Might it it not be said that the only works observing the precise laws of a form or genre are those in which a certain limitation of time is imposed on the author? Such is the case with the oratorical form; and for this reason Bossuet's *Funeral Orations* and some of his sermons impress us as being exemplary. Such also is the case with all dramatic works; they must not exceed the time that people allot to theater-going, which is not the same in all countries. Spanish plays are perceptibly shorter than our classical tragedies, which in turn lack the elbow room that Wagner gave to his music dramas. All three, however, answer an expectation, a demand by the public. Claudel's dramas in verse answer a demand that has still to be made, a need that he hopes to create in the public at large, but one that has existed only sporadically until now, and in certain individuals. Hence the difficulties encountered in producing his works on the stage.

I.—Everything you say seems accurate. Moreover, I feel that the short story has gained the right to be called a genre chiefly because it is limited to the space available in newspapers and magazines. It is written to be read at one sitting. As soon as there is a "to be continued," as soon as the reader is left in suspense, it is encroaching on the genre "novel"—which is not a genre, strictly speaking, because it has no laws of its own.

HE.—So that the word "perfect," which seems out of place with a novel, might be applied to a short story.

I.—In any case it would seem less inappropriate; and I am ready to use it when speaking, for example, of Pushkin's "The Shot" and "The Queen of Spades," two masterpieces of their kind; of Maupassant's *Boule de Suif* and—

HE.—Excuse me. *Boule de Suif* couldn't be printed in one issue of a magazine.

I.—I was playing your cards; you might have let me cheat a little. But it's getting late, and we can come back to this subject after the new year begins. Let us hope that it will be less dismal than these two wretched years of disgrace.

HE.—Fortunately a few gleams of light are beginning to appear.

I.—In a tunnel artificial lighting serves as best it can. Before seeing daylight, I am afraid we shall have to plunge deeper into the shadows. Meanwhile, let us cling to hope.

Number 9

"What you said last week about the novel," I told him, "not only impressed me as being true but set me to thinking that works intended for an audience, for a group of people brought together for a definite time, are the only ones capable of constituting what I have called a genre. And if novels lack the strict rules that would make them a genre, I wonder whether it isn't chiefly because they are addressed to separate individuals, as poems are likewise. The task of a novel is to persuade or impress, to retain the charmed attention—but of a reader who takes his own time, lending himself to the game only when he feels so inclined; and this, I should say, explains why the game has no rules that the author is forced to observe. Before books had become a commodity, in the old days of rhapsodies, bards, minstrels, and public recitations, epic poetry could be called a genre, as could our *chansons de gestes*. But there is no good reason why the novel I read when sitting alone in my comfortable chair, at the moments that best suit my leisure, should bother itself with rules that the reader doesn't expect it to follow.

"The case is different when one reads a book aloud in the family circle, as I often used to do in my younger days. At such times the divagations of genius, the tedious expositions and sublime irrelevancies, seem out of place; and the chosen author must answer the expectations and desires of several persons at once. As a result of reading aloud to a group that included persons of different ages and sexes, all of whom were equally attentive and quite intelligent, I came to perceive rather clearly what the rules of the novel would be if it ever became a genre; and they are good rules too, in spite of Kléber Haedens. Nevertheless, when I had retired to my own room, they didn't keep me from greatly enjoying and admiring some pseudo-novel of genius that broke all the rules—whether the book was *Tristram Shandy*, *Pantagruel*, *Dead Souls*, *Green Heinrich*, *Marius the Epicurean*, or *Remembrance of Things Past*."

He.—The genre is addressed to a group; the novel is addressed to individuals. Is that the distinction?

I.—Yes; and after what we have just said, it is interesting to note that the novel as a topic for discussion is closely related to the question of individualism. Nations rich in novels are also nations in which the individual is most clearly distinguished, and tries hardest to distinguish himself, from the mass. *Par contre*, the form in which

Germany excels and triumphs is the lyrical drama, a synthetic form in which music and poetry collaborate toward a total effect. This form, which achieved its flowering in Wagner's *Ring,* is one to which an assembled throng listens religiously, and in which, I should judge, the great social fusion of our time can recognize its most appropriate expression.

HE.—You suggest that countries where the novel is at home are also countries marked by individualism; and yet the Russian novel—

I.—At first glance I seem to have been on the wrong track. Still, after a little reflection it occurs to me that in Russia under the czars there was little chance of assembling those vast audiences for which Dostoyevsky might have written the dramas he talked about in his early letters to his brother. He abandoned the project, knowing as he did that he would have to address each of his readers separately.

HE.—And we might add that the Russian novel has evolved since then, either by inner compulsion or, more likely, as a result of social upheavals; it has become, so to speak, disindividualized. It now seeks the support of whole communities. Crusoe is never alone in Russia; he is a group of pioneers. . . .   (1944)

MARK SCHORER (1908-   )

From *Technique as Discovery*

MODERN CRITICISM, through its exacting scrutiny of literary texts, has demonstrated with finality that in art beauty and truth are indivisible and one. The Keatsian overtones of these terms are mitigated and an old dilemma solved if for beauty we substitute form, and for truth, content. We may, without risk of loss, narrow them even more, and speak of technique and subject matter. Modern criticism has shown us that to speak of content as such is not to speak of art at all, but of experience; and that it is only when we speak of the *achieved* content, the form of the work of art as a work of art, that we speak as critics. The difference between content, or experience, and achieved content, or art, is technique.

When we speak of technique, then, we speak of nearly everything. For technique is the means by which the writer's experience, which is his subject matter, compels him to attend to it; technique is the only means he has of discovering, exploring, developing his subject, of conveying its meaning, and, finally, of evaluating it. And surely it

Reprinted by permission from *The Hudson Review,* Vol. I, No. 1,
Spring 1948. Copyright 1948 by *The Hudson Review,* Inc.

follows that certain techniques are sharper tools than others, and will discover more; that the writer capable of the most exacting technical scrutiny of his subject matter, will produce works with the most satisfying content, works with thickness and resonance, works which reverberate, works with maximum meaning.

We are no longer able to regard as seriously intended criticism of poetry which does not assume these generalizations; but the case for fiction has not yet been established. The novel is still read as though its content has some value in itself, as though the subject matter of fiction has greater or lesser value in itself, and as though technique were not a primary but a supplementary element, capable perhaps of not unattractive embellishments upon the surface of the subject, but hardly of its essence. Or technique is thought of in blunter terms than those which one associates with poetry, as such relatively obvious matters as the arrangement of events to create plot; or, within plot, of suspense and climax; or as the means of revealing character motivation, relationship, and development; or as the use of point of view, but point of view as some nearly arbitrary device for the heightening of dramatic interest through the narrowing or broadening of perspective upon the material, rather than as a means toward the positive definition of theme. As for the resources of language, these, somehow, we almost never think of as a part of the technique of fiction—language as used to create a certain texture and tone which in themselves state and define themes and meanings; or language, the counters of our ordinary speech, as forced, through conscious manipulation, into all those larger meanings which our ordinary speech almost never intends. Technique in fiction, all this is a way of saying, we somehow continue to regard as merely a means to organizing material which is "given" rather than as the means of exploring and defining the values in an area of experience which, for the first time *then*, are being given.

Is fiction still regarded in this odd, divided way because it is really less tractable before the critical suppositions which now seem inevitable to poetry? Let us look at some examples: two well-known novels of the past, both by writers who may be described as "primitive," although their relative innocence of technique is of a different sort— Defoe's *Moll Flanders* and Emily Brontë's *Wuthering Heights*; and three well-known novels of this century—*Tono-Bungay*, by a writer who claimed to eschew technique; *Sons and Lovers*, by a novelist who, because his ideal of subject matter ("the poetry of the immediate present") led him at last into the fallacy of spontaneous and un-changeable composition, in effect eschewed technique; and *A Portrait of the Artist as a Young Man*, by a novelist whose practice made claims for the supremacy of technique beyond those made by anyone in the past or by anyone else in this century.

Technique in fiction is, of course, all those obvious forms of it which are usually taken to be the whole of it, and many others; but for the present purposes, let it be thought of in two respects particularly: the uses to which language, as language, is put to express the quality of the experience in question; and the uses of point of view not only as a mode of dramatic delimitation, but more particularly, of thematic definition. Technique is really what T. S. Eliot means by "convention"—any selection, structure, or distortion, any form or rhythm imposed upon the world of action; by means of which —it should be added—our apprehension of the world of action is enriched or renewed. In this sense, everything is technique which is not the lump of experience itself, and one cannot properly say that a writer has no technique or that he eschews technique, for, being a writer, he cannot do so. We can speak of good and bad technique, of adequate and inadequate, of technique which serves the novelist's purpose, or disserves. . . .   (1948)

JOSÉ ORTEGA Y GASSET (1883-   )

From *Notes on the Novel*

UBLISHERS complain that novels do not sell well, and it is true that the reading public buys fewer novels while the demand for books of a theoretical character is relatively increasing. This statistical fact, even if there were no more intrinsic reasons, would suffice to make us suspect that something is amiss with the literary genre of the novel. When I hear a friend, particularly if he is a young writer, calmly announce that he is working on a novel I am appalled, and I feel that in his case I should be trembling in my boots. Perhaps I am wrong, but I cannot help scenting behind such an equanimity an alarming dose of incomprehension. To produce a good novel has always been a difficult thing. But while, before, it was enough to have talent the difficulty has now grown immeasurably, for to be a gifted novelist is no longer a guaranty for producing a good novel.

Unawareness of this fact is one component of the aforementioned incomprehension. Anyone who gives a little thought to the conditions of a work of art must admit that a literary genre may wear out. One

From *Notes on the Novel* by José Ortega y Gasset (Princeton University, 1948). Reprinted with permission of the publishers.

cannot dismiss the subject by comfortably assuming that artistic creation depends on nothing but the artist's personal power called inspiration or talent—in which case decadence of a genre would be due exclusively to an accidental lack of talents, and the sudden appearance of a man of genius would at any time automatically turn the tide. Better beware of notions like genius and inspiration; they are a sort of magic wand and should be used sparingly by anybody who wants to see things clearly. Imagine a woodsman, the strongest of woodsmen, in the Sahara desert. What good are his bulging muscles and his sharp ax? A woodsman without woods is an abstraction. And the same applies to artists. Talent is but a subjective disposition that is brought to bear upon a certain material. The material is independent of individual gifts; and when it is lacking genius and skill are of no avail.

Just as every animal belongs to a species, every literary work belongs to a genre. (The theory of Benedetto Croce who denies the existence of literary forms in this sense has left no trace in aesthetics.) A literary genre, the same as a zoological species, means a certain stock of possibilities; and since in art only those possibilities count which are different enough not to be considered replicas of one another, the resources of a literary genre are definitely limited. It is erroneous to think of the novel—and I refer to the modern novel in particular—as of an endless field capable of rendering ever new forms. Rather it may be compared to a vast but finite quarry. There exist a definite number of possible themes for the novel. The workmen of the primal hour had no trouble finding new blocks—new characters, new themes. But present-day writers face the fact that only narrow and concealed veins are left them.

With this stock of objective possibilities, which is the genre, the artistic talent works, and when the quarry is worked out talent, however great, can achieve nothing. Whether a genre is altogether done for can, of course, never be decided with mathematical rigor; but it can at times be decided with sufficient practical approximation. At least, that the material is getting scarce may appear frankly evident.

This, I believe, is now happening to the novel. It has become practically impossible to find new subjects. Here we come upon the first cause of the enormous difficulty, an objective not a personal difficulty, of writing an acceptable novel at this advanced stage.

During a certain period novels could thrive on the mere novelty of their subjects which gratuitously added an induced current, as it were, to the value proper of the material. Thus many novels seemed readable which we now think a bore. It is not for nothing that the novel is called "novel." The difficulty of finding new subjects is accompanied by another, perhaps more serious, dilemma. As the store of possible subjects is more and more depleted the sensibility of the reading public becomes subtler and more fastidious. Works that yesterday would still have passed, today are deemed insipid. Not only is the difficulty of finding new subjects steadily growing, but ever "newer" and more extraordinary ones are needed to impress the reader. This is the second cause of the difficulty with which the genre as such is faced in our time.

Proof that the present decline is due to more fundamental causes than a possibly inferior quality of contemporary novels is given by the fact that, as it becomes more difficult to write novels, the famous old or classical ones appear less good. Only a very few have escaped drowning in the reader's boredom.

This development is inevitable and need not dishearten the novelists. On the contrary; for they themselves are bringing it about. Little by little they train their public by sharpening the perception, and refining the taste, of their readers. Each work that is better than a previous one is detrimental to this and all others of the same level. Triumph cannot help being cruel. As the victor wins the battle at the cost of smashing the foe, thus the superior work automatically becomes the undoing of scores of other works that used to be highly thought of.

In short, I believe that the genre of the novel, if it is not yet irretrievably exhausted, has certainly entered its last phase, the scarcity of possible subjects being such that writers must make up for it by the exquisite quality of the other elements that compose the body of a novel.

Autopsy

It cannot be denied that to us the great Balzac, save for one or two of his books, makes rather difficult reading. Our perceptive apparatus, used to more distinct and genuine spectacles, detects at once the conventional, artificial and à-peu-près complexion of the world of the *Human Comedy*. Were I asked why I find fault with Balzac I should answer: Because he is a dauber. What distinguishes the dauber from the good painter? That on the latter's painting the object it represents is there in person, as it were, in the fullness of its being, in self-presence. Whereas the former, instead of presenting the object itself, sets down on his canvas only a few feeble and unessential allusions to it. The longer we look at his work, the clearer it becomes that the object is not there.

This difference between self-presence and mere allusion seems to me decisive in all art but very specially in the novel.

The subject of *Le rouge et le noir* could be told in a few dozen words. What is the difference between such a report and the novel itself? Certainly not the style. The crucial point is that when we say: "Madame Rênal falls in love with Julien Sorel" we merely allude to this fact while Stendhal presents it in its immediate and patent reality.

Now, an examination of the evolution of the novel from its beginnings to our day reveals that, from being pure narration which but alludes, the novel has advanced to strict presentation. At first, the narrative as such kept the reader amused through the novelty of the subject. He was as delighted to listen to the hero's adventures as we are to hear what has happened to a person we love. But soon adventures by themselves lose attraction, and what then pleases is not so much the fortunes of the personages as their self-presence. We enjoy seeing those people before us and being admitted to their inner life, understanding them, and living immersed in their world or atmosphere. From being narrative and indirect the novel has become direct and descriptive. The best word would be "presentative." The imperative of the novel is autopsy. No good telling us what a person is, we want to see with our own eyes.

Analyze such ancient novels as have survived in the appreciation of responsible readers, and it will appear that they all use the autoptic method. Above all *Don Quixote*. Cervantes fills all our senses with the genuine presence of his personages. We listen to their true conversations, we see their actual movements. Stendhal's greatness derives from the same cause.

No Definitions

We want to see the life of the figures in a novel, not to be told it. Any reference, allusion, narration only emphasizes the absence of what it alludes to. Things that are there need not be related.

Hence one of the major errors a novelist can commit consists in attempting to define his personages.

It is the task of science to work out definitions. All scientific endeavor lastly consists in the systematic effort to leave behind the object and to arrive at its definition. Now, a definition is nothing if not a series of concepts, and a concept is nothing else than a mental allusion to an object. The concept "red" contains no red; it is merely a movement of the mind toward the color of this name, a sign pointing in the direction of this color.

It has been said by Wundt, if I remember right, that the most primitive form of a concept is the pointing gesture of the index finger. An infant still tries to take hold of any object that enters his field of vision because his undeveloped sense of perspective prevents him from judging distances. After many failures he gives up and contents himself with indicating the object with his outstretched hand—a symbolic capture. The true function of concepts is to point or to indicate. Science is concerned not with things but with the system of signs it can substitute for things.

Art, on the other hand, urged by a magnificent impulse to see, turns from the conventional signs to the things themselves. There is a good deal of truth in Fiedler's assertion that the aim of painting is to furnish a fuller and completer view of things than can be obtained in the ordinary intercourse with them.

The same, I believe, applies to the novel. In its beginnings the plot may have seemed to form its most important part. Later it appeared that what really matters is not the story which is told but that the story, whatever it might be, should be told well. From our present-day standpoint the primitive novel seems more narrative than the modern. However, this impression may have to be revised. Perhaps a primitive reader resembled a child in that he was capable of seeing in a few lines, in a bare pattern the integral object with vigorous presence. (Primitive sculpture and certain new psychological discoveries of great importance corroborate this belief.) In that case the novel would, strictly speaking, not have changed; its present descriptive, or rather presentative, form would merely be the means that had to be used in order to produce in a limp sensibility the same effect which in more springy souls had been obtained by narration.

When I read in a novel "John was peevish" it is as though the writer invited me to visualize, on the strength of his definition, John's peevishness in my own imagination. That is to say, he expects me to be the novelist. What is required, I should think, is exactly the opposite: that he furnish the visible facts so that I obligingly discover and define John to be peevish. A novelist must proceed in the same way as the impressionistic painters who set down on the canvas such elements as the spectator needs for seeing an apple, and leave it to him to give to this material the finishing touches. Hence the fresh taste of all impressionistic painting. We seem to see the objects of the picture in a perpetual *status nascendi*. In the career of every thing there are two moments of supreme drama: birth and death— *status nascens* and *status evanescens*. Nonimpressionistic painting, superior though it may be in other respects, suffers from one shortcoming: that it presents its objects altogether finished, mummified and, as it were, past. That actuality, that existence in the present tense, which things possess in impressionistic pictures is irremediably missing.

The Novel a Sluggish Genre

Hence the present-day novel must be the opposite of a story. A story relates events; the accent is on action. The fresh mind of a child is interested in adventure as such—perhaps, as we were saying, because the child sees in palpable presence what our imagination is too weak to visualize. Adventures do not interest us; or at least, they interest only the child that, as a somewhat barbarous residue, we all carry inside. The rest of our person is not susceptible to the mechanical thrill of, say, a dime novel; and so we feel, after having finished reading such products, a bad taste in our mouth as though we had indulged in a base pleasure. It is not easy nowadays to invent adventures capable of stirring the superior portion of our sensibility.

Action thus becomes a mere pretext—the string, as it were, that makes the beads into a necklace. Why that string cannot be dispensed with, will appear later on. At this point I wish to draw attention to the fact that when a novel bores us it is not, as an insufficient analysis may lead us to believe, because "its subject is uninteresting." If that were so we might as well declare the entire species dead and buried. For the impossibility of inventing new "interesting subjects" is all too patent.

No, when we are fascinated by a novel it is not because of its subject, not because we are curious to know what happened to Mr. So-and-so. The subject of any novel can be told in a few words and in this form holds no interest. A summary narration is not to our taste; we want the novelist to linger and to grant us good long looks at his personages, their being, and their environment till we have had our fill and feel that they are close friends whom we know thoroughly in all the wealth of their lives. That is what makes of the novel an essentially slow-moving genre, as either Goethe or Novalis observed. I will go even further and say that today the novel is, and must be, a sluggish form—the very opposite therefore of a story, a "serial," or a thriller.

I have sometimes tried to explain the pleasure—a mild pleasure, to be sure—aroused by certain American films that consist of a long series of episodes. (But the word "episode" is absurd; a work made of episodes would be like a meal composed of side dishes.) And I found to my great surprise that I felt entertained not by the stupid subject but by the personages themselves. A film in which the detective and the young American girl are attractive may go on indefinitely and never become boring. It does not matter what they do; we simply enjoy watching them. They interest us not because of what they are

doing; rather the opposite, what they do interests us because it is
they who do it.

Let the reader recall the great novels of former days that have
lived up to the high standards of our time, and he will observe that his
attention is turned to the personages themselves, not to their adventures. We are fascinated by Don Quixote and Sancho, not by
what is happening to them. In principle, a *Don Quixote* as great as
the original is conceivable in which the knight and his servant go
through entirely different experiences. And the same holds for Julien
Sorel or David Copperfield.

Function and Substance

Our interest has shifted from the plot to the figures, from actions
to persons. Now, this transference—let it be noted parenthetically—
finds a counterpart in what has, these last twenty years, been happening in physics and, above all, in philosophy. From Kant to about
1900 we observe a determinate tendency in theoretical thought to
eliminate substances and to replace them by functions. In Greece
and in the Middle Ages it was believed that *operari sequitur esse*—
actions follow, and derive from, being. The nineteenth century may
be said to have established the opposite principle: *esse sequitur operari*
—the being of a thing is nothing else than the sum total of its
actions and functions.

Should we, by any chance, now be again in the process of turning
from action to the person, from function to substance? Such a
transition would be indicative of an emerging classicism. . . .   (1948)

ELIZABETH BOWEN (1899-   )
From *Notes on Writing a Novel*

PLOT—*Essential. The Pre-Essential.*

LOT MIGHT seem to be a matter of choice. It is not. The
particular plot is something the novelist is driven to. It
is what is left after the whittling-away of alternatives. The
novelist is confronted, at a moment (or at what appears to be the
moment: actually its extension may be indefinite) by the impossibility
of saying what is to be said in any other way.

He is forced towards his plot. By what? By the 'what is to be

Reprinted from *Notes on Writing a Novel*, by Elizabeth Bowen,
by permission of Alfred A. Knopf, Inc., and Longmans, Green & Co.,
Ltd. Published in U.S.A., 1950, by Alfred A. Knopf, Inc.

said.' What is 'what is to be said?' A mass of subjective matter that has accumulated—impressions received, feelings about experience, distorted results of ordinary observation, and something else—*x*. This matter is *extra* matter. It is superfluous to the non-writing life of the writer. It is luggage left in the hall between two journeys, as opposed to the perpetual furniture of rooms. It is destined to be elsewhere. It cannot move till its destination is known. Plot is the knowing of destination.

Plot is diction. Action of language, language of action.

Plot is story. It is also 'a story' in the nursery sense = lie. The novel lies, in saying that something happened that did not. It must, therefore, contain uncontradictable truth, to warrant the original lie.

Story involves action. Action towards an end not to be foreseen (by the reader) but also towards an end which, having *been* reached, must be seen to have been from the start inevitable.

Action by whom? The Characters (see CHARACTERS). Action in view of what, and because of what? The 'what is to be said.'

What about the idea that the function of action is to *express* the characters? This is wrong. The characters are there to provide the action. Each is created, and must only be so created, as to give his or her action (or rather, contributory part in the novel's action) verisimilitude.

What about the idea that plot should be ingenious, complicated —a display of ingenuity remarkable enough to command attention? If more than such a display, what? Tension, or mystification towards tension, are good for emphasis. For their own sakes, bad.

Plot must further the novel towards its object. What object? The non-poetic statement of a poetic truth.

Have not all poetic truths been already stated? The essence of a poetic truth is that no statement of it can be final.

Plot, story, is in itself un-poetic. At best it can only be not anti-poetic. It cannot claim a single poetic licence. It must be reasoned —onward from the moment when its non-otherness, its only-possibleness has become apparent. Novelist must always have one foot, sheer circumstantiality, to stand on, whatever the other foot may be doing. (N.B.—Much to be learnt from story-telling to children. Much to be learnt from the detective story—especially non-irrelevance. [See RELEVANCE])

Flaubert's '*Il faut intéresser.*' Stress on manner of telling: keep in mind, 'I will a tale *unfold.*' Interest of watching silk handkerchief drawn from a conjuror's watch.

Plot must not cease to move forward. (See ADVANCE.) The *actual* speed of the movement must be even. *Apparent* variations in speed

are good, necessary, but there must be no actual variations in speed.
To obtain those apparent variations is part of the illusion-task of the
novel. Variations in texture can be made to give the effect of variations
in speed. Why are *apparent* variations in speed necessary? (a) For
emphasis. (b) For non-resistance, or 'give,' to the nervous time-
variations of the reader. Why is *actual* evenness, non-variation, of
speed necessary? For the sake of internal evenness for its own sake.
Perfection of evenness = perfection of control. The evenness of the
speed should be the evenness inseparable from tautness. The tautness
of the taut string is equal (or even) all along and at any part of the
string's length.

CHARACTERS

Are the characters, then, to be constructed to formula—the
formula pre-decided by the plot? Are they to be drawn, cut out,
jointed, wired, in order to be manipulated for the plot?

No. There is no question as to whether this would be right or
wrong. It would be impossible. One cannot 'make' characters, only
marionettes. The manipulated movement of the marionette is not the
'action' necessary for plot. Characterless action is not action at all, in
the plot sense. It is the indivisibility of the act from the actor, and
the inevitability of *that* act on the part of *that* actor, that gives action
verisimilitude. Without that, action is without force or reason. Force-
less, reasonless action disrupts plot. The term 'creation of character'
(or characters) is misleading. Characters pre-exist. They are *found*.
They reveal themselves slowly to the novelist's perception—as might
fellow-travellers seated opposite one in a very dimly-lit railway carriage.

The novelist's perceptions of his characters take place *in the
course of the actual writing of the novel*. To an extent, the novelist
is in the same position as his reader. But his perceptions should be
always just in advance.

The ideal way of presenting character is to invite perception.

In what do the characters pre-exist? I should say, in the mass
of matter (see PLOT) that had accumulated before the inception of
the novel.

(N.B.—The unanswerability of the question, from an outsider:
'Are the characters in your novel invented, or are they from real life?'
Obviously, neither is true. The outsider's notion of 'real life' and the
novelist's are hopelessly apart.)

How, then, is the pre-existing character—with its own inner
spring of action, its contrarieties—to be made to play a preassigned
rôle? In relation to character, or characters, once these have been
contemplated, *plot* must at once seem over-rigid, arbitrary.

What about the statement (in relation to Plot) that 'each character is created in order, and only in order, that he or she may supply the required action?' To begin with, strike out 'created.' Better, the character is *recognized* (by the novelist) by the signs he or she gives of unique capacity to act in a certain way, which 'certain way' fulfills a need of the plot.

The character is there (in the novel) for the sake of the action he or she is to contribute to the plot. Yes. But also, he or she exists *outside* the action being contributed to the plot.

Without that existence of the character outside the (necessarily limited) action, the action itself would be invalid.

Action is the simplification (for story purposes) of complexity. For each one act, there are an x number of rejected alternatives. It is the palpable presence of the alternatives that gives action interest. Therefore, in each of the characters, while he or she is acting, the play and pull of alternatives must be felt. It is in being seen to be capable of alternatives that the character becomes, for the reader, valid.

Roughly, the action of a character should be unpredictable before it has been shown, inevitable when it has been shown. In the first half of a novel, the unpredictability should be the more striking. In the second half, the inevitability should be the more striking.

(Most exceptions to this are, however, masterpiece-novels. In *War and Peace, L'Education Sentimentale* and *Le Recherche du Temps Perdu*, unpredictability dominates up to the end.)

The character's prominence in the novel (pre-decided by the plot) decides the character's range—of alternatives. The novelist must allot (to the point of rationing) psychological space. The 'hero,' 'heroine' and 'villain' (if any) are, by agreement, allowed most range. They are entitled, for the portrayal of their alternatives, to time and space. Placing the characters in receding order to their importance to the plot, the number of their alternatives may be seen to diminish. What E. M. Forster has called the 'flat' character has no alternatives at all.

The ideal novel is without 'flat' characters.

Characters must *materialize*—i.e., must have a palpable physical reality. They must be not only see-able (visualizable); they must be to be felt. Power to give physical reality is probably a matter of the extent and nature of the novelist's physical sensibility, or susceptibility. In the main, English novelists are weak in this, as compared to French and Russians. Why?

Hopelessness of categoric 'description.' Why? Because this is static. Physical personality belongs to action: cannot be separated from it. Pictures must be in movement. Eyes, hands, stature, etc., must appear, and only appear, *in play*. Reaction to physical personality is part of action—love, or sexual passages, only more marked application of this general rule.

(Conrad an example of strong, non-sexual use of physical personality.)

The materialization (in the above sense) of the character for the novelist must be instantaneous. It happens. No effort of will—and obviously no effort of intellect—can induce it. The novelist can *use* a character that has not yet materialized. But the unmaterialized character represents an enemy pocket in an area that has been otherwise cleared. This cannot go on for long. It produces a halt in plot.

When the materialization *has* happened, the chapters written before it happened will almost certainly have to be recast. From the plot point of view, they will be found invalid.

Also, it is essential that for the reader the materialization of the character should begin early. I say begin, because for the *reader* it may, without harm, be gradual.

Is it from this failure, or tendency to fail, in materialization that the English novelist depends so much on engaging emotional sympathy for his characters?

Ruling sympathy out, a novel must contain at least one *magnetic* character. At least one character capable of keying the reader up, as though he (the reader) were in the presence of someone he is in love with. This is not a rule of salesmanship but a pre-essential of *interest*. The character must do to the reader what he has done to the novelist—magnetize towards himself perceptions, sense-impressions, desires.

The unfortunate case is, where the character has, obviously, acted magnetically upon the author, but fails to do so upon the reader.

There must be combustion. Plot depends for its movement on internal combustion.

Physically, characters are almost always copies, or composite copies. Traits, gestures, etc., are searched for in, and assembled from, the novelist's memory. Or, a picture, a photograph or the cinema screen may be drawn on. Nothing physical can be *invented*. (Invented physique stigmatizes the inferior novel.) Proust (in last volume) speaks of this assemblage of traits. Though much may be lifted from a specific person in 'real life,' no person in 'real life' could supply everything (physical) necessary for the character in the novel. No such person could have just that exact degree of physical intensity required for the character.

Greatness of characters is the measure of the unconscious greatness of the novelist's vision. They are 'true' in so far as he is occupied with poetic truth. Their degrees in realness show the degrees of his concentration.

SCENE—*Is a derivative of Plot. Gives actuality to Plot.*

Nothing can happen nowhere. The locale of the happening always colours the happening, and often, to a degree, shapes it.

Plot having pre-decided what is to happen, scene, scenes, must be so found, so chosen, as to give the happening the desired force.

Scene, being physical, is, like the physical traits of the characters, generally a copy, or a composite copy. It, too, is assembled—out of memories which, in the first place, may have had no rational connection with one another. Again, pictures, photographs, the screen are sources of supply. Also dreams.

Almost anything drawn from 'real life'—house, town, room, park, landscape—will almost certainly be found to require *some* distortion for the purposes of the plot. Remote memories, already distorted by the imagination, are most useful for the purposes of scene. Unfamiliar or once-seen places yield more than do familiar, often-seen places.

Wholly invented scene is as unsatisfactory (thin) as wholly invented physique for a character.

Scene, much more than character, is inside the novelist's conscious power. More than any other constituent of the novel, it makes him conscious *of* his power.

This can be dangerous. The weak novelist is always, compensatorily, scene-minded. (Jane Austen's economy of scene-painting, and her abstentions from it in what might be expected contexts, could in itself be proof of her mastery of the novel.)

Scene is only justified in the novel where it can be shown, or at least felt, to act upon action or character. In fact, where it has dramatic use.

Where not intended for dramatic use, scene is a sheer slower-down. Its staticness is a dead weight. It cannot make part of the plot's movement by being shown *in play*. (Thunderstorms, the sea, landscape flying past car or railway-carriage windows are not scene but happenings.)

The deadeningness of straight and prolonged 'description' is as apparent with regard to scene as it is with regard to character. Scene must be evoked. For its details relevance (see RELEVANCE) is essential. Scene must, like the characters, not fail to materialize. In this it follows the same law—instantaneous for the novelist, gradual for the reader.

In 'setting a scene' the novelist directs, or attempts to direct, the reader's visual imagination. He must allow for the fact that the reader's memories will not correspond with his own. Or, at least, not at all far along the way.

DIALOGUE—*Must* (1) Further Plot. (2) Express Character.

Should not on any account be a vehicle for ideas for their own sake. Ideas only permissible where they provide a key to the character who expresses them.

Dialogue requires more art than does any other constituent of the novel. Art in the *celare artem* sense. Art in the trickery, self-justifying distortion sense. Why? Because dialogue must appear realistic without being so. Actual realism—the lifting, as it were, of passages from a stenographer's take-town of a 'real life' conversation—would be disruptive. Of what? Of the illusion of the novel. In 'real life' everything is diluted; in the novel everything is condensed.

What are the realistic qualities to be imitated (or faked) in novel dialogue?—Spontaneity. Artless or hit-or-miss arrival at words used. Ambiguity (speaker not sure, himself, what he means). Effect of choking (as in engine): more to be said than can come through. Irrelevance. Allusiveness. Erraticness: unpredictable course. Repercussion.

What must novel dialogue, behind mask of these faked realistic qualities, really be and do? It must be pointed, intentional, relevant. It must crystallize situation. It must express character. It must advance plot.

During dialogue, the characters confront one another. The confrontation is in itself an occasion. Each one of these occasions, throughout the novel, is unique. Since the last confrontation, something has changed, advanced. What is being said is the effect of something that has happened; at the same time, what is being said *is in itself something happening*, which will in turn, leave its effect.

Dialogue is the ideal means of showing what is between the characters. It crystallizes relationships. It *should*, ideally, so be effective as to make analysis of explanation of the relationships between the characters unnecessary.

Short of a small range of physical acts—a fight, murder, love-making—dialogue is the most vigorous and visible inter-action of which characters in a novel are capable. Speech is what the characters *do to each other*.

Dialogue provides means for the psychological materialization of the characters. It should short-circuit description of mental traits. Every sentence in dialogue should be descriptive of the character who is speaking. Idiom, tempo, and shape of each spoken sentence should be calculated by novelist, towards this descriptive end.

Dialogue is the first case of the novelist's need for notation from real life. Remarks or turns of phrase indicatory of class, age, degree of intellectual pretension, *idées reçues*, nature and strength of governing fantasy, sexual temperament, persecution-sense or acumen (fortuitous arrival at general or poetic truth) should be collected. (N.B.—Proust, example of this semi-conscious notation and putting to use of it.)

All the above, from *class to acumen*, may already have been established, with regard to each character, by a direct statement by the novelist to the reader. It is still, however, the business of dialogue to show these factors, or qualities, in play.

There must be present in dialogue—*i.e.*, in each sentence spoken by each character—*either* (a) calculation, or (b) involuntary self-revelation.

Each piece of dialogue *must* be 'something happening.' Dialogue *may* justify its presence by being 'illustrative'—but this secondary use of it must be watched closely, challenged. Illustrativeness can be stretched too far. Like straight description, it then becomes static, a dead weight—halting the movement of the plot. The 'amusing' for its *own* sake, should above all be censored. So should infatuation with any idiom.

The functional use of dialogue for the plot must be the first thing in the novelist's mind. Where functional usefulness cannot be established, dialogue must be left out.

What is this functional use? That of a bridge.

Dialogue is the thin bridge which must, from time to time, carry the entire weight of the novel. Two things to be kept in mind—(a) the bridge is there to permit *advance*, (b) the bridge must be strong enough for the weight.

Failure in any one piece of dialogue is a loss, at once to the continuity and the comprehensibility of the novel.

Characters should, on the whole, be under rather than over articulate. What they *intend* to say should be more evident, more striking (because of its greater inner importance to the plot) than what they arrive at *saying*.

ANGLE

The question of *angle* comes up twice over in the novel.

Angle has two senses—(a) visual, (b) moral.

(a) *Visual Angle.*—This has been much discussed—particularly I think by Henry James. Where is the camera-eye to be located? (1)

In the breast or brow of *one* of the characters? This is, of course, simplifying and integrating. But it imposes on the novel the limitations of the 'I'—whether the first person is explicitly used or not. Also, with regard to any matter that the specific character does not (cannot) know, it involves the novelist in long cumbrous passages of cogitation, speculation and guesses. E.g.—of any character other than the specific (or virtual) 'I' it must always be 'he appeared to feel,' 'he could be seen to see,' rather than 'he felt,' 'he saw.' (2) In the breast or brow of a succession of characters? This is better. It *must*, if used, involve very careful, considered division of the characters, by the novelist, in the *seeing* and the *seen*. Certain characters gain in importance and magnetism by being only *seen*: this makes them more romantic, fatal-seeming, sinister. In fact, no character in which these qualities are, for the plot, essential should be allowed to enter the *seeing* class. (3) In the breast or brow of omniscient story-teller (the novelist)? This, though appearing naïve, would appear best. The novelist should retain right of entry, at will, into any of the characters: their memories, sensations and thought-processes should remain his, to requisition for appropriate use. What conditions 'appropriateness'? The demands of the plot. Even so, the novelist must not lose sight of point made above—the gain in necessary effect, for some characters, of their remaining *seen*—their remaining closed, apparently, even to the omniscience of the novelist.

The cinema, with its actual camera-work, is interesting study for the novelist. In a good film, the camera's movement, angle and distance have all worked towards one thing—the fullest possible realization of the director's idea, the completest possible surrounding of the subject. Any trick is justified if it adds a statement. With both film and novel, plot is the pre-imperative. The novelist's relation to the novel is that of the director's relation to the film. The cinema, cinema-going has no doubt built up in novelists a great authoritarianism. This seems to me good.

(b) *Moral Angle.*—This too often means, pre-assumptions—social, political, sexual, national, aesthetic, and so on. These may all exist, sunk at different depths, in the same novelist. Their existence cannot fail to be palpable; and their nature determines, more than anything else, the sympatheticness or antipatheticness of a given novel to a given circle of readers.

Pre-assumptions are bad. They limit the novel to a given circle of readers. They cause the novel to act immorally *on* that given circle. (The lady asking the librarian for a 'nice' novel to take home is, virtually, asking for a novel whose pre-assumptions will be identical with her own.) Outside the given circle, a novel's pre-assumptions must invalidate it for all other readers. The increasingly bad smell of most pre-assumptions probably accounts for the growing prestige of the detective story: the detective story works on the single, and universally acceptable, pre-assumption that an act of violence is anti-social, and that the doer, in the name of injured society, must be traced.

Great novelists write without pre-assumption. They write from outside their own nationality, class or sex.

To write thus should be the ambition of any novelist who wishes to state poetic truth.

Does this mean he must have no angle, no moral view-point? No, surely. Without these, he would be (a) incapable of maintaining the *conviction* necessary for the novel; (b) incapable of *lighting* the characters, who to be seen at all must necessarily be seen in a moral light.

From what source, then, must the conviction come? and from *what* morality is to come the light to be cast on the characters?

The conviction must come from certainty of the validity of the truth the novel is to present. The 'moral light' has not, actually, a moral source; it is moral (morally powerful) according to the strength of its power of revelation. Revelation of what? The virtuous-ness of the action of the character. What is virtue in action? Truth in action. Truth by what ruling, in relation to what? Truth by the ruling of, and in relation to, the inherent poetic truth that the novel states.

The presence, and action, of the poetic truth is the motive (or motor) morality of the novel.

The direction of the action of the poetic truth provides—in fact, *is*—the moral angle of the novel. If he remains with that truth in view, the novelist has no option as to his angle.

The action, or continuous line of action, of a character is 'bad' in so far as it runs counter to, resists, or attempts to deny, the action of the poetic truth. It is predisposition towards such action that constitutes 'badness' in a character.

'Good' action, or 'goodness' in the character, from predisposition towards such action, is movement along with, expressive of and con-tributory to, the action of the poetic truth.

If the novelist's moral angle is (a) decided by recognition of the poetic truth, and (b) maintained by the necessity of stating the truth by showing the truth's action, it will be, as it should be, im-personal. It will be, and (from the 'interest' point of view) will be able to stand being, pure of pre-assumptions—national, social, sexual, etc.

(N.B.—'Humour' is the weak point in the front against pre-assumptions. Almost all English humour shows social (sometimes, now, backed by political) pre-assumptions. (Extreme cases—that the lower, or employed, classes are quaint or funny—that aristocrats, served by butlers, are absurd. National pre-assumptions show in treatment of foreigners.)

ADVANCE

It has been said that plot must advance; that the underlying (or inner) speed of the advance must be even. How is this arrived at?

(1) Obviously, first, by the succession, the succeedingness, of events or happenings. It is to be remembered that *everything* put on record at all—an image, a word spoken, an interior movement of thought or feeling on the part of a character—is an event or happening. These proceed out of one another, give birth to one another, in a continuity that must be (a) obvious, (b) unbroken.

(2) Every happening cannot be described, stated. The reader must be made to feel that what has not been described or stated has, none the less, happened. How? By the showing of subsequent events or happenings whose source *could* only have been in what has not actually been stated. Tuesday is Tuesday by virtue of being the day following Monday. The stated Tuesday must be shown as a derivative of the unstated Monday.

(3) For the sake of emphasis, time must be falsified. But the novelist's consciousness of the subjective, arbitrary and emotional nature of the falsification should be evident to the reader. Against this falsification—in fact, increasing the force of its effect by contrast—a clock should be heard always impassively ticking away at the same speed. The passage of time, and its demarcation, should be a factor in plot. The either concentration or even or uneven spacing-out of events along time is important.

The statement 'Ten years had passed,' or the statement 'It was now the next day'—each of these is an event.

(4) Characters most of all promote, by showing, the advance of the plot. How? By the advances, from act to act, in their action. By their showing (by emotional or physical changes) the effects both of action and of the passage of time. The diminution of the character's alternatives shows (because it is the work of) advance—by the end of a novel the character's alternatives, many at the beginning, have been reduced to almost none. In the novel, everything that happens either *to* or *because* of one of the characters. By the end of the novel, the character has, like the silk worm at work on the cocoon, spun itself out. Completed action is marked by the exhaustion (from one point of view) of the character. Throughout the novel, each character

is expending potentiality. This expense of potentiality must be felt.

(5) Scene promotes, or contributes to, advance by its freshness. Generically, it is fresh, striking, from being unlike the scene before. It is the new 'here and now.' Once a scene ceases to offer freshness, it is a point-blank enemy to advance. Frequent change of scene *not* being an imperative of the novels—in fact, many novels by choice, and by wise choice, limiting themselves severely in this matter—how is there to continue to be freshness? By means of ever-differing presentation. Differing because of what? Season of year, time of day, effects of a happening (*e.g.*, with house, rise or fall in family fortunes, an arrival, a departure, a death), beholding character's mood. At the first presentation, the *scene* has freshness; afterwards, the freshness must be in the *presentation*. The same scene can, by means of a series of presentations, each having freshness, be made to ripen, mature, to actually advance. The *static* properties in scene can be good for advance when so stressed as to show advance by contrast—advance on the part of the characters. Striking 'unchangingness' gives useful emphasis to change. Change should not be a factor, at once, in *both* scene and character; either unchanged character should see, or be seen against, changed scene, or changed character should see, or be seen, against unchanged scene. *Two* changes obviously cancel each other out, and would cancel each other's contribution to the advance of plot.

RELEVANCE

Relevance—the question of it—is the headache of novel writing.

As has been said, the model for relevance is the well-constructed detective story: nothing is 'in' that does not tell. But the detective story is, or would appear to be, simplified by having *fact* as its kernel. The detective story makes towards concrete truth; the novel makes towards abstract truth.

With the detective story, the question 'relevant to *what?*' can be answered by the intelligence. With the novel, the same question must constantly, and in every context, be referred to the intuition. The intelligence, in a subsequent check over, may detect, but cannot itself put right, blunders, lapses or false starts on the part of the intuition.

In the notes on Plot, Character, Scene and Dialogue, everything has come to turn, by the end, on relevance. It is seen that all other relevances are subsidiary to the relevance of the plot—*i.e.*, the relevance to itself that the plot demands. It is as contributory, in fact relevant, to plot that character, scene and dialogue are examined. To be perfectly contributory, these three must be perfectly relevant. If character, scene or dialogue has been weakened by anything irrelevant *to itself*, it can only be imperfectly relevant—which must mean, to a degree disruptive—to the plot.

The main hope for character (for each character) is that it should be magnetic—*i.e.*, that it should *attract* its parts. This living propensity of the character to assemble itself, to integrate itself, to make itself in order to *be* itself will not, obviously, be resisted by the novelist. The magnetic, or magnetizing, character can be trusted as to what is relevant to *itself*. The trouble comes when what is relevant to the character is found to be not relevant to the plot. At this point, the novelist must adjudicate. It is possible that the character may be right; it is possible that there may be some flaw in the novelist's sense of what is relevant to the plot.

Again, the character may, in fact must, decide one half of the question of relevance in dialogue. The character attracts to itself the right, in fact the only possible, idiom, tempo and phraseology for *that* particular character in speech. In so far as dialogue is *illustrative*, the character's, or characters', pull on it must not be resisted.

But in so far as dialogue must be 'something happening'—part of action, a means of advancing plot—the other half of the question of dialogue-relevance comes up. Here, the pull from the characters may conflict with the pull from the plot. Here again the novelist must adjudicate. The recasting and recasting of dialogue that is so often necessary is, probably, the search for ideal compromise.

Relevance in scene is more straightforward. Chiefly, the novelist must control his infatuation with his own visual power. No non-contributory image, must be the rule. Contributory to what? To the mood of the 'now,' the mood that either projects or reflects action. It is a good main rule that objects—chairs, trees, glasses, mountains, cushions—introduced into the novel should be stage-properties, necessary for 'business.' It will be also recalled that the well-set stage shows many objects *not* actually necessary for 'business,' but that these have a right to place by being descriptive—explanatory. In a play, the absence of the narrating voice makes it necessary to establish the class, period and general psychology of the characters by means of objects that can be seen. In the novel, such putting of objects to a descriptive (explanatory) use is excellent—alternative to the narrator's voice.

In scene then, relevance demands either usefulness for action or else explanatory power in what is shown. There is no doubt that with some writers (Balzac, sometimes Arnold Bennett) categoricalness, in the presentation of scene, is effective. The aim is, usually, to suggest, by multiplication and exactitude of detail, either a scene's material oppressiveness or its intrinsic authority. But in general, for the purposes of most novelists, the number of objects genuinely necessary for explanation will be found to be very small.

Irrelevance, in any part, is a cloud and a drag on, a weakener of, the novel. It dilutes meaning. Relevance crystallizes meaning.

The novelist's—any writer's—object is, to whittle down his meaning to the exactest and finest possible point. What, of course, is fatal is when he does not know what he does mean: he has no point to sharpen.

Much irrelevance is introduced into novels by the writer's vague hope that at least some of this *may* turn out to be relevant, after all. A good deal of what might be called provisional writing goes to the first drafts of first chapters of most novels. At a point in the novel's progress, relevance becomes clearer. The provisional chapters are then recast.

The most striking fault in work by young or beginning novelists submitted for criticism, is irrelevance—due either to infatuation or indecision. To direct such an author's attention to the imperative of relevance is certainly the most useful—and possibly the only—help that can be given.   (1950)

HARRY LEVIN (1912-   )

What Is Realism?

N STATING an issue which others will then be called upon to face, propounding very sketchily the terms to which their articles will lend concrete significance, perhaps I should invoke the special protection of jesting Pilate—that patron saint of profound inquiries superficially pursued. For the problem that I have undertaken to pose brings up a number of incidental and ultimate questions which we could not stop for, even if we knew the answers, within a single issue of the present journal. The most we can hope for is to focus, upon the main tendency of modern literature, the same sort of analytic and evaluative discussion that has already been concentrated upon the topic of romanticism. At the outset we can answer Pilate's question, positivistically and tautologically, by defining truth as the accurate correspondence between reality itself and a given account of reality. We are thereupon confronted by the question, "What is reality?" Since it cannot bear precisely the same significance for any two human beings, Carlyle declared that "reality escapes us." Let us concede the point; let it stand as *x*, the unknown element in whatever

From *Comparative Literature*, Vol. III, No. 3, Summer, 1951; reprinted with permission of the author.

formulation we may reach. We come closer by approaching the problem from the other side—by sorting out the testimony that various witnesses have deposed, charting the general direction they seem to indicate, and tentatively calling this process of approximation "realism."

But here another difficulty arises, insofar as some of them lead in opposite directions. For example, the trend of modern thought toward empiricism, materialism, pragmatism, naturalism came to a head a generation ago when two schools of philosophers all but agreed: the so-called "New Realists" and the so-called "Critical Realists." V. L. Parrington broadened the area of agreement by applying the term "critical realism" to the recent period in American literature. More recently, however, there have been accumulating signs of re-version to an older kind of realism, the scholastic kind that proceeded from the doctrine of *universalia ante rem*. Shunted between two ex-treme positions which claim the same title, we may turn from epistemology to etymology, and take the Latin root word *res* as our starting point. It is well to remember that the word contains, as it were, the thing. It is not altogether far-fetched to observe that, semantically speaking, "realism" is distantly connected with "real estate." That quasi-legal connection is tangibly supported by the bonds of interest that tie so many novelists to the realistic tradition: by Balzac's sense of property, Dickens's inventories and Tolstoy's estates, Henry James's preoccupation with "things."

We lose little by confining our attention to that terrain of experi-ence which philosophical sophistication would label "naïve realism." Its classic gesture occurred when Dr. Johnson kicked the stone. Char-acteristically it manifests itself by repudiating some manifestation of idealism. When publicists tell us to look at a situation realistically, we can be fairly certain that we are about to be asked to condone some piece of moral skulduggery. Instead of an appeal to principle, we are presented with a repudiation of principle. Thus the realistic attitude derives its meaning from the conditions of its application. Like the concept of liberty, it cannot exist in a vacuum; in the abstract it means virtually nothing. History defines our liberties in terms of the specific constraints they sought to overcome; free speech and free trade presuppose unjust imprisonment and arbitrary taxation, the *lettre de cachet* and the *gabelle*. The purport of President Roosevelt's Four Freedoms lay in their counterattack against four tyrannies. In this respect as in others, realism closely parallels the development of liberalism—another protean phenomenon which can only be pinned down by firmly grasping its varied responses to particular issues.

So much is clear, as Karl Mannheim has said: "Realism means different things in different contexts." Its would-be historians may well be deterred by the object-lesson of Lord Acton's uncompleted *History of Liberty*. But students of literature have the measurable advantage of working from texts as well as contexts, and Erich Auerbach's *Mimesis* has lately shown what stylistic analysis can do, when trained upon the descriptive techniques of selected authors from Homer to Virginia Woolf. When Professor Auerbach finds no formula for the presentation of actuality (*dargestellte Wirklichkeit*) in different languages at different epochs, he impressively documents our need for assuming a relativistic point of view. Possibly an absolute standard could be set up in the plastic arts, where the actual object can be directly compared with its artistic treatment. Yet even there the realism seems to be a matter of degree, varying with choice of subject and emphasis on detail. Even when we speak of "photographic reproduction," we cannot take for granted its objectivity. The very phrase *trompe-l'œil* gives it away. The camera's eye is relatively less subjective than the eye of the beholder; yet it was photography which opened the way for impressionistic painting, which in turn has angled and composed and highlighted the art of the photographer.

Perhaps, like students of the diverging "romanticisms," we should pluralize our subject; but we should not, like some of them, allow divergences to obscure a fundamental impetus. Art has continually adapted itself to man's changing conceptions of reality—that is to say, his successive adjustments to society and nature. In a static culture, where his position is fixed and his world-view unchanging, expression is likely to be conventionalized. But Occidental culture has been dynamic, and its arts have endeavored to keep pace with its accelerating changes. This distinction, which is broadly exemplified in the contrast between East and West, sharply emerged from the Iconoclastic Controversy, when Eastern orthodoxy prescribed a rigid convention while Western artists were free to move toward secularization, individuality, realism—from the symbolic, in short, to the representational. Now, if, as Aristotle maintains, art springs from the interplay of two complementary instincts, μίμησις and ἁρμονία, there are times when the imitation of nature predominates and other times when it is subordinated to the imposition of a pattern. When Plato condemned poetry for its unreality (in the most idealistic and paradoxical sense of that term), Aristotle proposed a compromise in the name of poetic truth and higher reality, and thence handed on the doctrine of verisimilitude to the neo-classical critics.

Meanwhile the sphere of the probable expanded, while much that the ancients regarded as universal was seen by the moderns to be more limited. Against such limitations romanticism protested, when Wordsworth and Coleridge set out to write about lower ranks of society and stranger wonders of nature than classicism seemed willing to recognize. Not that the classicists excluded realism, but they relegated it to the comic stage; comedy was the *imago veritatis,* and the common man was no hero but a figure of fun. The medium that most completely mirrors the increasing stature of the middle class has been, of course, the major vehicle of literary realism, the novel. The novel originated, with a characteristic gesture, by repudiating its mediaeval predecessor; the picaresque tale overtook the knightly romance; and Cervantes, by pitting the daily realities of the developing city against the chivalric ideals of the declining castle, provided an archetype for all novelists and future realists. "La rivalité du monde réel et de la représentation que nous nous en faisons"—this might be a French critic's description of *Don Quixote.* It happens to be André Gide's description of what his novelist is attempting in *Les Faux-monnayeurs.*

Conversely, looking backward from Gide, we can see how every great novel has attempted—*mutatis mutandis*—to distinguish what is real from what is counterfeit. Defoe's narrations, he invariably assured his readers, are not fiction but fact; and Diderot pointedly entitled one of his stories *Ceci n'est pas un conte.* To convince us of his essential veracity, the novelist must always be disclaiming the fictitious and breaking through the encrustations of the literary. "La vraie éloquence se moque de l'éloquence." It is no coincidence that, from Rabelais to Jane Austen, so many realists have begun as parodists; it has even been argued, by Viktor Shklovsky, that parody is the basis of the novelistic form. We must not assume that, because it is polymorphous, the novel is formless; nor that writers very easily or spontaneously express themselves in a realistic mode. "No more literary school than the realists has ever existed," as George Moore, their leading British apologist, allowed. But we must first go—as Moore did—to France, where most of the problems of modern literature have been formulated, if we would track the critical usage down to its historical context. (If we would trace it to its metaphysical chrysalis, we should have to look even farther back to Germany, to Schiller's *Über naïve und sentimentalische Dichtung,* where antique *Realismus* is contrasted with the idealistic outlook of the romantics.)

The earliest applications of the term that we encounter in the *New English Dictionary* are cited from Emerson in 1856 and Ruskin in 1857: the first is roughly synonymous with "materialism," the second with "grotesquerie," and both are decidedly pejorative. In France, on the other hand, the latter year marks the trial and vindication of *Madame Bovary*—a date as important for realism as the *première* of *Hernani* is for romanticism. The relationship between the two movements, as we acknowledge more and more, is continuous rather than antithetical. The realism of the romanticists has its dialectical counterpart in the romanticism of the realists, and it would be hard to say under which category we should classify *La Chartreuse de Parme* or *Les Misérables*. As early as 1826, investigation has shown, *le romantisme* and *le réalisme* echoed interchangeably through contemporary periodicals. But in the phrase of its journalistic fugleman, Champfleury, realism was one of "those religions in -ism" which came into the world in 1848. Its preparation had been technical as well as ideological; it profited from Daguerre's epoch-making invention, which entered the public domain in 1839, as well as from Houssaye's history of Flemish painting published in 1846. It reached its artistic climax when Courbet, whose paintings were rejected by the Salon of 1855, set up his own exhibition of these solidly executed studies in humble life, which he called his *Pavillon du Réalisme*.

The critic Duranty summed up objectives when he called for "the exact, complete, and sincere reproduction of the social milieu in which we live." His little magazine, *Réalisme*, coincided with a collection of essays under the same title, brought out by Champfleury in 1857. By then the catchword was becoming popular; even M. Prudhomme, the bourgeois incarnate, could sign his letters with assurances of his "distinguished consideration and realism." However, Duranty believed that the realists were too individualistic to establish a school, while Champfleury considered them transitional and expected them to give way before another movement in thirty years. Within half that time, in the 1870's, Zola was putting out manifestoes for naturalism. Where the older group had posthumously venerated Balzac, the naturalists paid homage to Flaubert, but he remained indifferent to schools and slogans. When Zola amiably admitted that these were devices to gain publicity for younger writers, he scarcely did justice to the grimmer implications of the newer term—the boundless distance between Robinson Crusoe's easy control over his environment and the crushed victims of Hardy's cosmic irony or Dreiser's chemical determinism.

Naturalism found its inspiration in science rather than art, its exemplar in Darwin rather than Courbet. In contrast to the accumulation of things, the jumbled catalogues of realism, its objects were meticulously selected and related through the chain of cause and effect. Seeking to complete the process of identification between literature and life, it conceived a book as a *document humain* and a play as a *tranche de vie*. But Zola's novels were experimental in quite a different sense from the physiological experimentation of Claude Bernard. Their twofold aim is reflected in their subtitle: *Histoire naturelle et sociale d'une famille sous le Second Empire*. As natural history, they demonstrate nothing; they simply illustrate the obsolescent theories of Zola's scientific contemporaries. Their social story is something else again, combining the exposure of bureaucracy with a plea for the underdog, each volume covering another field of documentation. Zola, writing in retrospect, gave voice to the political opposition that the Second Empire vainly tried to silence. Similarly in Russia, under the tsars, in spite of censorship, suppression, and regimentation, writers were able to lodge their protest against an even more autocratic régime. Perhaps because Russians had to live a lie, as Turgenev suggested, their novels were so intensely devoted to truth.

Into the second half of the nineteenth century, realists and naturalists carried augmenting burdens of social criticism and humanitarian sympathy. The brothers Goncourt, for all their aristocratic tastes, furthered the advance of proletarian fiction; they urged, in the preface to *Germinie Lacerteux*, the right of the lower class to a novel of its own. The spread of democracy, the rise in the standard of living, the exploitation of typography and literacy brought pressure for further extensions of the literary franchise. Hence Harriet Beecher Stowe announced that *Uncle Tom's Cabin* (*or Life among the Lowly*) would treat a theme "hitherto ignored by the associations of polite and refined society." Politeness and refinement inevitably hold a vested interest in the *status quo*, which is loudly outraged by the depiction of uncomfortable facts and ignoble existences, and would outlaw them by invoking the ambiguous sanction of universality. Official and academic sponsorship, reducing the dynamic to the static, produce what William Dean Howells termed "a petrification of taste." Resistance is no less inevitable than movement, and repeats itself over the years. Just as Brunetière deprecated the naturalistic school, just as the disillusioned novels of the First World War were attacked by propagandists for the Second, so the hired moralists of *Life* magazine have latterly been editorializing against *From Here to Eternity* and *The Naked and the Dead.*

None the less realism, heralded by romanticism and continued by naturalism, has been the animating current of nineteenth-century literature. Today it no longer operates as an *avant-garde*; it has acquired tradition and even academies. Watchwords continue to become outmoded and novelties must be rediscovered again and again; the naturists supersede the naturalists and the verists yield to self-proclaimed veritists; and yet the real thing seems even more remote than before. Can it be that this progression, which has moved on so rapidly from generation to generation, is slowing down to an impasse? The next step, to judge from *surréalisme* (or "superrealism"), seems to be less a new projection of the old realism than a sharp reaction against it—against representation in favor of symbolism. Such land-marks as Joyce's *Ulysses*, pointing in two directions, lead forward—or is it backward?—via psychology toward fantasy and myth. The tech-nological obsolescence of the novel itself is predictable in an era when fiction can hardly keep up with fact, when the reporter turns novelist and the novelist turns reporter, when the instinct for imitation is more efficiently satisfied by journalism, radio, film, and above all television. Within the abstracted realm now left to the purer arts, it may be that the instinct for harmony—for order, degree, and arrangement —will again prevail.

Whatever happens is bound to register the adaptation to change, but the quality of change may prove so far-reaching as to undermine the tendencies upon which realism has been grounded: a democratic attitude toward society, an experimental attitude toward nature. The forces that work against social mobility and scientific inquiry are those that steer writers back into the province of convention. Much of the writing that confronts us, at this midpoint of the twentieth century, seems transitional in character: conventional in pattern, realistic in detail. Yet an art which must submit itself, either to production codes or party lines, is basically unrealistic. Witness, on the one hand, the cinema. And, on the other, the neo-Marxist slogan of "socialist realism" is, in the light of historical definition, a contradiction in terms. The role of the great realists—as who but Gorki pointed out?— has been to transcend their own class, to criticize the bourgeoisie. It does not necessarily follow that their successors ought to panegyrize the proletariat. Middle-class culture, with all its faults, has had its virtue—the redeeming virtue of self-criticism. "Kunst wird Kritik," Thomas Mann has lately remarked, and the bourgeois novel is nothing if not critical. It may have told the whole truth very rarely, and in-cluded many other things than the truth; but it has kept open the question "What is truth?" in the teeth of dogmas and systems that strive to close it.

In reducing our theme to a handful of historical and critical generalizations, I am aware that these preliminary comments do much less than justice to its large diversity and striking particularity; and, for this reason and others, I have greater confidence in the major part of our collective undertaking, which is embodied in the five essays that follow. These are by no means intended as a comprehensive survey, enumerating the many and far-flung titles that have been ticketed as realistic. Rather they constitute a tentative inquiry as to what is meant when certain works are so designated, what traits their authors share, and wherein they differ. To test how far these differences may be pushed, and how much consistency of intention and execution

remains, we have subdivided our endeavor along the lines of the
various national literatures. The question has in each case been put to
an accomplished scholar, for consideration in the special light of his
field. The fields, as they are represented here, require no explanation
or apology; but it is regrettable that other literary traditions could
not, for reasons of space, also be discussed. We could scarcely pretend
to completeness without some appraisal of the early and vital developments in Italy and Spain or of the late and unique flowering in the
Scandinavian countries. And it would be useful to verify our premises,
which derive from a closely related group of cultures, by considering
parallels among the Classics or in the Near and Far East. Our task,
however, is not conclusive but introductory; we merely wish to open
a discussion which, we sincerely hope, others will broaden and
deepen.   (1951)

ROBERT LIDDELL (1908-   )

From *The Subject of Fiction*

1. *The Difficulty of Choosing a Subject*
at the Present Day

THERE IS, no doubt, too much written and said about the
present day, too much speculation about what the novelist
must do today, and will *have* to do tomorrow. In the arts
it is not very important to be up-to-date, and nothing looks more
out-of-date today than the book that was up-to-date a year or two
ago. And it is not an intelligent exercise to ask such questions as:
'What is the future of the novel?' or: 'Has the novel a future?'

A very few words on this point should be enough. While English
remains a living language, in which prose can be read and written
fluently, and so long as people live, and there are personal relations
between them—then English fiction is possible. Reasons may make it
more difficult to write at one time than another—it is probably now,
for several reasons, as difficult as it has been at any time since the
life-time of Richardson. It is especially difficult to find a suitable
subject.

2. *The Insecurity of Life*

The chief difficulty today is caused by the crushing impact of
public affairs. 'There is no private life which has not been determined

From *Some Principles of Fiction* (London: Jonathan Cape, 1953).
Reprinted with permission of the publishers.

by a wider public life,' says George Eliot—but since her day the determination has been very much more rigid. No one in Middlemarch, after all, ever had to join the armed forces, ever had to leave Middlemarch if he did not like it. And those who remained in Middlemarch never had to fear that their lives might be cut short or their homes destroyed by a bomb.

Nowadays, if a hero and heroine marry at the end of a book, and live happily ever afterwards—although we know that fictional characters are only puppets, and that the toy-box is shut at the end of the book, yet we cannot help asking how long that happiness is likely to last. Writer and reader alike feel an insecurity: we only half believe in the happiness or unhappiness of real persons, and therefore of fictional characters which are their *simulacra*—it seems such a frail thing.

On the other hand, if we read one of those bluff, middlebrow writers who seem to pride themselves on having escaped the jaded nerves of our epoch—then we believe even less in the characters or in the world that they have created. They seem to have been incapable of sensitively imagining what it is like to be alive today.

Already, after the first world war, Katherine Mansfield was complaining of writers who wrote as if it had not occurred. 'I don't want (God forbid!) mobilization and the violation of Belgium, but the novel can't just leave the war out. There must have been a change of heart.'

Today we do not ask for pages about the Spanish war (God forbid!) or the Munich agreement—which loom too large as it is in contemporary fiction.

What we do demand of an author is rather, perhaps, a feeling of sadness, a lack of faith in simple or easy solutions to human problems, a sense of the frailty of life ... no loud, hearty songs of innocence, but quiet songs of experience; and a great part of the experience of our time is expressed in a few, sad little words of Mr. Stephen Spender's:

> Who live under the shadow of a war,
> What can I do that matters?

There is no attempt here to lay a moral or social duty upon the writer; it is an attempt to define an artistic duty for the novelist who is trying in any way to represent contemporary life. One can hardly write truthfully about characters living in this age without showing that many of them live in perpetual fear that their world is in imminent danger of falling to pieces round their ears. It would be like writing a novel about the Middle Ages, and leaving out the fear of

Hell. This is not to suggest that the novelist could or should have a scheme for saving the world; if he thinks he knows how to save the world, then he had better go to work about it, and leave off writing fiction, for fiction will not hold the world together. Nor do we much want to read the views of his characters upon public events, for they will be very stale by the time the book is in print. We only require sadness, scepticism and a feeling of insecurity.

Those novels which people used to write at one time, about consumptive patients in sanatoria, would not be a bad model for present-day novelists, if they were better novels—for all characters nowadays are sick, with 'this strange disease of modern life', and it will probably carry them off. Whether characters are, for example, *Munichois* or *anti-Munichois* is only a question of which way they have got the disease: we do not want to know, for clinical details are boring.

In this unfortunate age in which we live, since everything is insecure, some people think it does not much matter how they behave —these people become criminals. Others, less extreme in their application of a similar point-of-view, still think that it does not very much matter what an individual does or suffers: these people are apt to be impatient with fiction. What can it matter, they argue, what an imaginary person does or suffers, when the world's fate hangs in the balance? Are not novelists fiddling while Rome is burning?

This is not so sensible an attitude as it might at first appear. The fate of the world, after all, is only important in so far as it affects the people in it. We may speak, if we like, of Poland, Spain or wherever suffering; but of course it means nothing: it is only Poles, Spaniards or whoever that can suffer. Moreover we cannot even say that two Poles, for example, can suffer twice as much as one. Suffering is not a thing that can be added up or multiplied, like horsepower. There is never more suffering, or worse suffering at any one time in the world than the worst than can be contained in one human consciousness.

If we think that it does not matter what happens to the individual, then we have no reason to think that it matters what happens to the world, for it is the individual who feels what happens to the world.

If we think the individual matters, then our sympathy can as easily be extended to the imaginary individual—for other people are to us for the most part imaginary individuals. And if the novelist seems to be fiddling while Rome is burning, it may be a useful service to pay to the firemen while they have their luncheon.

St. Augustine says that he could not weep for his sins, which might plunge him into Hell, but he could weep for Dido's unhappy love. He thought this a sign of his own perversity, but we may also regard it as a sign of Vergil's artistry: Vergil made him weep for Dido. A novelist may still hope to make us weep for his heroine, and to forget for a while the things that may plunge us in ruin; but his Dido, if she is a woman living in the world of today, will have a shakier throne to sit on, and a more unstable background than that of the Queen of Carthage. This is one of the things that will make her story more difficult to tell. The novelist not only has to keep his eye on his character, and no interesting characters keep still for very long—he has also to keep his eye upon a surrounding world that will not keep still, as it kept (comparatively) still for Jane Austen or for Trollope—to see steadily what is, itself, unsteady.

3. *The Standardization of Life*

Not only is life insecure, it may also be said that it is less interesting than it used to be, and that people are not so interesting as they used to be. When people profess to find that Dickens's characters are wild exaggerations, and when they say that they have never seen anyone remotely like Mrs. Gamp or Mr. Pecksniff, it is to be feared that they are often telling the truth—they haven't. Those of us who have been more fortunate, must sorrowfully admit that the most Dickensian people of our acquaintance are now elderly, or in their graves.

The standardization of life, alas, requires no proof. The progress of machinery has made the working-lives of industrial labourers infinitely less interesting, as everyone knows. It may be possible to avoid the uglification of life—well-designed things can be made by machines; it may be possible, by use of machinery, so to cut down working hours that industrial labourers may (on the balance) be happier. This is no consolation to the novelist as such, who does not care whether they are happy or not, or whether what they make is beautiful or hideous. He would like their working-lives to be interesting and significant as a subject for fiction—and that they will never be again. If we look, on the contrary, at the lives of stone-masons or woodlanders in the Wessex novels, we can see at once how rich their working-lives were in material for the novelist.

Again, big businesses, multiple stores and the like may be able to do much for their work-people, but one thing they cannot give them, an interesting working-life. Yet for anyone who had worked for Mrs. Todgers or for Poll Sweedlepipe or for any of the little shops and businesses in Dickens, life would have been full of drama.

The standardization of life does not only blight people's working-lives, but also their amusements. A big household, like that of Mansfield Park, would be unlikely today to get up private theatricals—with all those wonderful scenes of jealousy and passion that result. The Bertrams, and Rushworths, and Crawfords, and Fanny Price and Mrs. Norris would drive into Northampton, and go to the cinema. The wrong people might sit together, or Henry Crawford might press Fanny's hand in the dark: but there is little there for a novelist to get his teeth into.

4. The Removal of Obstacles to Love

There has been in this century such a relaxation of people's ideas about sexual morality, and, in particular, about marriage, that most people's emotional lives are very much freer and less complicated than they used to be. People may or may not be happier or better for this change—but for the novelist as such it is a change for the worse, for life is less interesting.

In *Sense and Sensibility* Edward Ferrars is unhappy through three-quarters of the book because, while he was under twenty-one, and not even legally bound by his promise, he had offered marriage to an underbred young woman, who has since appeared a worthless character to his more mature judgment. Life with Lucy must be unhappy; moreover Edward has now fallen in love seriously, and with a very superior woman in his own class, and has reason to believe that she is attached to him—but he may take no steps to break off his engagement.

Much later in the nineteenth century, it is thought dishonourable for the hero of *The Spoils of Poynton* not to fulfil his engagement to a most odious young woman, after he has come to dislike her as she deserves. He may not even play a waiting game, and hope that she will tire of him and give him up, though there is every chance of success in this line. He has to behave as if he were even impatient to marry her.

These two great novels must today be read with a 'willing suspension of disbelief' in the standards of honour maintained. Neither of these situations could occur today—or, if they did, the man would be thought so absurdly scrupulous that he would forfeit all sympathy.

It seems easier now, at any rate in fiction, to put an end to a marriage, than it was then to put an end to an engagement—and the social consequences are less disagreeable. It is therefore harder for a novelist to convince his readers by a picture of a desperately unhappy married life. Formerly husband or wife might cry: *'I can't get out!*' like Sterne's starling. That is not true any more: the door is open. Formerly there was no way out but Death, and that door could only be forced by Suicide or Murder—wonderful climaxes to a plot. A husband or wife who escapes by Suicide is now thought feeble; if either rids himself of a partner by Murder, it looks brutal and pointless.

There is a very good essay on this subject by Mr. Aldous Huxley, called *Obstacle Race*. He begins by a brief analysis of that strange novel by Stendhal, *Armance*, in which religion, convention, honour, delicacy and money one after another keep the lovers apart.

'Poor Octave!' says Mr. Huxley, 'Unhappy Armance! Their whole life was a kind of obstacle race—a climbing over and a crawling under barriers, a squeezing through narrow places. And the winning-post? For Octave the winning-post was a dose of laudanum; for Armance, a cell in a nunnery.

'If they had run their course today, they would have run it on the flat, or at any rate over a course irregular only by nature, not artificially obstructed. The going is easier now.'

Mr. Huxley went on to give as an example of flat-racing the love-stories of a Russian writer, whose sexual morality was merely that of the farmyard. Since the date of Mr. Huxley's essay, those who direct the destinies of Russia are said to have ordered many changes in these things—so much the better for the future of the Russian novel.

The most beautiful and skilful obstacle-racing in English fiction is probably to be found in *The Wings of the Dove*. The lovers' meeting in the park, at the beginning of this novel, is one of the most splendid in prose literature, simply because of the obstacles in their way. They themselves are fully aware of them, and Kate Croy almost glories in them—she is about to devise yet another obstacle, and one which will in the end, though she little knows it, keep them permanently apart. 'Yes,' she says, 'we're hideously intelligent. But there's fun in it too. We must get our fun where we can. I think our relation's beautiful. It isn't a bit *banal*. I cling to some saving romance in things.'

In too many recent novels the characters have only the most banal and unbeautiful relationships, and couple like animals, without the intelligence ever coming into play. There is no 'saving romance.'

Some French novelists have avoided the banality of flat-racing. Proust and Gide deal with sexual abnormality, which is still ringed round with complications; M. Mauriac deals with Catholics, who still recognize the existence of obstacles. Here are two fields for obstacle-racing indeed, but they have disadvantages. Those who write about Catholic or homosexual characters usually are consciously, rather too self-consciously, presenting them to a public which is neither homosexual nor Catholic, and from which a more or less 'willing suspension of disbelief' is therefore required: the difficulty of tone is quite exceptional. These are probably safer fields for French writers: a French novelist can without so much difficulty regard Catholic standards as a norm—and he is not awed by British criminal laws, or by British methods of banning books. It is sad to see these promising courses for obstacle-racing being levelled by some novelists into the dullest of flat race courses. . . .   (1953)

ROBERT HUMPHREY (1919-   )

From *Stream of Consciousness in the Modern Novel*

> The discovery that memories, thoughts, and feelings exist outside the primary consciousness is the most important step forward that has occurred in psychology since I have been a student of that science.
>
> WILLIAM JAMES

TREAM of consciousness is one of the delusive terms which writers and critics use. It is delusive because it sounds concrete and yet it is used as variously—and vaguely—as "romanticism," "symbolism," and "surrealism." We never know whether it is being used to designate the bird of technique or the beast of genre—and we are startled to find the creature designated is most often a monstrous combination of the two. The purpose of this study is to examine the term and its literary implications.

Stream of Consciousness Defined

Stream of consciousness is properly a phrase for psychologists. William James coined it. The phrase is most clearly useful when it is applied to mental processes, for as a rhetorical locution it becomes doubly metaphorical; that is, the word "consciousness" as well as the word "stream" is figurative, hence, both are less precise and less stable. If, then, the term stream of consciousness (I shall use it since it is already established as a literary label) is reserved for indicating an approach to the presentation of *psychological* aspects of character in fiction, it can be used with some precision. This reservation I shall make, and it is the basis from which the contradicting and often

From *Stream of Consciousness in the Modern Novel* (Berkeley: University of California Press, 1954). Reprinted with permission of the Regents of the University of California.

meaningless commentary on the stream-of-consciousness novel can be resolved.[1]

The stream-of-consciousness novel is identified most quickly by its subject matter. This, rather than its techniques, its purposes, or its themes, distinguishes it. Hence, the novels that are said to use the stream-of-consciousness *technique* to a considerable degree prove, upon analysis, to be novels which have as their essential subject matter the consciousness of one or more characters; that is, the depicted consciousness serves as a screen on which the material in these novels is presented.

"Consciousness" should not be confused with words which denote more restricted mental activities, such as "intelligence" or "memory." The justifiably irate comments of the psychology scholars deplore the layman's use of the term. One of these scholars writes: "It has been said that no philosophical term is at once so popular and so devoid of standard meaning as *consciousness*; and the layman's usage of the term has been credited with begging as many metaphysical questions as will probably be the privilege of any single word." The area which we are to examine here is an important one in which this confusion has been amassed. Since our study will concern persons who are lay-men in psychology, it is necessary that we proceed with the "layman's usage." Naturally, the stream-of-consciousness writers have not defined their label. We readers who have stamped it on them must try to do it.

Consciousness indicates the entire area of mental attention, from preconsciousness on through the levels of the mind up to and includ-ing the highest one of rational, communicable awareness. This last area is the one with which almost all psychological fiction is concerned. Stream-of-consciousness fiction differs from all other psychological fiction precisely in that it is concerned with those levels that are more inchoate than rational verbalization—those levels on the margin of attention.

So far as stream-of-consciousness fiction is concerned, it is point-less to try to make definite categories of the many levels of conscious-ness. Such attempts demand the answers to serious metaphysical ques-tions, and they put serious questions about the stream-of-consciousness writers' concepts of psychology and their aesthetic intentions—ques-tions which the epistemologists, the psychologists, and the literary

[1] At least two writers, Frederick Hoffman and Harry Levin, have recog-nized this loose use of "stream of consciousness." Levin employs in its place the French rhetorical term *monologue intérieur*. Although Levin uses even this term too loosely for any general discussion of that technique, it serves well for his special purposes. I am indebted to him for the basic distinction between the terms in question.

historians have not yet answered satisfactorily. It is desirable for an analysis of stream-of-consciousness fiction to assume that there are levels of consciousness from the lowest one just above oblivion to the highest one which is represented by verbal (or other formal) communication. "Low" and "high" simply indicate degrees of the rationally ordered. The adjectives "dim" and "bright" could be used just as well to indicate these degrees. There are, however, two levels of consciousness which can be rather simply distinguished: the "speech level" and the "prespeech level." There is a point at which they overlap, but otherwise the distinction is quite clear. The prespeech level, which is the concern of most of the literature under consideration in this study, involves no communicative basis as does the speech level (whether spoken or written). This is its salient distinguishing characteristic. In short, the prespeech levels of consciousness are not censored, rationally controlled, or logically ordered. By "consciousness," then, I shall mean the whole area of mental processes, including especially the prespeech levels. The term "psyche" I shall use as a synonym for "consciousness," and at times, even the word "mind" will serve as another synonym. These synonyms, although they are handicapped by the various evocative qualities they possess, are convenient to use because they lend themselves well to the forming of adjectives and adverbs.

Hence, "consciousness" must not be confused with "intelligence" or "memory" or any other such limiting term. Henry James has written novels which reveal psychological processes in which a single point of view is maintained so that the entire novel is presented through the intelligence of a character. But these, since they do not deal at all with prespeech levels of consciousness, are not what I have defined as stream-of-consciousness novels. Marcel Proust has written a modern classic which is often cited as an example of stream-of-consciousness fiction, but A la recherche du temps perdu is concerned only with the reminiscent aspect of consciousness. Proust was deliberately recapturing the past for the purposes of communication; hence he did not write a stream-of-consciousness novel. Let us think of consciousness as being in the form of an iceberg—the whole iceberg and not just the relatively small surface portion. Stream-of-consciousness fiction is, to follow this comparison, greatly concerned with what lies below the surface.

With such a concept of consciousness, we may define stream-of-consciousness fiction as a type of fiction in which the basic emphasis is placed on exploration of the prespeech levels of consciousness for the purpose, primarily, of revealing the psychic being of the characters.

When some of the novels which fall into this classification are considered, it becomes immediately apparent that the techniques by which the subjects are controlled and the characters are presented are palpably different from one novel to the next. Indeed, there is no stream-of-consciousness technique. Instead, there are several quite different techniques which are used to present stream of consciousness.

The Self-Conscious Mind

It is not an uncommon misconception that many modern novels, and particularly the ones that are generally labeled stream of consciousness, rely greatly upon private symbols to represent private confusions. The misconception comes primarily from considering whatever is "internal" or "subjective" in characterization as arrant fantasy, or, at best, as psychoanalytical.[2] Serious misreadings and unsound evaluations result from this initial misunderstanding, particularly in discussion of major twentieth-century novels. I refer to such subjective fiction as *Ulysses, Mrs. Dalloway, To the Lighthouse,* and *The Sound and the Fury.* These novels may very well be within a category we can label stream of consciousness, so long as we know what we are talking about. The evidence reveals that we never do—or never have done so.

It is meaningless to label all of the novels stream of consciousness that are generally named as such, unless we mean by that phrase simply "inner awareness." The expression of this quality is what they have in common. It is, however, apparent that that is not what has been meant when they have been so labeled and forced to share the same categorical niche. It is not what William James meant when he coined the term. James was formulating psychological theory and he had discovered that "memories, thoughts, and feelings exist outside the primary consciousness" and, further, that they appear to one, not as a chain, but as a stream, a flow. Whoever, then, first applied the phrase to the novel did so correctly only if he was thinking of a *method* of representing inner awareness. What has actually happened is that *monologue intérieur* was clumsily translated into English. But it is palpably true that the methods of the novels in which this device is used are different, and that there are dozens of other novels which use internal monologue which no one would seriously classify as stream of consciousness. Such are, for example, *Moby Dick, Les Faux-monnayeurs,* and *Of Time and the River.* Stream of consciousness, then, is not a synonym for *monologue intérieur.* It is not a

2 It is, of course, true that there are several attempts to represent character in fiction in psychoanalytical terms—notably in Conrad Aiken's novels, *Blue Voyage* and *Great Circle*—but these attempts are for the most part curiosities, and they are finally insignificant.

term to name a particular method or technique; although it probably was used originally in literary criticism for that purpose. One can safely conjecture that such a loose and fanciful term was a radiant buoy to well-meaning critics who had lost their bearings. The natural, and historically accurate, association of the term with psychology, along with the overwhelming psychoanalytical trend of twentieth-century thought, has resulted in giving all novels that could be loosely associated with the loose phrase "stream of consciousness" a marked Viennese accent.

The word "stream" need not concern us immediately, for representation of the flow of consciousness is, provided one is convinced that consciousness flows, entirely a matter of technique. The approach to take is to consider the word "consciousness" and to attempt to formulate what, to the various writers, is the ultimate significance of what consciousness contains. It is, in short, a psychological and a philosophical question. Stream-of-consciousness literature is psychological literature, but it must be studied at the level on which psychology mingles with epistemology. Immediately the question confronts us: What does consciousness contain? Then, too, what does it contain so far as philosophy and psychology have investigated it *and* what does it contain so far as the novelists in question have represented it? These may be mutually exclusive questions; they are certainly different ones. But the concern here is not with psychological theory; it is with novelistic subject matter. The question for this study is a phenomenological one: What does consciousness contain in the sense of what has it contained so far as the consciousness of the novelists have experienced it? Any answer must respect the possible range of a creative writer's sensitivity and imagination. No answer needs proving beyond the gesture of saying: There it is in Virginia Woolf; there it is in James Joyce. It should be remembered that, first, we are attempting to clarify a literary term; and second, we are trying to determine how fictional art is enriched by the depiction of inner states.

The attempt to create human consciousness in fiction is a modern attempt to analyze human nature. Most of us will be convinced, now, that it can be the starting point of that most important of all intellectual functions. We have, for example, Henry James's word for it that "experience is never limited, and it is never complete." He continues in the same context to point to the "chamber of consciousness" as the chamber of experience. Consciousness, then, is *where* we are aware of human experience. And this is enough for the novelist. He, collectively, leaves nothing out: sensations and memories, feelings and conceptions, fancies and imaginations—and those very unphilosophic, but consistently unavoidable phenomena we call intuitions, visions, and insights. These last terms, which usually embarrass the epistemologist, unlike the immediately preceding series, are not always included under the label "mental life." Precisely for this reason it is important to point them up here. Human "knowledge" which comes not from "mental" activity but from "spiritual" life is a concern of novelists, if not of psychologists. Knowledge, then, as a category of consciousness must include intuition, vision, and sometimes even the occult, so far as twentieth-century writers are concerned.

Thus, we may, on inductive grounds, conclude that the realm of life with which stream-of-consciousness literature is concerned is mental and spiritual experience—both the whatness and the howness of it. The whatness includes the categories of mental experiences: sensations, memories, imaginations, conceptions, and intuitions. The howness includes the symbolizations, the feelings, and the processes of association. It is often impossible to separate the what from the how. Is, for example, memory a part of mental content or is it a mental process? Such fine distinctions, of course, are not the concern of novelists as novelists. Their object, if they are writing stream of consciousness, is to enlarge fictional art by depicting the inner states of their characters.

The problem of character depiction is central to stream-of-consciousness fiction. The great advantage, and consequently the best justification of this type of novel, rests on its potentialities for presenting character more accurately and more realistically. There is the example of the *roman expérimental* behind James Joyce, Virginia Woolf, and Dorothy Richardson, and though a little farther removed, behind William Faulkner. But there is a difference, and it is a tremendous one, between Zola and Dreiser, say, two novelists who attempted a kind of laboratory method in fiction, and the stream-of-consciousness writers. It is indicated chiefly in the difference in subject matter— which is, for the earlier novelists, motive and action (external man) and for the later ones, psychic existence and functioning (internal man). The difference is also revealed in the psychological and philosophical thinking in back of this. Psychologically it is the distinction between behavioristic concepts and psychoanalytical ones; philosophically, it is that between a broad materialism and a generalized existentialism. Combined, it is the difference between being concerned about what one does and being concerned about what one is.

I do not offer a Freudian or Existential brief for stream-of-consciousness literature. All of its authors doubtless were familiar, more or less, with psychoanalytical theories and with the twentieth-century recrudescence of personalism and were directly or indirectly influenced by them. Even more certain can we be that these writers were influenced by the broader concepts of a "new psychology" and a "new philosophy"—a nebulous label for all postbehavioristic and non-positivistic thinking, including any philosophy or psychology which emphasized man's inner mental and emotional life (e.g., Gestalt psychology, psychoanalytical psychology, Bergsonian ideas of *durée* and the *élan vital*, religious mysticism, much symbolic logic, Christian existentialism, etc.). It is this background which led to the great difference between Zola's subject matter and Joyce's; between Balzac's and Dorothy Richardson's. Yet as novelists all of these writers were concerned with the problem of characterization. There is naturalism in character depiction found in the work of both the late and the early of the above novelists, but there is a contrast and it is determined by the difference in psychological focusing. In short, the stream-of-consciousness novelists were, like the naturalists, trying to depict life accurately; but unlike the naturalists, the life they were concerned with was the individual's psychic life.

In examining the chief stream-of-consciousness writers in order to discover their diverse evaluations of inner awareness, we need to keep in mind two important questions: What can be accomplished by presenting character as it exists psychically? How is fictional art enriched by the depiction of inner states? The direction of the following discussion will be toward answering these questions. . . .   (1954)

MALCOLM COWLEY (1898-   )
From *The Literary Situation*

THE NEW FICTION can be recognized in the bookstores without reading a page of the text. Almost always it consists of thin books about the size of printed plays and hardly thicker than volumes of poetry. Fat novels are either naturalistic or else they are historical romances.

On the back of the dust wrapper there is a posed cabinet-size photograph of the author, who usually wears an intent and other-worldly look around the eyes. Beneath the photograph—if it doesn't fill the page, like the famous picture of Truman Capote brooding on a couch—there are critical comments, often calling attention to the depth or inwardness of the novel, its graceful irony, its meanings "on different levels," and its effective use of symbols. Naturalistic novels wear a different type of dressing gown. They give the blurb writer so much to talk about that there is room for only a small photograph, and the advance critical comments are supposed to be written by booksellers on order blanks.

Opening the book to the front matter, we usually find an epigraph or inscription. If it consists of a quotation from Rimbaud or Dante (in French or Italian), or from a seventeenth-century English author, or if there are several quotations, including one from T. S. Eliot, and another from a Greek or Roman classic, preferably Longinus' *On the Sublime*, then we can be certain that the book is new-fictional and can go on to examine the text. Let us see what remarks are suggested by its various features, including time, setting, point of view, characters, themes, structure, and style.

The *time* of the new fiction is vaguely the present, or rather it is a recent but undated yesterday. Not much time elapses from beginning to end of the action; it may be a few days or weeks, perhaps a summer (*Wait, Son, October Is Near*), at most an academic year of two semesters. Sometimes the foreground of the novel is confined to a single day, but in that case it is rounded out with memories, so that we learn to know the principal character from birth.

The *setting* is seldom one of the centers where policy decisions are made; it is never Capitol Hill or the Pentagon or the boardroom of any corporation or political London or Paris or Army headquarters in the field. These are backgrounds for novels with public or social subjects. Preferring to deal with private lives, the new fiction is likely to have a remote and peripheral scene, for example—as I think of some recent novels—a lonely ranch in Colorado, a village in East Texas, a small town in Georgia, various plantation houses in Louisiana and Mississippi (all rotting into the dank loam), a country house in Maine, a "happy rural seat" in Ontario that haunts a house in Cleveland (don't ask how), an abandoned summer hotel, two beach resorts full of homosexuals, several freshwater colleges, a private asylum, the international colony in Rome, the still more international colony in Tangier, and a caravan crossing the Sahara under the sheltering sky. There is always an excuse for assembling the characters in one of these out-of-the-way places. Sometimes it is merely the accidents of travel; more often it is a house party, a vacation, a deathbed, a wedding (dozens of weddings), a family reunion—at any rate the device permits the novelist to present his story without any of the frayed edges that are so irritating when we encounter them in life.

The *point of view* from which the story will be told is chosen with extreme care so as to give an effect of depth and immediacy. The author with X-ray eyes who could look at a scene and know what everybody was thinking—but without penetrating deeply into anyone's mind—has practically vanished from American fiction. With him has vanished the museum-guide type of author who kept judging his characters and explaining them to the reader. The new author hides his personality in the background, like a dramatist. He tries to submerge himself in one or more of the characters and he tells the story as the character sees, hears, and feels it.

This concern with point of view is not exclusively a mark of the new fiction, since it extends to almost all our postwar writing. The "new" novelists, however, have devices and refinements of their own. One device is to describe a series of events through the eyes of a first character, then of a second, then of a third, then back to the first again, and so to the end of the novel (which might be *The Disguises of Love*, by Robie Macauley). Each character offers a different picture of the situation, and the author makes no explanatory comments, thus leaving the reader with a much-desired effect of irony or ambiguity, or plain confusion. Another device is for the novelist to pretend that he is a very young or stupid person who watches the behavior of grown-ups with an innocent eye. Very often the young person is a pre-adolescent girl vaguely resembling Henry James's Maisie; there are heroines of about her age in *The Member of the Wedding*, by Carson McCullers, *The Mountain Lion*, by Jean Stafford, and *The Strange Children*, by Caroline Gordon. Again the central intelligence may be a boy, also pre-adolescent, as in Truman Capote's *Other Voices, Other Rooms* and Peter Taylor's *A Woman of Means*. The hero of *Wait, Son, October is Near*, by John Bell Clayton, is a bright ten-year-old. In *The Caged Birds*, by Leroy Leatherman, an adult drama is rather dimly registered on the rather dim consciousness of a little boy of eight. All these books, except the last, are effectively written, and two or three of them are distinguished, but there are others in the same genre that give the effect of a country-club masquerade where busty debutantes and hairy-legged attorneys come dressed as babies.

The *characters* in the new fiction are distinguished by their lack of a functional relationship with American life. They don't sow or reap, build, mine, process, promote or sell, repair, heal, plead, administer, or legislate. In a still broader sense they don't join or belong. One widely observed feature of present-day America is that the lives of most individuals are defined by their relations with an interlocking series of institutions—for example, government bureaus, churches, schools and universities, the armed services, labor unions, chambers of commerce, farm bureaus, veterans' organizations, and, for most of us, that center of our daily activities, the office. But characters in the new fiction are exceptional persons who keep away from offices—at least for the duration of the novel—and are generally as unattached as Daniel Boone.

It is true that some of them are teachers, but they don't engage in faculty politics and seldom enter a classroom. Some are housewives who never cook or clean, and some are businessmen who have retired or are on vacation or play subordinate roles as fathers of the heroes and heroines. The characters likely to be treated at length are students of both sexes, young artists and writers, gentlemen on their travels, divorced or widowed mothers, gay boys, neurotic bitches, virtuous grandfathers, old women on their deathbeds, and preternaturally wise little girls. As compared with the population at large, the characters include an abnormally large number of persons living on inherited incomes. They also include more than the average proportion of very old people and children, with a smaller proportion of men and women in the active or money-earning ages. The women, down to the age of six, are more forceful or malignant and less inhibited than the men, most of whom are victims rather than heroes or villains. Some of the men are likely to be symbolic figures—for example, a scientist as prototype of evil, a doctor or a priest to represent spiritual wisdom, and a reformer as an object of scorn.

Instead of political or social subjects the new fiction has *themes* that are taken from individual lives. The distinction becomes clear if you ask one of the authors what is the subject of his next book. "It's hard to say," he will answer; then, after a pause, he will add brightly, "I guess it's just about people." On reading the manuscript you will find that it is about people in some private crisis or dilemma that serves as the novelist's theme and his excuse for presenting a picture of human destinies.

So far the themes considered suitable for the new fiction have proved to be limited in number, and many of them keep reappearing in one book after another. One of the most popular is the initiation of a pre-adolescent girl or boy into the knowledge of sex or evil (as in *The Mountain Lion* and *Other Voices, Other Rooms*). Another is the mad infatuation of a middle-aged man or woman with a predatory younger person (as in *The Disguises of Love,* and in *The Roman Spring of Mrs. Stone,* by Tennessee Williams). Still another is the heroine's flight from reality, involving her surrender to drugs, nymphomania, or catatonic dementia (as in Paul Bowles' *The Sheltering Sky*). Some of the novels deal with the interplay between a religiously inspired character and a group of unbelievers; some show the hero or heroine struggling toward and finally reaching maturity; others, by contradiction, exalt the innocent world of childhood and depict grown persons as dangerous hypocrites. Later I shall have more to say about the novels—there are scores of them circulating in manuscript—that describe the ruin of a sensitive and truly artistic young man by his possessive mother.

The new fiction seldom deals with the familiar American theme of social mobility. In the old fiction one expected the hero (or the heroine, if she was the central character) to rise in the world like Silas Lapham and Sister Carrie and Susan Lenox. Sometimes he surprised us by falling, like Sister Carrie's lover and Dr. Richard Diver of *Tender Is The Night,* but in any case there was a vertical movement through different layers of society. In the new fiction there is little movement of the sort. Both the hero and the heroine can be expected to stay in the same position, socially speaking, though sometimes one of them suffers a moral decline. If the other characters include a man making his fortune, he is likely to be presented as a disagreeable person. Often the novelist seems to be making a plea for social stability and inherited position.

That is not the only social or political idea implied by the new fiction. Another idea suggested in many novels, including some but not all of those with a Southern background, is the foolishness of racial prejudice. Still another is the weakness and cowardice of liberals, and a fourth, expressed in terms of character, is the selfishness of reformers. Very old men and women are often depicted admiringly, as if to demonstrate that the past, with its widely accepted values and simple code of conduct, is better than the present. It remains true, however, that most of the ideas to be deduced from the new fiction are moral rather than social or political. Usually they can be translated into statements of a highly generalized type: for example, "Evil is in the human heart," "We must have compassion," "Let us be content with our lot," "Ripeness is all," "Little children, love one another!" or simply, "Mother was to blame."

The *structure* of the novels is usually balanced, efficient, economical, and tightly joined. A reader is left with the impression—which may be false in some cases—that the author has made a complete plan for the novel before setting to work on the first chapter. That is a comparatively safe method of writing novels and it has been followed by many distinguished authors. There are others, perhaps including more of the great, who have started with characters involved in a situation and have allowed them to work out their own destinies. "I write the first sentence," said Laurence Sterne, "and trust in God for the next." Dickens and most of the famous Victorians began publishing their novels by installments before they were finished and before the novelists knew how the stories would end. Jean Giraudoux said that he liked to go to the country with a ream of paper and an empty mind; when he came back to Paris his novel would be ready for publication.

There are all sorts of middle courses for novelists, but I am trying to suggest the two extremes. The second, that of Sterne and Giraudoux, implies a great deal of self-confidence, or trust in God. Even when followed by men of talent it is likely to produce formless, wasteful, inconsistent books, but the stories will flow like rivers or music and the characters may be a continual surprise to the author as well as the reader. The other method, that of the new fictionists, involves so much planning and preparation that the characters are no longer free to develop as in life. At best the stories will have an architectural form; their music is frozen and has ceased to flow; their economic structure is balanced in repose.

As for the *style* of the new fiction, there seems to be an impression that it is precious and hard to understand. The impression is justified in the case of a very few authors. Frederick Buechner, for example, likes to use glittering phrases that seem to have been picked from a jeweler's tray with a pair of tweezers. William Goyen (*The House of Breath*) writes as if from a twilight region where extreme sensitivity is on the point of being transformed into simple hallucination. Neither of them is typical of the "new" novelists. The typical style is simple and correct; often it is the sort of language that one of the characters, chosen as observer, would use in his daily life. The storytelling character is seldom or never a foul-mouthed person, and it is safe to assume that any novel peppered with obscenities belongs to the old-fictional or naturalistic school. The tone of the new writing is decorous, subdued, in the best of taste, and every sentence is clear in itself. The difficulty for the reader lies in recognizing the symbols and what the author intends by them, or—in view of the author's aloof and ironic attitude—in finding the meaning of the story as a whole.

(1954)

WILLIAM FAULKNER (1897-   )

From *An Interview*, by Jean Stein vanden Heuvel

INTERVIEWER: Mr. Faulkner, you were saying a while ago that you don't like interviews.

FAULKNER: The reason I don't like interviews is that I seem to react violently to personal questions. If the questions are about the work, I try to answer them. When they are about me, I may answer

From *Writers at Work* (*Paris Review Interviews*) edited by Malcolm Cowley (New York: Viking Press, 1959). Reprinted by permission of the publishers and Jean Stein vanden Heuvel.

or I may not, but even if I do, if the same question is asked tomorrow, the answer may be different.

INTERVIEWER: How about yourself as a writer?

FAULKNER: If I had not existed, someone else would have written me, Hemingway, Dostoevski, all of us. Proof of that is that there are about three candidates for the authorship of Shakespeare's plays. But what is important is *Hamlet* and *Midsummer Night's Dream*, not who wrote them, but that somebody did. The artist is of no importance. Only what he creates is important, since there is nothing new to be said. Shakespeare, Balzac, Homer have all written about the same things, and if they had lived one thousand or two thousand years longer, the publishers wouldn't have needed anyone since.

INTERVIEWER: But even if there seems nothing more to be said, isn't perhaps the individuality of the writer important?

FAULKNER: Very important to himself. Everybody else should be too busy with the work to care about the individuality.

INTERVIEWER: And your contemporaries?

FAULKNER: All of us failed to match our dream of perfection. So I rate us on the basis of our splendid failure to do the impossible. In my opinion, if I could write all my work again, I am convinced that I would do it better, which is the healthiest condition for an artist. That's why he keeps on working, trying again; he believes each time that this time he will do it, bring it off. Of course he won't, which is why this condition is healthy. Once he did it, once he matched the work to the image, the dream, nothing would remain but to cut his throat, jump off the other side of that pinnacle of perfection into suicide. I'm a failed poet. Maybe every novelist wants to write poetry first, finds he can't, and then tries the short story, which is the most demanding form after poetry. And, failing at that, only then does he take up novel writing.

INTERVIEWER: Is there any possible formula to follow in order to be a good novelist?

FAULKNER: Ninety-nine per cent talent . . . 99 per cent discipline . . . 99 per cent work. He must never be satisfied with what he does. It never is as good as it can be done. Always dream and shoot higher than you know you can do. Don't bother just to be better than your contemporaries or predecessors. Try to be better than yourself. An artist is a creature driven by demons. He don't know why they choose him and he's usually too busy to wonder why. He is completely amoral in that he will rob, borrow, beg, or steal from anybody and everybody to get the work done.

INTERVIEWER: Do you mean the writer should be completely ruthless?

FAULKNER: The writer's only responsibility is to his art. He will be completely ruthless if he is a good one. He has a dream. It anguishes him so much he must get rid of it. He has no peace until then. Everything goes by the board: honor, pride, decency, security, happiness, all, to get the book written. If a writer has to rob his mother, he will not hesitate; the "Ode on a Grecian Urn" is worth any number of old ladies.

INTERVIEWER: Then could the *lack* of security, happiness, honor, be an important factor in the artist's creativity?

FAULKNER: No. They are important only to his peace and contentment, and art has no concern with peace and contentment.

INTERVIEWER: Then what would be the best environment for a writer?

FAULKNER: Art is not concerned with environment either; it doesn't care where it is. If you mean me, the best job that was ever offered to me was to become a landlord in a brothel. In my opinion it's the perfect milieu for an artist to work in. It gives him perfect economic freedom; he's free of fear and hunger; he has a roof over his head and nothing whatever to do except keep a few simple accounts and to go once every month and pay off the local police. The place is quiet during the morning hours, which is the best time of the day to work. There's enough social life in the evening, if he wishes to participate, to keep him from being bored; it gives him a certain standing in his society; he has nothing to do because the madam keeps the books; all the inmates of the house are females and would defer to him and call him "sir." All the bootleggers in the neighborhood would call him "sir." And he could call the police by their first names.

So the only environment the artist needs is whatever peace, whatever solitude, and whatever pleasure he can get at not too high a cost. All the wrong environment will do is run his blood pressure up; he will spend more time being frustrated or outraged. My own experience has been that the tools I need for my trade are paper, tobacco, food, and a little whisky.

INTERVIEWER: Bourbon, you mean?

FAULKNER: No, I ain't that particular. Between scotch and nothing, I'll take scotch.

INTERVIEWER: You mentioned economic freedom. Does the writer need it?

FAULKNER: No. The writer doesn't need economic freedom. All he needs is a pencil and some paper. I've never known anything good in writing to come from having accepted any free gift of money. The good writer never applies to a foundation. He's too busy writing something. If he isn't first rate he fools himself by saying he hasn't got time or economic freedom. Good art can come out of thieves, boot-leggers, or horse swipes. People really are afraid to find out just how much hardship and poverty they can stand. They are afraid to find out how tough they are. Nothing can destroy the good writer. The only thing that can alter the good writer is death. Good ones don't have time to bother with success or getting rich. Success is feminine and like a woman; if you cringe before her, she will override you. So the way to treat her is to show her the back of your hand. Then maybe she will do the crawling.

INTERVIEWER: Can working for the movies hurt your own writing?

FAULKNER: Nothing can injure a man's writing if he's a first-rate writer. If a man is not a first-rate writer, there's not anything can help it much. The problem does not apply if he is not first rate, because he has already sold his soul for a swimming pool.

INTERVIEWER: Does a writer compromise in writing for the movies?

FAULKNER: Always, because a moving picture is by its nature a collaboration, and any collaboration is compromise because that is what the word means—to give and to take.

INTERVIEWER: Which actors do you like to work with most?

FAULKNER: Humphrey Bogart is the one I've worked with best. He and I worked together in *To Have and Have Not* and *The Big Sleep*.

INTERVIEWER: Would you like to make another movie?

FAULKNER: Yes, I would like to make one of George Orwell's 1984. I have an idea for an ending which would prove the thesis I'm always hammering at: that man is indestructible because of his simple will to freedom.

INTERVIEWER: How do you get the best results in working for the movies?

FAULKNER: The moving-picture work of my own which seemed best to me was done by the actors and the writer throwing the script away and inventing the scene in actual rehearsal just before the camera turned. If I didn't take, or feel I was capable of taking, motion-picture work seriously, out of simple honesty to motion pictures and myself too, I would not have tried. But I know now that I will never be a good motion-picture writer; so that work will never have the urgency for me which my own medium has. . . .

INTERVIEWER: You say that the writer must compromise in work-ing for the motion pictures. How about his writing? Is he under any obligation to his reader?

FAULKNER: His obligation is to get the work done the best he can do it; whatever obligation he has left over after that he can spend any way he likes. I myself am too busy to care about the public. I have no time to wonder who is reading me. I don't care about John Doe's opinion on my or anyone else's work. Mine is the standard which has to be met, which is when the work makes me feel the way I do when I read *La Tentation de Saint Antoine,* or the Old Testament. They make me feel good. So does watching a bird make me feel good. You know that if I were reincarnated, I'd want to come back a buzzard. Nothing hates him or envies him or wants him or needs him. He is never bothered or in danger, and he can eat anything.

INTERVIEWER: What technique do you use to arrive at your standard?

FAULKNER: Let the writer take up surgery or bricklaying if he is interested in technique. There is no mechanical way to get the writing done, no short cut. The young writer would be a fool to follow a theory. Teach yourself by your own mistakes; people learn only by error. The good artist believes that nobody is good enough to give him advice. He has supreme vanity. No matter how much he admires the old writer, he wants to beat him.

INTERVIEWER: Then would you deny the validity of technique?

FAULKNER: By no means. Sometimes technique charges in and takes command of the dream before the writer himself can get his hands on it. That is *tour de force* and the finished work is simply a matter of fitting bricks neatly together, since the writer knows probably every single word right to the end before he puts the first one down. This happened with *As I Lay Dying.* It was not easy. No honest work is. It was simple in that all the material was already at hand. It took me just about six weeks in the spare time from a twelve-hour-a-day job at manual labor. I simply imagined a group of people and subjected them to the simple universal natural catastrophes, which are flood and fire, with a simple natural motive to give direction to their progress. But then, when technique does not intervene, in another sense writing is easier too. Because with me there is always a point in the book where the characters themselves rise up and take charge and finish the job—say somewhere about page 275. Of course I don't know what would happen if I finished the book on page 274. The quality an artist must have is objectivity in judging his work, plus the honesty and courage not to kid himself about it. Since none of my work has met my own standards, I must judge it on the basis of that one which caused me the most grief and anguish, as the mother loves the child who became the thief or murderer more than the one who became the priest.

INTERVIEWER: What work is that?

FAULKNER: *The Sound and the Fury.* I wrote it five separate times, trying to tell the story, to rid myself of the dream which would continue to anguish me until I did. It's a tragedy of two lost women: Caddy and her daughter. Dilsey is one of my own favorite characters, because she is brave, courageous, generous, gentle, and honest. She's much more brave and honest and generous than me. . . .

INTERVIEWER: Are there any artistic advantages in casting the novel in the form of an allegory, as the Christian allegory you used in *A Fable?*

FAULKNER: Same advantage the carpenter finds in building square corners in order to build a square house. In *A Fable* the Christian allegory was the right allegory to use in that particular story, like an oblong square corner is the right corner with which to build an oblong rectangular house.

INTERVIEWER: Does that mean an artist can use Christianity simply as just another tool, as a carpenter would borrow a hammer?

FAULKNER: The carpenter we are speaking of never lacks that hammer. No one is without Christianity, if we agree on what we mean by the word. It is every individual's individual code of behavior by means of which he makes himself a better human being than his nature wants to be, if he followed his nature only. Whatever its symbol —cross or crescent or whatever—that symbol is man's reminder of his duty inside the human race. Its various allegories are the charts against which he measures himself and learns to know what he is. It cannot teach man to be good as the textbook teaches him mathematics. It shows him how to discover himself, evolve for himself a moral code and standard within his capacities and aspirations, by giving him a matchless example of suffering and sacrifice and the promise of hope. Writers have always drawn, and always will draw, upon the allegories of moral consciousness, for the reason that the allegories are matchless —the three men in *Moby Dick*, who represent the trinity of conscience: knowing nothing, knowing but not caring, knowing and caring. The same trinity is represented in *A Fable* by the young Jewish pilot officer, who said, "This is terrible. I refuse to accept it, even if I must refuse life to do so"; the old French Quartermaster General, who said, "This is terrible, but we can weep and bear it"; and the English battalion runner, who said, "This is terrible, I'm going to do something about it."

INTERVIEWER: Are the two unrelated themes in *The Wild Palms* brought together in one book for any symbolic purpose? Is it as certain critics intimate a kind of esthetic counterpoint, or is it merely haphazard?

FAULKNER: No, no. That was one story—the story of Charlotte Rittenmeyer and Harry Wilbourne, who sacrificed everything for love, and then lost that. I did not know it would be two separate stories until after I had started the book. When I reached the end of what is now the first section of *The Wild Palms*, I realized suddenly that something was missing, it needed emphasis, something to lift it like counterpoint in music. So I wrote on the "Old Man" story until "The Wild Palms" story rose back to pitch. Then I stopped the "Old Man" story at what is now its first section, and took up "The Wild Palms" story until it began again to sag. Then I raised it to pitch again with another section of its antithesis, which is the story of a man who got his love and spent the rest of the book fleeing from it, even to the extent of voluntarily going back to jail where he would be safe. They are only two stories by chance, perhaps necessity. The story is that of Charlotte and Wilbourne.

INTERVIEWER: How much of your writing is based on personal experience?

FAULKNER: I can't say. I never counted up. Because "how much" is not important. A writer needs three things, experience, observation, and imagination, any two of which, at times any one of which, can supply the lack of the others. With me, a story usually begins with a single idea or memory or mental picture. The writing of the story is simply a matter of working up to that moment, to explain why it happened or what it caused to follow. A writer is trying to create believable people in credible moving situations in the most moving way he can. Obviously he must use as one of his tools the environment which he knows. I would say that music is the easiest means in which to express, since it came first in man's experience and history. But since words are my talent, I must try to express clumsily in words what the pure music would have done better. That is, music would express better and simpler, but I prefer to use words, as I prefer to read rather than listen. I prefer silence to sound, and the image produced by words occurs in silence. That is, the thunder and the music of the prose take place in silence.

INTERVIEWER: Some people say they can't understand your writing, even after they read it two or three times. What approach would you suggest for them?

FAULKNER: Read it four times.

INTERVIEWER: You mentioned experience, observation, and imagination as being important for the writer. Would you include inspiration?

FAULKNER: I don't know anything about inspiration, because I don't know what inspiration is—I've heard about it, but I never saw it. . . .

INTERVIEWER: How did you get your background in the Bible?

FAULKNER: My Great-Grandfather Murry was a kind and gentle

man, to us children anyway. That is, although he was a Scot, he was (to us) neither especially pious nor stern either: he was simply a man of inflexible principles. One of them was, everybody, children on up through all adults present, had to have a verse from the Bible ready and glib at tongue-tip when we gathered at the table for breakfast each morning; if you didn't have your scripture verse ready, you didn't have any breakfast; you would be excused long enough to leave the room and swot one up (there was a maiden aunt, a kind of sergeant-major for this duty, who retired with the culprit and gave him a brisk breezing which carried him over the jump next time).

It had to be an authentic, correct verse. While we were little, it could be the same one, once you had it down good, morning after morning, until you got a little older and bigger, when one morning (by this time you would be pretty glib at it, galloping through without even listening to yourself since you were already five or ten minutes ahead, already among the ham and steak and fried chicken and grits and sweet potatoes and two or three kinds of hot bread) you would suddenly find his eyes on you—very blue, very kind and gentle, and even now not stern so much as inflexible; and next morning you had a new verse. In a way, that was when you discovered that your childhood was over; you had outgrown it and entered the world.

INTERVIEWER: Do you read your contemporaries?

FAULKNER: No, the books I read are the ones I knew and loved when I was a young man and to which I return as you do to old friends: the Old Testament, Dickens, Conrad, Cervantes—*Don Quixote*. I read that every year, as some do the Bible. Flaubert, Balzac —he created an intact world of his own, a bloodstream running through twenty books—Dostoevski, Tolstoi, Shakespeare. I read Melville occasionally, and of the poets Marlowe, Campion, Jonson, Herrick, Donne, Keats, and Shelley. I still read Housman. I've read these books so often that I don't always begin at page one and read on to the end. I just read one scene, or about one character, just as you'd meet and talk to a friend for a few minutes.

INTERVIEWER: And Freud?

FAULKNER: Everybody talked about Freud when I lived in New Orleans, but I have never read him. Neither did Shakespeare. I doubt if Melville did either, and I'm sure Moby Dick didn't.

INTERVIEWER: Do you ever read mystery stories?

FAULKNER: I read Simenon because he reminds me something of Chekhov.

INTERVIEWER: What about your favorite characters?

FAULKNER: My favorite characters are Sarah Gamp—a cruel, ruthless woman, a drunkard, opportunist, unreliable, most of her character was bad, but at least it was character; Mrs. Harris, Falstaff, Prince Hal, Don Quixote, and Sancho of course. Lady Macbeth I always admire. And Bottom, Ophelia, and Mercutio—both he and Mrs. Gamp coped with life, didn't ask any favors, never whined. Huck Finn, of course, and Jim. Tom Sawyer I never liked much—an awful prig. And then I like Sut Lovingood, from a book written by George Harris about 1840 or '50 in the Tennessee mountains. He had no illusions about himself, did the best he could; at certain times he was a coward and knew it and wastn't ashamed; he never blamed his misfortunes on anyone and never cursed God for them.

INTERVIEWER: Would you comment on the future of the novel?

FAULKNER: I imagine as long as people will continue to read novels, people will continue to write them, or vice versa; unless of course the pictorial magazines and comic strips finally atrophy man's capacity to read, and literature really is on its way back to the picture writing in the Neanderthal cave.

INTERVIEWER: And how about the function of the critics?

FAULKNER: The artist doesn't have time to listen to the critics. The ones who want to be writers read the reviews, the ones who want to write don't have the time to read reviews. The critic too is trying to say "Kilroy was here." His function is not directed toward the artist himself. The artist is a cut above the critic, for the artist is writing something which will move the critic. The critic is writing something which will move everybody but the artist.

INTERVIEWER: So you never feel the need to discuss your work with anyone?

FAULKNER: No, I am too busy writing it. It has got to please me and if it does I don't need to talk about it. If it doesn't please me, talking about it won't improve it, since the only thing to improve it is to work on it some more. I am not a literary man but only a writer. I don't get any pleasure from talking shop.

INTERVIEWER: Critics claim that blood relationships are central in your novels.

FAULKNER: That is an opinion and, as I have said, I don't read critics. I doubt that a man trying to write about people is any more interested in blood relationships than in the shape of their noses, unless they are necessary to help the story move. If the writer concentrates on what he does need to be interested in, which is the truth and the human heart, he won't have much time left for anything else, such as ideas and facts like the shape of noses or blood relationships, since in my opinion ideas and facts have very little connection with truth.

INTERVIEWER: Critics also suggest that your characters never consciously choose between good and evil.

FAULKNER: Life is not interested in good and evil. Don Quixote was constantly choosing between good and evil, but then he was choosing in his dream state. He was mad. He entered reality only when he was so busy trying to cope with people that he had no time to distinguish between good and evil. Since people exist only in life, they must devote their time simply to being alive. Life is motion, and motion is concerned with what makes man move—which is ambition, power, pleasure. What time a man can devote to morality, he must take by force from the motion of which he is a part. He is compelled to make choices between good and evil sooner or later, because moral conscience demands that from him in order that he can live with himself tomorrow. His moral conscience is the curse he had to accept from the gods in order to gain from them the right to dream.

INTERVIEWER: Could you explain more what you mean by motion in relation to the artist?

FAULKNER: The aim of every artist is to arrest motion, which is life, by artificial means and hold it fixed so that a hundred years later, when a stranger looks at it, it moves again since it is life. Since man is mortal, the only immortality possible for him is to leave something behind him that is immortal since it will always move. This is the artist's way of scribbling "Kilroy was here" on the wall of the final and irrevocable oblivion through which he must someday pass. . . .

(1956)

JOYCE CARY (1888-1957)

From *An Interview*,
by John Burrows and Alex Hamilton

NTERVIEWERS: Have you by any chance been shown a copy of Barbara Hardy's essay on your novels in the latest number of *Essays in Criticism?*

CARY: On "Form." Yes I saw it. Quite good, I thought.

INTERVIEWERS: Well, setting the matter of form aside for the moment, we were interested in her attempt to relate you to the tradition of the family chronicle. Is it in fact your conscious intention to re-create what she calls the pseudo-saga?

CARY: Did she say that? Must have skipped that bit.

INTERVIEWERS: Well, she didn't say "consciously," but we were interested to know whether this was your intention.

CARY: You mean, did I intend to follow up Galsworthy and Walpole? Oh, no, no, no. Family life, no. Family life just goes on. Toughest thing in the world. But of course it is also the microcosm of a world. You get everything there—birth, life, death, love and jealousy, conflict of wills, of authority and freedom, the new and the old. And I always choose the biggest stage possible for my theme.

INTERVIEWERS: What about the eighteenth-century novelists? Someone vaguely suggested that you recaptured their spirit, or something of that kind.

CARY: Vaguely is the word. I don't know who I'm like. I've been called a metaphysical novelist, and if that means I have a fairly clear and comprehensive idea of the world I'm writing about, I suppose that's true.

INTERVIEWERS: You mean an idea about the nature of the world which guides the actions of the characters you are creating?

CARY: Not so much the ideas as their background. I don't care for philosophers in books. They are always bores. A novel should be an experience and convey an emotional truth rather than arguments.

INTERVIEWERS: Background—you said background.

CARY: The whole set-up—character—of the world as we know it. Roughly, for me, the principal fact of life is the free mind. For good and evil, man is a free creative spirit. This produces the very queer world we live in, a world in continuous creation and therefore continuous change and insecurity. A perpetually new and lively world, but a dangerous one, full of tragedy and injustice. A world in everlasting conflict between the new idea and the old allegiances, new arts and new inventions against the old establishment.

INTERVIEWERS: Miss Hardy complains that the form shows too clearly in your novels.

CARY: Others complain that I don't make the fundamental idea plain enough. This is every writer's dilemma. Your form is your meaning, and your meaning dictates the form. But what you try to convey is reality—the fact plus the feeling, a total complex experience of a real world. If you make your scheme too explicit, the framework shows and the book dies. If you hide it too thoroughly, the book has no meaning and therefore no form. It is a mess.

INTERVIEWERS: How does this problem apply in *The Moonlight*?

CARY: I was dealing there with the contrast between conventional systems in different centuries—systems created by man's imagination to secure their lives and give them what they seek from life.

INTERVIEWERS: Didn't the critics call Rose a tyrant?

CARY: Oh, they were completely wrong about Rose. She was a Victorian accepting the religion and the conventions of her time and sacrificing her own happiness to carry them out. A fine woman. And no more of a tyrant than any parent who tries to guide a child in the right path. That religion, that system, has gone, but it was thoroughly good and efficient in its own time. I mean, it gave people good lives and probably all the happiness that can be achieved for anybody in this world.

INTERVIEWERS: Are the political aspects of your work controlled by the same ideas?

CARY: Religion is organized to satisfy and guide the soul— politics does the same thing for the body. Of course they overlap —this is a very rough description. But the politician is responsible for law, for physical security, and in a world tumult, of perpetual conflict, he has the alternatives, roughly again, of persuading people or shooting them. In the democracies, we persuade. And this gives great power to the spellbinder, the artist in words, the preacher, the demagogue, whatever you call him. Rousseau, Marx, Tolstoi, these were great spellbinders—as well as Lacordaire. My Nimmo is a typical spellbinder. Bonser was a spellbinder in business, the man of imagination. He was also a crook, but so are many spellbinders. Poets have started most of the revolutions, especially nationalist revolutions. On the other hand, life would die without poets, and democracy must have its spellbinders.

INTERVIEWERS: Roosevelt?

CARY: Yes, look what he did—and compare him with Wilson. Wilson was a good man, but he hadn't the genius of the spellbinder— the art of getting at people and moving the crowd.

INTERVIEWERS: Is Nimmo based on Roosevelt?

CARY: No, he belongs to the type of all of them—Juárez, Lloyd George, Bevan, Sankey and Moody, Billy Graham.

INTERVIEWERS: Do you base your characters on people you know?

CARY: Never, you can't. You may get single hints. But real people are too complex and too disorganized for books. They aren't simple enough. Look at all the great heroes and heroines, Tom Jones, Madame Bovary, Anna Karenina, Baron Charlus, Catherine Linton: they are essentially characters from fable, and so they must be to take their place in a formal construction which is to have a meaning. A musician does not write music by trying to fit chords into his whole. The chords arise from the developments of his motives.

INTERVIEWERS: In one of your prefaces you said, didn't you, that Jimson's father came from life?

CARY: I met an old man, an artist who had been in the Academy and a success, and was then ruined by the change of taste when the impressionists created their new symbolic school. But I didn't use him in my book, I don't know anything about his character, only his tragedy. A very common one in this world. (*Suddenly*) The French seem to take me for an existentialist in Sartre's sense of the word. But I'm not. I am influenced by the solitude of men's minds, but equally by the unity of their fundamental character and feelings, their sympathies which bring them together. I believe that there is such a thing as unselfish love and beauty. I am obliged to believe in God as a person. I don't suppose any church would accept me, but I believe in God and His grace with an absolute confidence. It is by His grace that we know beauty and love, that we have all that makes life worth living in a tough, dangerous, and unjust world. Without that belief I could not make sense of the world and I could not write. Of course, if you say I am an existentialist in the school of Kierkegaard, that is more reasonable. But existentialism without a god is nonsense—it atomizes a world which is plainly a unity. It produces merely frustration and defeat. How can one explain the existence of personal feelings, love and beauty, in nature, unless a person, God, is there? He's there as much as hydrogen gas. He is a fact of experience. And one must not run away from experience. I don't believe in miracles. I'm not talking here of faith cures—but some breach in the fundamental consistency of the world character which is absolutely impossible. I mean absolutely. (*With emphasis*) God is a character, a real and consistent being, or He is nothing. If God did a miracle He would deny His own nature and the universe would simply blow up, vanish, become nothing. And we can't even conceive nothingness. The world is a definite character. It *is*, and therefore it is *something*. And it can't be any other thing. Aquinas tells you all the things that God can't do without contradicting himself.

INTERVIEWERS: But about existentialism.

CARY: Kierkegaard states the uniqueness of the individual and I stand by that.

INTERVIEWERS: That's what you meant, then, when you said that what makes men tick should be the main concern of the novelist? The character's principle of unity?

CARY: And action, their beliefs. You've got to find out what people *believe*, what is pushing them on.... And of course it's a matter, too, of the simpler emotional drives—like ambition and love. These are the real stuff of the novel, and you can't have any sort of real form unless you've got an ordered attitude towards them.

INTERVIEWERS: But the fundamental beliefs are not always the most apparent, or, it seems to us, the most successful of the achievements in the novel. We were expecting, for instance, a much closer analysis of the religious beliefs of Brown in *To Be a Pilgrim*. But we felt, in fact, that what came across most successfully were the emotional responses of people to people—compelling, for instance, Lucy to follow Brown.

CARY: The details were there once. That is, Brown's arguments were there, and Lucy's response. But Lucy was only one character, one motive in the symphony. And also I was up against the problem of explicit statement. I may have cut too much, but the book is long and packed already. The essence of Lucy was her deep faith. She wasn't the kind of person who can float along from day to day like a piece of newspaper or a banana skin in the gutter. And in the book, I had her feelings expressed. But I cut them somewhere in the rewriting. I rewrite a great deal and I work over the whole book and cut out anything that does not belong to the emotional development, the texture of feeling. I left too much of the religious argument in *Except the Lord* and people criticize it as too explicit or dull.

INTERVIEWERS: Do you find in those later stages that you're primarily concerned with the more technical side of "form"? With, for example, managing the flashback? And do you think, incidentally, that you owe that particular trick to the films? I believe that you worked on a film in Africa.

CARY: No, I don't really think it has anything to do with films. The flashback in my novels is not just a trick. In, for example, *The Moonlight*, I used it in order to make my theme possible. It was essential to compare two generations. You can't do that without a flashback contrast; the chronological run-through by itself is no good.

INTERVIEWERS: In the preface to *Herself Surprised* you mentioned a technical difficulty you found yourself in. You wanted to show everything through the eyes of Sara, but found that to make her see everything diluted her character. This was the soliloquy as flashback. This struck us as the same dilemma that James found himself in when writing *What Maisie Knew*. Is this a just parallel? Do you read James?

CARY: Yes, but James is not very remarkable technically. He's one of our very greatest novelists, but you will not learn much by studying his technique. *What Maisie Knew*, that was one of the packed ones, wasn't it? Almost too packed. I enjoyed its intense appreciation of the child's nature, and the cruel imbecility of the world in which she was thrown about. But on the whole I prefer the beautifully clear atmosphere of a book like *The Europeans* or *Daisy Miller*—all James is in *Daisy Miller*.

INTERVIEWERS: Have you read *The Bostonians?* There was the spellbinder.

CARY: No, I haven't read that.

INTERVIEWERS: *The Princess Casamassima?*

CARY: I'm afraid I haven't read that either. Cecil is always telling me to read her and I must. But I read James a good deal. There are times you need James, just as there are times when you must have Proust—in his very different world of change. The essential thing about James is that he came into a different, a highly organized, a hieratic society, and for him it was not only a very good and highly civilized society, but static. It was the best the world could do. But it was already subject to corruption. This was the center of James' moral idea—that everything good was, for that reason, specially liable to corruption. Any kind of goodness, integrity of character, exposed that person to ruin. And the whole civilization, because it was a real civilization, cultivated and sensitive, was fearfully exposed to frauds and go-getters, brutes and grabbers. This was his tragic theme. But my world is quite different—it is intensely dynamic, a world in creation. In this world, politics is like navigation in a sea without charts and wise men live the lives of pilgrims.

INTERVIEWERS: Have you sympathy with those who most uncompromisingly pursue their own free idea whatever the opposition?

CARY: I don't put a premium on aggression. Oh, no, no, no. I'm no life-force man. Critics write about my vitality. What is vitality? As a principle it is a lot of balls. The life force is rubbish, an abstraction, an idea without character. Shaw's tale of life force is either senseless rubbish or he really means Shaw—Shaw as God's mind. The life force doesn't exist. Show me some in a bottle. The life of the world is the nature of God, and God is as real as the trees.

INTERVIEWERS: Which novelists do you think have most influenced you?

CARY: Influenced? Oh, lots. Hundreds. Conrad had a great deal at one point. I've got a novel upstairs I wrote forty years ago in Africa, under his influence. But I read very few novels nowadays. I read memoirs and history. And the classics. I've got them at my fingertips and I can turn up the points I want. I don't read many modern novels, I haven't time, but those I do read are often very good. There is plenty of good work being done, and in Britain the public for good work has enormously increased in my liftime—especially in the last thirty years.

INTERVIEWERS: Do you find, then, that conversation with the novelists of today helps?

CARY: Conversation?

INTERVIEWERS: I mean apart from the personal stimulus, do you find that what they have to say helps to resolve technical problems?

CARY: Oh, no. Not particularly. We chatter. But you have to work problems out for yourself, on paper. Put the stuff down and read it—to see if it works. Construction is a complicated job—later I'll show you my apparatus.

INTERVIEWERS: Is there only one way to get a thing right? How close is form?

CARY: That's a difficult question. Often you have very little room for maneuver. See Proust's letter to Mme. Schiff about Swann, saying he had to make Swann ridiculous. A novelist is often in Proust's jam.

INTERVIEWERS: You are a determinist—you think even novelists are pushed by circumstances?

CARY: Everyone but a lunatic has reason for what he does. Yes, in that sense I am a determinist. But I believe, with Kant, that the mind is self-determined. That is, I believe intensely in the creative freedom of the mind. That is indeed absolutely essential to man's security in a chaotic world of change. He is faced all the time with unique complex problems. To sum them up for action is an act of creative imagination. He fits the different elements together in a coherent whole and invents a rational act to deal with it. He requires to be free, he requires his independence and solitude of mind, he requires his freedom of mind and imagination. Free will is another matter—it is a term, or rather a contradiction in terms, which leads to continual trouble. The will is never free—it is always attached to an object, a purpose. It is simply the engine in the car—it can't steer. It is the mind, the reason, the imagination that steers.

Of course, anyone can deny the freedom of the mind. He can argue that our ideas are conditioned. But anyone who argues so must not stop there. He must deny all freedom and say that the world is simply an elaborate kind of clock. He must be a behaviorist. There is no alternative, in logic, between behaviorism, mechanism, and the personal God who is the soul of beauty, love, and truth. And if you believe in behaviorism, none of these things has any real existence. They are cogwheels in the clock, and you yourself do not exist as a person. You are a delusion. So take your choice. Either it is personal or it is a delusion—a delusion rather difficult to explain. . . .   (1955)

JACK KEROUAC (1922-   )
Essentials of Spontaneous Prose

 ET-UP   The object is set before the mind, either in reality, as in sketching (before a landscape or teacup or old face) or is set in the memory wherein it becomes the sketching from memory of a definite image-object.

PROCEDURE   Time being of the essence in the purity of speech, sketching language is undisturbed flow from the mind of personal secret idea-words, *blowing* (as per jazz musician) on subject of image.

METHOD   No periods separating sentence-structures already arbitrarily riddled by false colons and timid usually needless commas— but the vigorous space dash separating rhetorical breathing (as jazz musician drawing breath between outblown phrases)—"measured pauses which are the essentials of our speech"—"divisions of the *sounds* we hear"—"time and how to note it down." (William Carlos Williams)

SCOPING   Not "selectivity" of expression but following free deviation (association) of mind into limitless blow-on-subject seas of thought, swimming in sea of English with no discipline other than rhythms of exhalation and expostulated statement, like a fist coming down on a table with each complete utterance, bang! (the space dash)—Blow as deep as you want—write as deeply, fish as far down as you want, satisfy yourself first, then reader cannot fail to receive telepathic shock and meaning-excitement by same laws operating in his own human mind.

LAG IN PROCEDURE   No pause to think of proper word but the infantile pileup of scatalogical buildup words till satisfaction is gained, which will turn out to be a great appending rhythm to a thought and be in accordance with Great Law of timing.

TIMING   Nothing is muddy that *runs in time* and to laws of *time* —Shakespearian stress of dramatic need to speak now in own unalterable way or forever hold tongue—*no revisions* (except obvious rational mistakes, such as names or *calculated* insertions in act of not writing but *inserting*).

CENTER OF INTEREST   Begin not from preconceived idea of what to say about image but from jewel center of interest in subject of image at *moment* of writing, and write outwards swimming in sea of language to peripheral release and exhaustion—Do not afterthink except for poetic or P. S. reasons. Never afterthink to "improve" or defray impressions, as the best writing is always the most painful personal wrung-out tossed from cradle warm protective mind—tap from yourself the song of yourself, *blow!—now!—your* way is your only way— "good"—or "bad"—always honest, ("ludicrous"), spontaneous, "confessional" interesting, because not "crafted." Craft *is* craft.

STRUCTURE OF WORK   Modern bizarre structures (science fiction, etc.) arise from language being dead, "different" themes give illusion of "new" life. Follow roughly outlines in outfanning movement over subject, as river rock, so mindflow over jewel-center need (run your mind over it, *once*) arriving at pivot, where what was dim-formed "beginning" becomes sharp-necessitating "ending" and language shortens in race to wire of time-race of work, following laws of Deep Form, to conclusion, last words, last trickle—Night is The End.

MENTAL STATE   If possible write "without consciousness" in semi-trance (as Yeats' later "trance writing") allowing subconscious to admit in own uninhibited interesting necessary and so "modern" language what conscious art would censor, and write excitedly, swiftly, with writing-or-typing-cramps, in accordance (as from center to periphery) with laws of orgasm, Reich's "beclouding of consciousness." *Come* from within, out—to relaxed and said.   (1958)

Belief and Technique for Modern Prose

LIST OF ESSENTIALS

1. Scribbled secret notebooks, and wild typewritten pages, for yr own joy
2. Submissive to everything, open, listening
3. Try never get drunk outside yr own house
4. Be in love with yr life
5. Something that you feel will find its own form
6. Be crazy dumbsaint of the mind
7. Blow as deep as you want to blow

Reprinted from *Evergreen Review*, Vol. 2, No. 8 (Spring, 1959). Copyright © 1960 by Jack Kerouac. Reprinted by permission of The Sterling Lord Agency.

8. Write what you want bottomless from bottom of the mind
9. The unspeakable visions of the individual
10. No time for poetry but exactly what is
11. Visionary tics shivering in the chest
12. In tranced fixation dreaming upon object before you
13. Remove literary, grammatical and syntactical inhibition
14. Like Proust be an old teahead of time
15. Telling the true story of the world in interior monolog
16. The jewel center of interest is the eye within the eye
17. Write in recollection and amazement for yourself
18. Work from pithy middle eye out, swimming in language sea
19. Accept loss forever   (1959)

ALAIN ROBBE-GRILLET (1922-   )
Old "Values" and the New Novel
(Nature, Humanism, Tragedy)

> Tragedy is but a means of accepting human misfortune,
> of subsuming human misery, and therefore of justifying it
> as necessary, as a kind of wisdom or purification. To reject
> this salvage operation and to seek out technical means not
> to yield treasonably to it (for nothing is more insidious than
> tragedy) is in our time a necessary undertaking.
>   —ROLAND BARTHES

wo YEARS AGO, in an article entitled "A Fresh Start for Fiction," I made an effort to define the direction which might be taken by a new and as yet hesitant spirit of research in fiction. One point which I took for granted was the complete rejection of the old myths of *profondeur*, or depth of meaning in objects. The almost unanimously violent reactions of critics, the objections raised by esteemed friends proved, however, that I had proceeded much too hastily. Aside from a few persons who were themselves engaged in similar artistic, literary, or philosophic endeavors, no one was willing to concede that such a position did not lead necessarily to a denial of man himself. It became apparent, in fact, that there existed a quite tenacious fidelity to those old "myths."

That writers as different as François Mauriac and André Rousseaux should, for example, agree in denouncing the exclusive description of *surfaces* as a gratuitous mutilation of the novelist's art, as a result of

Translated by Bruce Morisette, *Evergreen Review*, Vol. III, No. 9, Summer 1959 and reprinted with permission of the Grove Press.

blindness on the part of a young literary revolutionary caught up in some sort of sterile despair, was not after all too surprising. More unexpected, and more disturbing, was the position—identical in many respects—taken by certain materialistic critics who did not hesitate to rely, in judging my programme, on certain "values" dangerously similar to the traditional values of Christianity. (And yet one could scarcely accuse this group of religious bias!) In both camps the fundamental principle was the same: an unabandonable solidarity between the human spirit and the world. Art had to play its "natural," reassuring role of mediator; and I was condemned in the name of "humanity."

Besides, they said, I was being rather naïve in claiming to deny depth of meaning; my own novels, it appeared, were only interesting, or readable, to the extent—to what extent was a matter of argument —that they expressed such depths without my realizing it.

It is obvious that there is only a rather loose parallelism between the three works I have published to date and my theoretical views on the possible future of the novel. Surely everyone will agree that a two- or three-hundred page novel must necessarily be more complex than a ten page article, and that it is always easier to point out a new path than to follow it. It does not ensue, however, that a partial—or even complete—failure in such an effort must be construed as decisive proof that the direction itself was wrong.

Finally, it must be emphasized that Humanism—Christian or otherwise—characteristically strives to reach out for and salvage *everything*, including whatever may attempt to restrict it, or to challenge it in its entirety. This salvaging of the opposition is in fact one of the mainsprings of its action.

It is not that I insist on justifying myself at any cost; I am merely trying to clarify the issues. The various positions outlined above are extremely useful for this purpose. What I am attempting here is less to refute certain arguments than to define their true import, and to state precisely how and why I must differ. Polemics are always useless; but the opportunity to engage in real dialogue should be accepted. And if dialogue is impossible, we must know the reason why. In any case we are all, I believe, sufficiently interested in these problems to warrant further open discussion.

Is there not, first of all, something faintly fraudulent about this term "humanity" that is constantly being thrown up to us? If the word is not entirely devoid of meaning, just what does it signify?

Apparently those who use it constantly, who employ it as their single criterion for praise or blame, confuse (voluntarily, perhaps) the precise and strict consideration of man in his situation in the world—the phenomena of man's existence—with a certain anthropocentric atmosphere, vague yet all-encompassing, that confers on everything its so-called "meaning," that is, that sends out through the interior of everything a more or less crafty network of feelings and thoughts. By simplifying the position of these new inquisitors, we may summarize it in two sentences. If I say, "The world is mankind," I shall always obtain absolution; but if I say, "Things are things, and man is only man," I shall be immediately judged guilty of a crime against humanity.

The crime is to state that something exists in the world which is not mankind, which makes no signs to man, which has nothing in common with him. From their viewpoint, the crime lies especially in recognizing this separation, this distance, without making any effort to transcend or to sublimate it.

Let us try another approach. How can a work of art be "inhuman," or "anti-human"? How can they, in particular, accuse a novel of turning against or away from man when it follows from page to page each of his steps, describing only what he does, what he sees, or what he imagines? And let it be made clear at once that it is not the character in the novel who is under attack from the critics. In so far as he is a "character," an individual moved by torments and passions, no one will ever accuse *him* of being inhuman, even if he should be a sadistic psychopath and a criminal—rather the contrary, many would say.

But in the novel the eye of this man comes to rest on things with a hard insistence: he sees them, but refuses to make them part of him, refuses to enter into any conniving or doubtful relationship with them, refuses to ask anything of them or to feel towards them any agreement or disagreement whatsoever. He may even, by chance, make them a support for his passion, for the line of sight that he directs at the world. But his glance limits itself to taking precise measurements; and his passion, likewise, stops at the surface of objects, without trying to penetrate them, since there is nothing inside, and without pretending to address to them the least emotional appeal, since they would not answer.

To condemn in the name of "humanity" a novel that presents such a character is to adopt the viewpoint of Humanism, which decrees that it is not enough to depict man as *there*, where he is, but commands us to proclaim that man is everywhere. Under the pretext that man can have only a subjective knowledge of the world, Humanism chooses man as the justification of everything. Like a "soul bridge" erected between man and things, the vision of Humanism is, above all, a pledge of solidarity.

In the realm of literature this solidarity is expressed mainly through the systematic search for analogies, or for analogical relationships.

Metaphor, in fact, is never an innocent figure of speech. To say that time is "capricious" or a mountain "majestic," to speak of the "heart" of the forest, of a "pitiless" sun, of a village "crouching" in the hollow of a valley is, to some extent, to furnish information about the things themselves: forms, dimensions, situations, etc. But the choice of an analogical vocabulary, however simple, always goes beyond giving an account of purely physical data; and what is added cannot be attributed to literary concerns only. The height of the mountain takes on, regardless of the writer's intention, a moral value; the heat of the sun becomes the result of an implied volition. In almost all contemporary literature these anthropomorphic analogies are reiterated too insistently, too coherently, not to be regarded as clues to a whole metaphysical system.

One must conclude that the writers who use such terminology are more or less consciously setting up a constant *rapport* between the universe and the human being who inhabits it. Thus the feelings of man are made to appear to originate one by one from his contacts with the world, and to find in the world their natural correspondences, if not their fulfillment.

Metaphor, which is supposed to express only comparison without concealed meaning, always introduces in fact a subterranean communication, a movement of sympathy—or of antipathy—which is its true *raison d'être*. As far as comparison is concerned, metaphor is nearly always useless, adding nothing new to the description. What loss would the village suffer if it were merely "situated" in the hollow of the valley? The word "crouching" gives no additional information. It does, on the other hand, transport the reader (guided by the author) into the hypothetical soul of the village. If I accept the word "crouching" I am no longer merely a spectator; I become myself the village (for the duration of the phrase), and the hollow of the valley functions as a sort of pit in which I seek refuge.

Taking these adhesive possibilities of the metaphor as their stronghold, the defenders of metaphor will reply that it thus possesses the advantage of bringing out an element not previously felt. Becoming the village—they say—the reader will project himself into the situation of the village, and therefore understand it better. Similarly for the mountain: I will depict it better, they claim, by stating that it is majestic than by measuring the angle at which my sight must be lifted to judge its height. . . . And this is sometimes true; but such procedure always implies a more serious counterpart. It is precisely this participation that is dangerous, because it leads directly to the idea of a hidden unity.

In truth, one must add, this additional benefit in descriptive value is only an excuse: the true practitioners of the metaphor aim only at the idea of a non-descriptive communication. If they lacked the verb "crouch" they would not even mention the position of the village. The heights of the mountain would mean nothing to them if it did not offer the moral spectacle of "majesty." . . .

Everything is contaminated. Above all the novel, which is the primary domain in our days of the tragic spirit. From women in love who become nuns to policemen who become gangsters, including along the way tormented criminals, prostitutes with pure souls, righteous men constrained by their conscience to commit injustices, sadists motivated by love, lunatics led by logic, the typical "character" of the novel must be, above all else, a *double* being. The plot will be "human" to the degree that it is equivocally dual, and the whole novel will be regarded as "true" in so far as it contains contradictions.

It is easy to laugh at this; it is less easy to free oneself from the conditioning effects imposed by tragedy on our mental patterns. One can go so far as to state that rejecting the ideas of "nature" and predestination leads *directly* to tragedy. There is no significant piece of contemporary literature that does not express at the same time the affirmation of our freedom and the "tragic" principle of its abandonment.

At least two great novels, in recent decades, have presented us with two new forms of this fatal complicity, under the names of *absurdity* and *nausea*.

Albert Camus, everyone knows, has designated as *absurdity* the impassable abyss that stands between man and the world, between the aspirations of the human spirit and the incapacity of the world to satisfy them. The "absurd" is therefore, for him, neither in man nor in things, but in the impossibility of establishing between the two any *rapport* other than "strangeness."

Readers must have noticed, however, that the hero of *L'Étranger* (*The Stranger*) carries on with the world an obscure kind of connivance, composed of bitterness and fascination. The relationships between this and the objects around him are in no way innocent: "absurdity" constantly leads to disappointment, withdrawal, revolt. It would hardly be an exaggeration to argue that it is actually *things* that finally draw the protagonist into his criminal act: the sun, the sea, the dazzling sand, the glistening knife, the spring gushing from the rocks, the revolver. . . . And, as to be expected, the principal role, among these things, is played by Nature.

Nor is the novel written in as *neutral* or "cleansed" style as the first pages might lead us to believe. Instead, only objects already burdened with a flagrantly obvious human significance are neutralized, carefully, and for moral reasons (thus the mother's coffin, described minutely with respect to the form and depth of penetration of its screws). Together with this we discover, more and more as the moment of the murder approaches, the most revealing classical metaphors, referring directly to man, or implying his omnipresence. The countryside is "gorged with sunlight," the evening is "like a melancholy truce," the holes in the roadway reveal the "shining flesh" of the tar, the earth is "blood colored," the sunlight is a "dazzling rain," its reflection on a shell is a "sword of light," the day has "cast anchor in an ocean of boiling metal." . . . Without counting the "breathing" of the "lazy" waves, the "sleeping" promontory, the "panting" sea and the "cymbals" of the sun. . . .

The central scene of the novel is the perfect image of a painful solidarity. The implacable sun is always "the same," its reflection on the knife blade held by the Arab "touches" the hero's forehead and "grinds into" his eyes. His hand clenches the revolver; he wishes to "shake" the sun; he fires repeatedly, four times. "And it was like four sharp knocks that I had struck upon the door of misfortune."

Thus "absurdity" turns out to be a form of tragic Humanism. It is not a recognition of the separation between man and objects. It is a lovers' quarrel between them, which leads to a crime of passion. The world is accused of complicity in murder.

When Sartre writes (in his *Explication de L'Étranger*) that the Stranger "refuses anthropomorphism," he gives us, as proved by the above citations, an incomplete view of the work. Sartre has certainly noticed these passages, but prefers to think that Camus, "unfaithful to his principles, is creating poetry." Could one not say, rather, that these metaphors are the real "explication" of the novel? Camus does not refuse anthropomorphism, but uses it with great economy and subtlety, in order to give it greater weight.

All of which fits into the pattern, since the real object is, as Sartre admits, to show us (in Pascal's words) "the natural misery of our condition." . . .   (1959)

BIOGRAPHICAL NOTES

AUDEN, WYNSTAN HUGH (1907-   ). English poet, editor, and teacher. Professor of Poetry at Oxford from 1955-1960; now an American citizen.

BALZAC, HONORÉ DE (1799-1850). French novelist, whose series of novels in the monumental *Human Comedy* (144 projected titles, 99 actually written in some 20 years) attempted to portray the whole of society in France, from the Empire through the July Monarchy.

BAUDELAIRE, CHARLES (1821-1867). French poet and critic, officially labeled a "Symbolist" by literary historians. His defense of Flaubert is an interesting effort to relate *avant-gardisme* in both poetry and the novel.

BOWEN, ELIZABETH (1899-   ). English novelist, whose carefully constructed books (*Friends and Relations*, 1931; *The Death of the Heart*, 1938; *The Heat of the Day*, 1949, etc.) mirror the technical concerns she treats in the passages we have selected for this volume.

BURNEY, FANNY (Frances Burney, 1752-1840). English novelist, whose epistolary novel *Evelina* (1778) won Dr. Johnson's praise. Her *Preface* is an early definition of the novel of manners.

CARY, JOYCE (1888-1957). English novelist, colonial officer; author of two trilogies (*Herself Surprised*, 1941; *To Be a Pilgrim*, 1942; *The Horse's Mouth*, 1944; and *A Prisoner of Grace*, 1952; *Except the Lord*, 1953; and *Not Honour More*, 1955) as well as other single novels. A book of critical lectures (*Art and Reality*, 1957) was completed just before his death.

CONRAD, JOSEPH (1857-1924). Polish-born English novelist, whose books (*Almayer's Folly*, 1895; *Lord Jim*, 1900; *Typhoon*, 1903; *Nostromo*, 1904; *The Secret Agent*, 1907; *The Arrow of Gold*, 1919, etc.) mark him as one of great craftsmen of the novel in English.

COWLEY, MALCOLM (1898-   ). American critic and editor; author of *Exile's Return* (1934)—a chronicle about expatriate writers in Paris after World War I; *After the Genteel Tradition* (1937), and *The Literary Situation* (1954).

DIDEROT, DENIS (1713-1784). French philosopher, chief editor of the *Encyclopédie*, novelist, literary and art critic. His piece on Richardson is typical of early criticism on the novel, with its stress on psychological accuracy and moral didacticism.

DOSTOIEVSKY, FYODOR (1821-1881). Russian novelist and critic, author of *Crime and Punishment* (1866), *The Idiot* (1869), *The Possessed* (1871-1872), and *The Brothers Karamazov* (1880), etc. His own works reflect the same moral concern that he attributes to George Sand.

DUNLOP, JOHN (1785-1842). English critic and one of the first to write a history of fiction, where—after the romance—the novel is treated as a serious form.

EDGEWORTH, MARIA (1767-1849). English novelist. Her *Castle Rackrent* (1800) has a claim to being one of the first local-color novels, since it aims to depict a truthful picture of life on an Irish estate.

ELIOT, GEORGE (Mary Ann Evans, 1819-1880). English novelist, author of *Adam Bede* (1859), *Silas Marner* (1861), *Middlemarch* (1871-1872), etc.

FAULKNER, WILLIAM (1897-   ). American novelist, Nobel Prize winner in 1950; author of *The Sound and the Fury* (1929), *Sanctuary* (1931), *Light in August* (1932), *The Hamlet* (1940), *Intruder in the Dust* (1948), *A Fable* (1954), etc.

FIELDING, HENRY (1717-1754). English novelist and playwight, best known for his novels *Joseph Andrews* (1742) and *Tom Jones* (1749). The *Preface* to the former attempts to define the laws for this "new" genre—the comic epic in prose, or the novel.

FLAUBERT, GUSTAVE (1821-1880). French novelist, whose excerpts from his letters demonstrate the immense difficulty he found in writing, and the care he devoted to his style in his prose fiction: *Madame Bovary* (1856), *The Sentimental Education* (1869), *Three Tales* (1877), and the posthumuous and incomplete *Bouvard and Pécuchet* (1881).

FORD, FORD MADOX (Ford Madox Hueffer, 1873-1939). English novelist, collaborator with Joseph Conrad, author of *The Good Soldier* (1915), *No More Parades* (1925), *A Man Could Stand Up* (1926), etc. His comments on the methods he and Conrad employed show their careful technical concerns.

FORSTER, E. M. (1879-   ). English novelist, critic, teacher at Cambridge; author of *Where Angels Fear to Tread* (1905), *The Longest Journey* (1907), *A Passage to India* (1924), etc. *Aspects of the Novel* has become one of the classics of criticism about the novel.

GIDE, ANDRÉ (1869-1951). French novelist, critic, essayist, and dramatist, whose novels dealt chiefly with adolescent revolt, the decline of bourgeois families, and the problem of creation in the arts: *The Immoralist* (1902), *Strait is the Gate* (1909), *The Caves of the Vatican* (1914—translated as *Lafcadio's Adventures*), *The Pastoral Symphony* (1919), *The Counterfeiters* (1925), etc. Awarded the Nobel Prize in 1947.

HAEDENS, KLÉBER (1913-   ). French critic and essayist, whose *Paradox about the Novel* (1941) assesses, among other things, techniques peculiar to the craft of the novel.

HAWTHORNE, NATHANIEL (1804-1864). American novelist and writer of romances, friend of Herman Melville, author of *Twice-Told Tales* (1837), *The Scarlet Letter* (1850), *The House of the Seven Gables* (1851), etc. His *Preface* to the latter book is an interesting and late defense of the romance against the more "realistic" novel.

HICKS, GRANVILLE (1901-   ). American critic and former Marxist, whose earlier writings placed the development of American literature within the context of the class struggle, and who applied the Marxist dialectic to contemporary novelists. His chief critical study during this earlier period was *The Great Tradition* (1933, revised 1935).

HOWELLS, WILLIAM DEAN (1837-1920). American novelist, editor of *The Atlantic Monthly*, friend of Mark Twain, advocate of French and Russian realism—although he maintained that American realism should portray American life in its "more smiling aspects." His best-known novel is *The Rise of Silas Lapham* (1885).

HUMPHREY, ROBERT (1919-   ). American teacher and critic.

JAMES, HENRY (1843-1916). American novelist, later a British citizen, brother of the pragmatist philosopher and psychologist William James. Among Henry James' novels are *Daisy Miller* (1879), *The Portrait of a Lady* (1881), *The Bostonians* (1886), *The Wings of the Dove* (1902), *The Ambassadors* (1903), *The Golden Bowl* (1904), etc. James continued the line of Flaubert, Turgenev and Conrad in his intense dedication to the conscious refinement of the art of writing prose fiction; and his device of employing a "detached observer" through whose consciousness we receive our impressions of characters and events has been emulated by many modern writers.

KEROUAC, JACK (1921-   ). American novelist and poet, one of the leaders of the "Beat Generation" or "Beat Movement," whose novels include *On the Road* (1957), *Visions of Cody* (1959), etc.

LEVIN, HARRY (1912-   ). American critic and scholar, Babbitt Professor at Harvard, a leading authority on both the English Renaissance and the nineteenth- and twentieth-century novel.

LIDDELL, ROBERT (1908-   ). English critic and novelist, whose two books about the novel—*A Treatise on the Novel* (1947), and *Some Principles of Fiction* (1953) are rich in insights about the limitations and potentialities of the novel as a genre.

LUBBOCK, PERCY (1879-   ). English critic, whose *Craft of Fiction* (1921) has become one of the classics of criticism on the novel. Ardent admirer of Henry James, Lubbock was chiefly occupied with the problem of narrative technique.

MANZONI, ALESSANDRO (1785-1873). Italian novelist, poet, playwright and critic. His most famous work was the novel *I promessi sposi* (*The Betrothed*, 1825-1827), which established him as the leader of Italian Romanticism. *Carmagnola* (1820) and *Adelchi* (1822) were two historical dramas. The essay *On the Historical Novel*, despite its occasional humor, is a serious defense of the genre and its practitioners.

MAUPASSANT, GUY DE (1850-1893). French novelist, disciple of Zola and member of the Médan group that worked under the aegis of the older writer; author of some 300 short stories as well as the novels *Une Vie* (*A Life*, 1883) and *Bel Ami* (*Dear Friend*, 1885).

MAURIAC, FRANÇOIS (1885-   ). French novelist and essayist, whose essentially Christian and Catholic concept of the novel is evident in such works as *Thérèse Desqueyroux* (1927), *Nest of Vipers* (1932), *End of the Night* (1935), *The Weakling* (1951), etc. He received a Nobel Prize in 1952.

ORTEGA Y GASSET, JOSÉ (1883-   ). Spanish essayist and philosopher, best known for his *Revolt of the Masses* (1930), most of whose works—such as the *Dehumanization of Art* (1925)—are con-concerned with what he considers to be the crisis in European culture.

ROBBE-GRILLET, ALAIN (1922-   ). French novelist and critic, whose books are sometimes referred to as examples of the "anti-novel."

ROUSSEAU, JEAN-JACQUES (1712-1778). French philosopher, musician, novelist and man of letters, among whose many writings were

The Social Contract (1762), *The Confessions* (1770-1788), and the epistolary novel *Julie, or the New Eloïse* (1761)—one of the eighteenth century's most influential novels.

SADE, MARQUIS DE (1740-1814). French essayist and writer of short novels, many of the latter strongly pornographic. The excerpts included in this volume from *The Sketch about Novels* (1800) point to the possibility of the novel enjoying sexual franchise without being labeled immoral. His fiction included *Justine, or Virtue's Sorrows* (1791), *Aline and Valcour* (1793), and *Philosophy in the Bedroom* (1795).

SCHLEGEL, FRIEDRICH (1772-1829). German critic and novelist (*Lucinda,* 1799), and a leading theorist for Romanticism, whose ideas were popularized by his brother August Wilhelm.

SCHORER, MARK (1908-   ). Novelist, critic, teacher, editor; Professor of English at the University of California at Berkeley. The portion of the essay we include concerns how a novelist manipulates "real" life to produce an organic whole in his work. Author of the monumental biography, *Sinclair Lewis* (1961).

SCOTT, SIR WALTER (1771-1832). Scottish poet, dramatist, novelist, and publisher. His historical novels such as *Waverley* (1814), *Ivanhoe* (1819), and *Kenilworth* (1821) set the pattern for most subsequent works in this genre during the nineteenth century. His tribute to Jane Austen is interesting, in that he acknowledges her talent for attaining what he was unable to perform.

SMOLLETT, TOBIAS (1721-1771). English surgeon, novelist, and translator of *Don Quixote* (1775). His novels include *Roderick Random* (1748), *Peregrine Pickle* (1751, revised 1758), and *Humphrey Clinker* (1771). The *Preface* to the first is an early discrimination between the romance and the "real" novel.

STAËL, MME. DE (1766-1817). French woman of letters whose chief contribution was to introduce German literature to France; friend of the Schlegel brothers. Her two novels were *Delphine* (1802) and *Corinne* (1807)—the latter a prime example of the artist-novel.

STENDHAL (Henri Beyle, 1783-1842). French novelist, music and art historian, and journalist. His novels—never popular in his own day—include *Armance* (1827), *The Red and the Black* (1830), *Lucien Leuwen* (1834, unfinished), *The Charterhouse of Parma* (1839), and *Lamiel* (1840).

TOLSTOI, COUNT LEO (1828-1910). Russian novelist (*War and Peace,* 1865-1869; *Anna Karenina,* 1875-1877; *The Resurrection,* 1899) whose concern for morality in art, evident in the essay on Maupassant, was augmented by his religious conversion in 1879.

TROLLOPE, ANTHONY (1815-1882). English novelist (*The Warden*, 1855; *Barchester Towers*, 1857; *Orley Farm*, 1862; *Phineas Finn*, 1869, etc.) whose immense literary output was achieved through a mechanical regularity in writing which he himself described in his *Autobiography* (1883).

VOGÜÉ, EUGÈNE MARIE MELCHIOR, VICOMTE DE (1848-1910). French diplomat and critic. His contribution to Russian studies to the *Revue des deux mondes* began in 1879, when he was stationed in St. Petersburg; and the collected essays became *The Russian Novel* (1886), written in part to display the weaknesses of Naturalism and to show the value of Christian suffering, so manifest in Dostoievsky and Tolstoi.

WOOLF, VIRGINIA (1882-1941). English novelist and critic, with Joyce an innovator with the stream of consciousness technique, whose novels included *Mrs. Dalloway* (1925), *To the Lighthouse* (1927), *Orlando* (1928), and *The Years* (1937).

ZOLA, ÉMILE (1840-1902). French critic, dramatist, and novelist; leading exponent of Naturalism and author of the immense cycle of novels, *The Rougon-Macquarts* (1871-1893)—twenty books chronicling "the natural and social history of a family under the Second Empire."

LOSSARY

Dr. Johnson once remarked with his customary, firm
common sense: "It is one of the maxims of civil law, that
definitions are hazardous." All the definitions that follow
are constructed with his cautionary advice in mind, and
the reader should examine them with some of Johnson's
own coolness. I have restricted the *Glossary* to literary terms
that center about the novel; and thus there has been a
deliberate omission of words like *comedy, tragedy, lyric,
biography,* etc., although as a catch-all form the novel
often incorporates these and other modes.

Allegory: A narrative which is actually a long and systematic extension
of a metaphor, item by item; and in which abstract ideas and doctrines
are made concrete. Allegorical prose narratives, while not common,
include Bunyan's *The Pilgrim's Progress* (1675) where Christian, en
route to the Celestial City, meets such characters as Hopeful and
Faithful, and George Orwell's *Animal Farm* (1946) with the pigs
Snowball and Napoleon representing Trotsky and Stalin. Allegorical
elements abound in the works of such novelists as Melville and Kafka.

Anagnorisis: Aristotle's term for the discovery or recognition in the
drama: simple when it involves the discovery of a long-lost brother,
more complex when it marks the moment when a character recognizes
his own true condition. The device is frequent in the novel: Dickens
was fond of the simpler type of recognition, as *Bleak House* (1852)
and *Great Expectations* (1861); Heathcliff's discovery of his own true
nature at the end of *Wuthering Heights* (1847) belongs to the second
type.

Antecedent action: As with the drama, the information provided the
reader in the exposition concerns what has occurred before the actual
action of the novel takes place. Lengthy examples would be the start
of Stendhal's *Charterhouse of Parma* (1839) or Balzac's *Eugénie
Grandet* (1833).

Apprenticeship novel: A novel where the theme is generally that of a young man maturing and learning the way of the world, often—but not necessarily—in the company of a teacher or a series of mentors. The "pedagogical novel" and in German the *Bildungsroman* (the formative novel, or novel of character-development) are equivalents. Notable examples include Voltaire's *Candide* (1759), Goethe's *Wilhelm Meister's Apprenticeship* (1795), Stendhal's *The Red and the Black* (1830), Samuel Butler's *The Way of All Flesh* (1903), Joyce's *A Portrait of the Artist as a Young Man* (1916), and Thomas Mann's *The Magic Mountain* (1924). These are merely outstanding instances. The pattern is far more universal than any casual inspection of the history of the novel would reveal.

Artist novel: In German, the *Künstlerroman*, where the protagonist (*q.v.*) is a writer, poet, painter, or musician, and the narrative shows his gradual aesthetic development. Naturally it is allied to the apprenticeship novel (*q.v.*). The Germans, from Romantics like Tieck, Mörike, Keller through Thomas Mann and Hesse, seem to have had a special proclivity for the genre. Modern examples include Romain Rolland's *Jean-Christophe* (1905-13), Joyce's *A Portrait of the Artist as a Young Man* (1916), Maugham's *The Moon and Sixpence* (1919), several of Thomas Wolfe's novels, and Joyce Cary's *The Horse's Mouth* (1944).

Bildungsroman: cf. *apprenticeship novel.*

Burlesque: A type of composition which excites laughter by ridiculing or caricaturing serious works. The word is related to "parody" and "travesty." Thus Cervantes' *Don Quixote* (1605-15) burlesques the chivalric romance (*q.v.*); Fielding's *Joseph Andrews* (1742) performs the same operation with certain elements in the epic (*q.v.*), as well as with a precedent serious novel, Richardson's *Pamela* (1740).

Character: (i) The name of a literary form popular in the seventeenth century (La Bruyère's *Les Caractères*, 1688, are perhaps best known), which was a brief sketch of a person who represented a distinct type of personality (*e.g.* the courtesan, the miser, the fop, etc.) or mode of living. (ii) One of the persons in a novel. (iii) The personality of such a figure. The type or stock character has been called "flat" by E. M. Forster, as against "round": the former given simple, easily discernible attributes and patterns of behavior, and generally one single trait. Thus in Dickens' novels we think of Mr. Pumblechook, Mr. Chadband, Mr. Turveydrop, etc.

Chorus character: In French, a *raisonneur*: a character who participates in the action of a novel, yet whose role is chiefly that of a commentator, and who seems to be a spokesman for the author (although this latter capacity is often dubious). Ishmael, in Melville's *Moby Dick* (1851), might be considered such; Marlowe, in several of Conrad's novels, likewise.

Climax: If, as in some dramas, a novel may be said to have a rising action, a climax, and a falling action, then the climax is the decisive turning point—generally a moment of great tension—when the fortunes of the hero are changed for better or for worse, or his attitude drastically altered.

Confidant (or female, **confidante**): A character, usually minor, to whom the leading character reveals his sentiments; more common in drama than in the novel, since on the stage it can supplant the use of the soliloquy.

Conflict: Naturally most plots contain elements of conflict, where the hero or protagonist comes up against opposing forces or persons.

Convention: Any specifically literary device which in effect departs from real life, and yet is tacitly accepted by the reader. In the novel, this is found in such procedures as the flashback (*q.v.*), the disclosure of a character's thought-processes by the author (*cf. inner monologue*), even the necessity for employing "He said" and "She remarked" in dialogue, etc.

Dénouement: French for "unknotting"; the resolution of the plot at the conclusion of a novel, which can also be accompanied by the discovery, recognition, anagnorisis (*q.v.*).

Detective story: In French, *le roman policier*; in German, *die Detektivgeschichte*. A short story or novel where a crime—usually murder—is committed at or near the beginning of the narrative, and the plot largely consists of attempts to discover the identity of the miscreant. It has been somewhat facetiously suggested that Sophocles' play *Oedipus the King* (*c.* 430 B.C.) is the paradigm for all detective stories, and a Hollywood subtitle for that tragedy might be "Murder at the Crossroads"; or "Who Killed King Laius?" Edgar Allan Poe's *The Murders in the Rue Morgue* (1841) is usually cited as the first example in prose fiction, although certain eighteenth-century novels—among them William Godwin's *Caleb Williams* (1794) and assorted Gothic novels (*q.v.*) seem prefigurations of the form, if not actual adherents. While today the detective novel goes under the slightly pejorative heading of light entertainment (*Who Cares Who Killed Roger Ackroyd?* is the title of an acerbic essay by Edmund Wilson), it is salutary to reflect that Dickens' *Bleak House* (1852), Victor Hugo's *Les Misérables* (1862), and Dostoievski's *The Brothers Karamazov* (1880) technically belong to this category. When elements of mystery and terror predominate and the type of analytical deduction made famous by Sherlock Holmes ("Elementary, my dear Watson") seems lacking, the phrase "mystery story" is often substituted.

Discovery: *cf. anagnorisis.*

Epic: A long, serious, narrative poem written in an elevated style ("nobleness and the grand manner" mark the epic, to quote Matthew

Arnold) relating the exploits of a hero, and often locating these historically in the distant or even mythic past. Distinctions can be made between the primary, primitive, folk, sometimes anonymous, and oral epic on the one hand—Homer's *Iliad* and *Odyssey* (900-750 B.C.?), the Old English *Beowulf* (6th century A.D., the manuscript dating from the 10th century); the *Chanson de Roland* (12th century), *El Cid* (12th century), the *Nibelungenlied* (13th century), the Finnish *Kalevala* (date unknown)—and on the other hand the secondary, art, literary, and written epic—Virgil's *Aeneid* (19 B.C.), Tasso's *Jerusalem Delivered* (1581-93), Camoens' *Lusiads* (1572), Milton's *Paradise Lost* (1667), Longfellow's *Hiawatha* (1858). Spenser's *Fairie Queene* (1596) and Dante's *Divine Comedy* (1315-21) share certain epic characteristics. We note a few major traits of the epic:

(1) The hero often enjoys superhuman and even divine attributes. God or the Gods have a stake in his destiny, which is embodied in adventures of legendary or historical importance: Virgil's Aeneas eventually founds Rome, Milton's poem deals with the creation of mankind, etc.

(2) The setting is huge in scope, alternating between heaven and earth, and usually including the entire known universe.

(3) Early epic heroes, reflecting societies where warfare was the customary order of existence, were valiant warriors in battle. Later epic heroes exhibit this same capacity for deeds of valor, although less martially.

(4) Supernatural forces (for Homer, the Pantheon of the Greek deities, God and Satan in Christian epics) frequently intervene in the situation.

(5) The emphasis is on stylistic sonority and grandeur, whether in the oral epic with its stock epithets and formulaic devices that facilitate the bard in his memorized recitation, or in the literary epic with its stylized syntax and ceremonial rhetoric.

(6) Particularly in early times, the epic poet tells his tale objectively and hence reflects the communal mood of the epic. (Both Dante and Milton represent movements toward subjectivity, in that each author occasionally intervenes in his poem.)

(7) Most epics employ certain literary conventions (*q.v.*): the epic question and invocation at the start, a story that begins *in medias res* (in the middle of things), trips to the Underworld or to the abode of some afterlife, catalogues of warriors and places, extended comparisons (the Homeric simile), and lengthy set-pieces by the principal characters.

Epistolary novel: A novel related through the medium of letters written by one or more of the characters, where the author ostensibly acts as a mere "editor" for his material, and thus does not seem to intrude in his own work. Richardson's *Pamela* (1740) is considered to be the first full-scale manifestation of the form; other eighteenth-century examples are Rousseau's *Julie, or the New Eloïse* (1761), Goethe's *Werther* (1774), Choderlos de Laclos' *Dangerous Liaisons* (1782). The epistolary novel as a form gradually has disappeared, when other techniques to display inner states of consciousness came to render this intimate device superfluous.

Erziehungsroman: (German) Essentially the pedagogical novel, or the novel dealing with the development of character. *Cf.* Apprenticeship novel.

Exemplum: Originally a tale told by preachers in the Middle Ages to illustrate the text of a sermon, and the *Pardoner's Tale* in Chaucer's *Canterbury Tales* (1387-1400) is a good example. Like the *fabliau* (*q.v.*), it may be regarded as one of the novel's antecedents. A case can be made for such works of prose fiction as Voltaire's *Candide* (1759) and Dr. Johnson's *Rasselas* (1759) as *exempla*.

Fabliau: Close to the word "fable" (where the characters, however, were generally animals and there was always some moral precept to be derived) the *fabliau* like the *exemplum* (*q.v.*) was one of the novel's humble ancestors. Popular in the twelfth century, probably originating in France, these were short tales written both in eight-syllable verse and in prose. Chaucer employed the form with variants throughout *Canterbury Tales* (1347-1400) in such stories as are told by the Reeve, Miller, Summoner, and Shipman. In the *fabliau* the characters are drawn from the middle and lower classes; the themes are satiric and realistic rather than idealized, often bawdy, and easily understood—all these qualities belonging to "low" literature rather than to "high" and classical letters. In short, the *fabliau* was one bridge between the fine fabling of the epic and the romance (*q.v.*) with their elegant *personae* and equally elegant audience, and the novel with its humbler characters and similarly middle-class readers.

Flashback: A scene describing events that have taken place before the time a novel actually begins.

Gothic novel: Officially inaugurated by Horace Walpole with *The Castle of Otranto* (1764), although there were earlier precedents, this was a genre where the decor was usually mediaeval, sometimes Oriental as in Beckford's *Vathek* (1786), and the atmosphere rich in ghosts, clanking chains, voluptuous monks, supernatural and mysterious events, hints of psychological aberrations, even sadism and masochism, and the entire apparatus of the "ghost story." Lewis's *The Monk* (1797), Mary Shelley's *Frankenstein* (1817), the tales of Poe and the novels of Charles Brockden Brown in America were later examples. Yet subsequent, more respectable writers attest to influences of the Gothic novel: Dickens, the Brontë sisters, Faulkner in our own time. Note also that it rose concurrently with the historical novel (*q.v.*).

Historical novel: A novel which recreates characters or events or the general setting of a past epoch, and where fictitious persons are often (but not necessarily) juxtaposed against real historical figures. Scott established the pattern with novels like *Waverley* (1814) and a whole series that followed his book, where the scene was Scotland around 1745, and the plot concerned with the Jacobite Rebellion. His other historical area, as in *Ivanhoe* (1819), was chiefly twelfth-century England and France. Thackeray, Dumas *père*, Vigny, Victor Hugo, Flaubert, Cooper, and Tolstoi were major contributors to the genre during the nineteenth century; Robert Graves, Kenneth Roberts, and Thomas Mann (*Joseph and His Brothers*, 1933-44) in the twentieth. The popularity of the historical novel is apparent from plethora of historical costume-pieces in recent years, and from Hollywood's delight in then converting these into super-colossal-extravaganzas: Margaret Mitchell's *Gone with the Wind* (1936), and the writings of Lloyd Douglas, Samuel Shellabarger, Hervey Allen, and Howard Fast.

Installment novel: In French, *le roman-feuilleton*; in German, *der Roman in Fortsetzungen*. A serialized novel, usually presented in monthly periodicals. Popular in the nineteenth century (Dickens, Balzac, and Thackeray published many of their books in this fashion), today it survives chiefly in such magazines as *The Saturday Evening Post* and similar purveyors of popular literature.

Interior monologue: One of the techniques employed in the stream of consciousness novel (*q.v.*), where the effort is made to record the thought processes of characters, rather than their physical actions, and the emphasis is away from a logical ordering of ideas toward pre-speech and non-verbalized levels of consciousness—all this to suggest the fluid activity of the mind. Thus James Joyce's *Ulysses* (1922) and *Finnegan's Wake* (1939) contain celebrated passages where the author seems not to exist and the stream of consciousness lacks any apparent intervention on his part. Virginia Woolf's *Mrs. Dalloway* (1925) and *To the Lighthouse* (1927) include scenes where the author is more evident as a guide and commentator.

Künstlerroman: cf. *Artist novel.*

Marchen: In German, a fairy-tale, fable, or legend. (*Die Märe* can mean news, tidings, rumor, tradition—all words, incidentally, with strong suggestions of oral transmission.) Generally the length of a long short story, although longer examples exist, the *Märchen* was favored by the German Romantics such as Novalis (Friedrich von Hardenberg), *Heinrich von Ofterdingen* (1802); Tieck, *Der blonde Eckbert* (1797), Fouqué, *Undine* (1811), and Chamisso, *Peter Schlemihl* (1814). Supernatural, occult, and occasionally mystical elements were prevalent. A type of prose-fiction ancillary to the main line of the novel, nevertheless the *Märchen* points to some tendencies in certain modern novels where the everyday world is invested with mystery, or where the author seems to be straining toward myth and symbol.

Mediaeval romance: *cf. Romance.*

Melodrama: Originally a stage-play with songs interspersed, and where the action had orchestral accompaniment. By the late eighteenth and early nineteenth century, melodrama came to mean a drama filled with sensational, violent effects and events, with the characters therein unbelievably good or wicked, and where virtue tended to triumph over seemingly insurmountable odds. (Here it was the direct ancestor of the modern radio, cinema, and television "soap opera.") But the popularity of melodramatic techniques contributed much to the novel, beginning with the Gothic novel (*q.v.*); and one easily notes melodramatic devices in the works of Dickens, the Brontë sisters, Edgar Allan Poe, Hugo, Balzac, *et al.*

Mystery story: *cf. Detective story.*

Naturalism: A word sometimes loosely applied to the Romantic movement, and the tendency starting in the mid- and later eighteenth century to "go back to nature." A more accurate and restrictive meaning relates naturalism to an intellectual current in the late nineteenth and early twentieth century, and there chiefly manifested in the novel and in the drama. Naturalism is a kind of heightened "realism" (*q.v.*); but naturalism is firmly rooted in certain post-Darwinian biological and deterministic theses. These posit that whatever is real is found in the order of nature—the causative world shorn of any idealistic, spiritual, religious, or metaphysical hypotheses. Hence man is merely a complex animal, differing only in degree and not in kind from the lower forms of life, and man is also the product of his heredity and environment (key words for naturalism), just as is any lower organism. But for man the environmental forces are generally seen as social and economic, and the heroes of naturalistic literature struggle—usually in vain—against these blind powers. The clinical frankness of much naturalism in matters concerning sex and hunger stems in part from the desire to reduce man to his material and "scientific" components, where these simpler elements are easier to examine and to regulate. The apparent brutality and callousness of many writers associated with the school results from their wish to be scientifically objective. Yet this same claim for a dispassionate documentation of a slice of life (*tranche de vie*, in Zola's phrase) paradoxically could produce a strong sense of social protest and a reforming zeal in many naturalists. The horrors of the "lower depths" (to use a title from a work by Maxim Gorki) elicited a demand for social change. Hence Marxism's claim that it viewed "scientific theory" as the struggle of social and economic forces was congenial to many naturalists. Yet it would seem that the ultimate utopian optimism of Marxism, and its vision of a final classless and presumably near-perfect society would clash with the basic moral pessimism implicit in the thinking of most naturalists. (The belated impact of the German philosopher Schopenhauer on many late nineteenth century French naturalists cannot be discounted. "Life is a pendulum which swings from Sorrow to Ennui," said Joris-Karl Huysmans.)

Zola and the Goncourt brothers were most responsible for illustrating and disseminating naturalistic doctrines in France during the 1880's; and the former's massive series of novels chronicling the fortunes—or the misfortunes—of a family (*The Rougon Macquarts: The Natural and Social History of a Family under the Second Empire, 1871-93*) are a monument to the movement. The line was continued after Zola in France, by Huysmans, Maupassant, and in our own time Barbusse, Romaine, Roger Martin du Gard, Céline and Jean-Paul Sartre; in Germany, by Gerhardt Hauptmann, Arno Holz, and Theodor Fontane; in England, by George Gissing and George Moore, with Hardy on the periphery; and in America, by the more familiar writings of Frank Morris, Theodore Dreiser, Eugene O'Neill, Stephen Crane, Jack London, James Farrell, and James M. Cain.

Novel: *The Oxford Universal Dictionary* defines the novel as "A fictitious prose narrative of considerable length, in which characters and actions representative of real life are portrayed in a plot of more or less complexity." This carefully qualified statement at least establishes the locus of the novel, although almost every component within the definition is liable to query and question. (1) "Considerable length" reminds us of purely quantitative difficulties in distinguishing between the novel, novelette, the tale, the German *Novelle*, the French *conte*, the short story, the long short story, etc. (2) "Prose narrative" recalls novels where language more akin to poetry than to the cool element of prose occasionally is the vehicle: Melville's *Moby-Dick* (1851) and Joyce's *Ulysses* (1922) are but two instances. (3) The historical novel (*q.v.*) can employ "real" history alongside its "characters and actions representative of real life"; and indeed the phrase "real life" raises a Pilate-like question as to what reality is. (4) Finally, the relatively plotless nature of certain modern experimental novels makes even the last portion of the statement dubious. To augment simple dictionary definition, perhaps the happiest way to attempt to grasp the protean contours of the novel is to sketch briefly its genesis and development.

The earliest extended narrative was the epic (*q.v.*), succeeded by the mediaeval or chivalric romance (*q.v.*)—both poetic ancestors of the prose novel. Both depicted exotic and often superhuman activity, where the gods often intervened in mortal affairs in the epic, and magic and enchantment were the apparatus of the romance. The protagonists were naturally noble and aristocratic: the common man only makes his entrance in classical literature as a figure of fun (Thersites in Homer's *Iliad*, or the subjects of the Roman *satira*, *q.v.*, or even Shakespeare's ludicrous clowns and rustics).

By the later Middle Ages and the early Renaissance, the *fabliau* (*q.v.*) and the Italian and French *novella* (*q.v.*) portrayed the everyday world of ordinary middle- and lower-class life, treating it both comically and seriously. On a large scale, such disparate works as Rabelais' *Gargantua* (1535) and Thomas Nashe's *The Unfortunate Traveller* (1594) show thematic and narrative tendencies we associate with the later full-blown novel. That the romance persisted within the limits of the new form (and its novelty is borne out by the French and Spanish words *novella* related to both newness and news, in the sense of journalism and reporting current events) is evident in books like d'Urfy's *Astrée* (1610), Mme. de Scudéry's *Artamène* (1649-53), Lyly's *Euphues* (1579), and Lodge's *Rosalynde* (1590)—where the very titles themselves evoke the artificial world of the romance and the pastoral. Indeed, as late as the mid-nineteenth century, Nathaniel Hawthorne could still discriminate between the novel and its concern with "the probable and ordinary course of man's experience." In the romances he chose to write, Italy became for him "a sort of poetic or fairy precinct, where actualities would not be so terribly insisted upon as they are . . . in America."

But the main line of the novel, manifest in the eighteenth-century novel when the form achieved maturation, has been to hew to the "probable." The simple growth of literacy among the middle class meant an increasing interest in reading journals and diaries (as well as in writing them), and a concern for history and biography. Even the increased production of newspapers implemented the public's desire to find in fiction a world not too remote from their own. The picaresque and the pedagogical novel (*q.v.*) are both firmly rooted in the here and now; and their typical heroes so often reflect the middle-class efforts to succeed in a shifting and unstable society, where feudal barriers to such rising were slowing being eroded.

Ever since the nineteenth century, it is safe to say that the novel has emerged as *the* popular form of literature. This is not to claim that the triumph is entirely salutary: the apparent ease (*cf.* the *Foreword*) with which novels can be read, as opposed to the attention and the quickness of mind that poetry and the theater often demand, may reflect a decline in intellectual standards. Certainly no literary form better demonstrates the uneasy amalgam of art and business, artistic creation and mass production. It is yet good to remember, however, that some of the greatest literary craftsmen (starting possibly with Flaubert) have turned their talents and genius to the novel; and the novel with its special resources—among them the ability to seem to enter into a human being's consciousness—has kept close company with two of the modern world's intellectual preoccupations, psychology and epistomology.

Novella: Italian for "a short new thing, a little new thing"—or "news," with suggestions of journalistic and immediate accounts of what has just occurred. The English word for *novel* derives from *novella;* French and German terms (*le roman* and *der Roman*) derive from *romance* (*q.v.*). By the fourteenth century the *novella* in Italy had come to mean a short tale in prose, either serious or comic or both (*cf. fabliau*). Boccaccio's *Decameron* (1348-58) is the best-known collection of *novelle.*

Novel of ideas: A loose phrase, since it is hard to imagine a novel without ideas. But some critics have chosen to place in this category those novels where the major portion of verbal interchanges between characters, or the descriptions of the characters' thought-processes, are concerned with abstract ideas of a metaphysical, sociological, or political nature. Thus Thomas Mann's *Magic Mountain* (1924), Aldous Huxley's *Point Counterpoint* (1928), André Malraux's *The Conquerors* (1928) and Camus' *The Plague* (1946) might qualify. In French, *roman à thèse* is a near-equivalent.

Novel of manners: Again a somewhat meaningless phrase, if "manners" are taken in the broadest sense. The phrase usually refers to those novels were a chief preoccupation is with the social customs, habits, and manners of a class or several classes within society. The category is made more explicit if one thinks of certain books by Jane Austen, Anthony Trollope, Henry James, Edith Wharton, and J. P. Marquand in our own day.

Picaresque novel: Basically the tale of a rogue (*picaro* is Spanish for "rogue") and a rascal, often satiric and always "realistic," insofar as it delineates the everyday world often in its more sordid aspects, and any idealization is avoided. The earlier picaro's exploits were often parodies of the deeds of derring-do found in the chivalric romance, and these were presented in the form of loosely-bound episodes. The first prominent picaresque novel, although actually a novelette by modern standards, was *The Life of Tormes: His Fortunes and Misfortunes* (anonymous, 1554), in which the Spain of the Golden Age was portrayed in all truth as a land of dire want and miserable hunger for the common people. Next greatest was Le Sage's *Gil Blas* (1715), although Cervantes used picaresque themes and devices in *Don Quixote* (1605-15). The picaresque line continued through such works as Fielding's *Joseph Andrews* (1742) and *Tom Jones* (1748), Smollett's *The Adventures of Roderick Random* in the same year; Dickens' *The Pickwick Papers* (1837), Stendhal's *The Red and the Black* (1830), Thackeray's *Vanity Fair* (1848)—with Becky Sharp as a female version of the picaro; Mark Twain's *The Adventures of Huckleberry Finn* (1884), Thomas Mann's *The Confessions of Felix Krull* (1911-37), and Saul Bellow's *The Adventures of Augie March* (1953). As with the pedagogical novel (*q.v.*) and other categories within the novel, the picaresque form (or at least some of its ingredients) is more common than a superficial inspection of the history of the novel would lead one to believe.

Plot: The plot can mean the abstract form that the action takes, quite separate from the characters within a play or a novel. Thus, on a fairly elementary level, the plot can be reduced to a series of answers to queries about what happens next: "and then . . . and then . . ." Progressing further, surely the plot is more than the mere story; for among other things, it represents an *arrangement* of the events or happenings by the author: not only selectivity of the occurrences, but—and this is particularly important for the novel—the manner in which the events are juxtaposed. (To be more concrete, consider Emily Brontë's *Wuthering Heights*, published in 1847. The story includes Catherine Earnshaw Linton's marriage to Edgar Linton, and her subsequent evident boredom with her husband. Both the act of the wedding and her growing discontent are not seen in the novel. The time span of the book runs from 1771 to 1803; yet the plot places the time of the narration of the story (by Nellie Dean to Lockwood, the person who tells us the tale) some thirty years after the bulk of the action takes place.

Aristotle's statements in the *Poetics* (Chapters VI and VII) about the nature of plot, controversial as their interpretations have been over the centuries, still are cogent with respect to the novel—although he, of course, was talking about the drama. (Indeed, L. J. Potts, in a recent translation of the *Poetics*, makes a good case for calling it *The Art of Fiction* because he maintains that Aristotle was actually dealing with fiction, rather than "what the word 'poetry' has represented to the common reader for the last hundred and fifty years.") When Aristotle spoke of plot (*mythos*, sometimes translated as "fable") as being "the soul of tragedy," in which case "character comes next," and when he stressed that the qualities of a character emerge from the action the author has conceived, it would seem that he was denigrating character at the expense of plot, and his remarks might seem a justification for mere action of melodramatic proportions. Yet his subsequent qualifications show that for Aristotle the thoughts and words of the characters, as well as their actions and deeds, composed the totality of the plot. In short, plot and character cannot actually be treated separately.

Conflict, suspense, surprise: these seem to be an author's principal devices to keep the plot moving. Other ingredients in the plot, glossed elsewhere, are anagnorisis (discovery, recognition), antecedent action, climax, dénouement, flashback, scene, and summary.

Point of view: A novelist really only has five choices by which he can narrate his story. If the narrator is a character within the novel, he can be the protagonist, or at least a main character; and he then speaks in the first person, as does Dickens' David Copperfield in that book (1850). Or he can appear as a minor character telling about the

principal figures: Ishmael, in Melville's *Moby-Dick* (1851). If the
narrator is *not* a character within his own book, he can play the role
of the omniscient, Olympian author as in Stendhal's *The Charterhouse
of Parma* (1839). Or he may speak as an actual observer to the actions
within his book, again writing in the first person as in categories one
and two, but severely limiting himself to what he has actually seen
and heard, and never entering into his character's minds. (This form,
incidentally, approaches real and fictionalized autobiography). Or he
may develop a third person narration through the eyes, ears, and mind
of one figure in the story, such as Strethers in Henry James' *The
Ambassadors* (1903).

Psychological novel: A controversial term (similar to "novel of ideas"
and "novel of manners," *q.v.*) since even the simplest prose tales
demonstrate an author's interest in human motivation. The name can
be reasonably applied to a novel where the inner lives of characters
receive more attention than their external actions. Choderlos de Laclos'
Dangerous Liaisons (1782) and Virginia Woolf's *Mrs. Dalloway*
(1925) fall into such a category more easily than do James Fenimore
Cooper's *The Last of the Mohicans* (1826) or Zola's *Germinal* (1885).

Realism: In its broadest sense, realism is merely an accurate representation of actual life through the medium of literature. Aristotle's
stress on *mimesis* (imitation) and his description of drama as the
imitation of an action can be interpreted as a plea for "realism."
Indeed, all literature can be said to be more or less "realistic"; yet obviously there is a wide stretch between Sophocles' stylized lines and
the speeches of Balzac's avaricious merchants. An opposition is again
often made between romantic and idealized literature and realistic
letters; giving to the former attributes of showing life somehow better
or more picturesque than it seems to be, reserving for the latter the
quality of a faithful portrayal of actuality. But once more the distinction seems to fall down, if we consider how much more improbable or
fanciful or heroic are the lives of some actual individuals when we
compare them to their nearest fictional counterparts.

True literary realism would seem to involve both the selection of
subject matter and a mode or manner in presenting it. From its inception the novel has seemed peculiarly committed to "realism," when
we recall the books of Defoe, Fielding, or Jane Austen. But to make
the word still more meaningful, it might be wise to restrict it to the
movement in the nineteenth century which arose—partly in opposition
to Romantic idealism—as an effort to record, mainly via the novel,
the experiences of everyday existence. Here even a reference to a sister
art may be helpful: Gustave Courbet set up his own *Pavilion of
Realism* when the Salon of 1855 in Paris rejected his painting, *The
Bathers* ("they dirty the very water they bathe in," said one critic).
Duranty's magazine *Realism* (1857) aimed at "the exact, complete,

and sincere reproduction of the social milieu in which we live." We spell out a few tendencies belonging to realism proper; although the critical reader will note that two of the nineteenth century's greatest "realists"—Balzac and Dickens—while they paid lip-service to such tenets, are also difficult to place within such neat categories.

(1) A concern for middle-class and (later in the century) lower-class life.

(2) A concentration on ordinary rather than extraordinary events.

(3) The author aims to render an impersonal and objective account of facts.

(4) A freedom from explicit moral and didactic instruction, and hence a bias against editorial intrusion (where the author comments in the first person on the ideas or the activities of his characters).

(5) A documentary impulse to record a large mass of physical detail, with a stress on phonographic and photographic reality.

(6) An effort to convince the reader that here is a part of the unselected flow of life, without the author's manipulating or contriving his material. "All is true," says Balzac near the start of *Père Goriot* (1835).

(7) An absence of apparent improbabilities, in the same effort to gain verisimilitude.

(8) An increasing awareness and projection of the motivating power of money and finance in the modern world.

(9) A certain degree of moral and social pessimism; allied to the conviction that the novel is no mere easy entertainment, but a serious critique of the social order.

(10) A similar degree of growing scientific pretension—Balzac's zoological analogies to the human species are an example. But it remained for Naturalism (*q.v.*) to apply nineteenth-century scientific ideas and principles to literature on a grand scale.

Recognition: *cf. anagnorisis.*

Regional novel: The novel restricted to a specific geographical locale, generally one outside the generalized contours of the city; where local color, habits of speech, peculiar *mores*, etc., are important. The term should be viewed with critical suspicion, since every novel seems to find its local habitation and a name in some *place*. Yet we associate the phrase with Hardy's Wessex novels, Arnold Bennett's novels, like *Clayhanger* (1910), that deal with the Five Towns, and the recent productions of William Faulkner and Robert Penn Warren, and J. P. Marquand's New England studies, etc.

Rising action: *cf. climax.*

Roman à clef: French, "novel with a key": the type of novel where we sense thinly-veiled biography or autobiography, and where all or some of the fictitious characters are portraits of real persons, whether contemporary or historical. Thus in Disraeli's *Coningsby* (1844), Oswald Millbank is really Gladstone; Jawster Sharp is John Bright, the agitator against the Corn Laws; Sidonia is Lionel Nathan de Rothschild, the great banker, etc. The statement that appears at the head of most modern novels, which ostensibly guards against charges of libel, amounts to saying that "nothing is really anybody." It may also be attributed to the novelist's concern that he create a fictive universe, free from any engagement with his own life. In this connection, it might be noted that many first novels by young authors come close to being *romans à clef*.

Romance: The mediaeval or chivalric romance descended from the classical epic (*q.v.*), and therefore the romance occupies a half-way role between the epic and the novel. First written in verse and later in prose, in the *lingua romantica* (that is, in vernacular rather than in classical or mediaeval Latin), some of the Old French romances were actually translations from the Latin. Unlike the ancient, heroic, and warlike epic, the theme of love prevailed in the romance. The *personae* were kings and queens, knights and ladies, with supernatural creatures —enchanters, fairies, etc.—in the background. The narrative took place in strange and exotic lands; magic and enchantment were routine occurrences; the theme of the romance, which often was based on the doctrine of Courtly Love (*Hohe Minne, Cortezia*), could be the quest of the knight to seek the lady from whom he is parted. Hints of allegory abounded. The Lady occasionally took on the lineaments of the Virgin Mary, and the Quest could partake of those same hazards attendant upon the search for the Holy Grail.

Satira: later form of the Latin word *Satura*: a work which was a medley or potpourri of mixed subjects in a variety of styles. Menippean satire blended prose narrative with verse and philosophy; and the most famous work to develop from this genre was the *Satyricon* attributed to Petronius Arbiter (d. 66 A.D.), the director ("Arbiter elegentiae") of the pleasures of the Imperial Court of the Emperor Nero.

Satire: A work that ridicules human failings and stupidity, and attempts to arouse in the reader scorn, contempt, and derision for its subject. The line between satire and mere comedy or amusement is thin; and generally the point is made that satire has a corrective aim, comedy simply tries to be funny. Voltaire's *Candide* (1759) is satiric; Evelyn Waugh's *Scoop* (1938) contains some satirical elements, but seems to be purely comic.

Scene: That which takes place before the reader's eyes in a novel, and entails description and dialogue. All novels are composed of "scene" and "summary" (*q.v.*), although the tendency in the development of the genre seems to have been to get away from excessive use of the latter.

Serialized novel: *cf. Installment novel.*

Short story: Narrative prose fiction, distinguished only by its length from the novel. Even here the *Novelle*, a popular form in German literature, destroys any easy definition: is it a long short story or a short novel? The 15,000 word limit assigned by some critics as the maximum length for the short story smacks of arbitrariness, as does Edgar Allan Poe's statement that what he called the "prose tale" could be read at one sitting, in a half hour up to two hours; and that such a work produced "a certain unique or single effect." Obvious antecedents for the short story are the older *fabliau, conte,* and *Märchen* (*q.v.*).

Slice of life: *cf. Naturalism.*

Sociological novel: Like many of the terms used to describe forms of of the novel, here is another to be regarded with suspicion. What novel does not mirror some aspect of the society that it purports to describe, and which in turn has produced it? As early as Goethe's *Werther* (1774), that author seemed compelled to demonstrate that his hero's tragedy was largely dictated by the constricting social conditions of eighteenth-century Germany. Yet there exist those novels where social conditions are emphasized, and some thesis about their errors and possible amelioration is advanced: Dickens' *Hard Times* (1854), Harriet Beecher Stowe's *Uncle Tom's Cabin* (1852), Zola's *Germinal* (1885); as well as asorted works by contemporary writers such as Upton Sinclair, John Steinbeck, Erskine Caldwell, John Dos Passos, etc.

Stream-of-consciousness novel: A phrase originally devised by William James (*Principles of Psychology*, 1890)—not concerning the novel, however—to describe the amorphous flowing of psychic activity. It has since been applied to those novels, or portions of novels, where the author tries to capture and to recreate the mental life of a character. Actually the earliest novelists—Cervantes, Fielding, and Sterne included—portray their protagonists' *thinking*. In the nineteenth century, one can locate brilliant examples in Stendhal, for instance, of what might be called mental monologues. The stream-of-consciousness technique has chiefly labored to project a more immediate presentation of the psyche, where laws of logic and reason seem to retreat before the vagrant and spontaneous onslaught of free-association; and we dwell in a world of pre-speech, where similarly the naked image antedates the more reflective and artificial concept and abstraction. Dujardin's *The Laurels are Cut* (1887) has generally been accepted as the first work to display this technique in embryo. Henry James and Marcel Proust tend to show the mind still working in a relatively orderly logical and syntactical pattern; Dorothy Richardson, Virginia Woolf, James Joyce, and William Faulkner move toward a more revolutionary description of unrestricted psychical activity. *Cf. Interior monologue.*

Summary: *Cf. Scene.* The other element, along with "scene" in the novel, where the author or one of his characters tells us about events that have occurred, but where we actually are not partner to the events. Hence dialogue, for instance, is lacking. Thus the beginning of Balzac's *Eugénie Grandet* (1833) opens with a long thirty-page summary to prior actions, with an immense amount of information about the characters, before we see or hear them.